Impact
Evaluation
in Practice

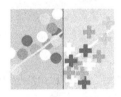

Impact Evaluation in Practice is available as an interactive textbook at **http://www.worldbank.org/pdt.** The electronic version allows communities of practice and colleagues working in sectors and regions, as well as students and teachers, to share notes and related materials for an enhanced, multimedia learning and knowledge-exchange experience.

Additional ancillary material specific to *Impact Evaluation in Practice* is available at **http://www.worldbank.org/ieinpractice**.

This book has been made possible thanks to the generous support from the Spanish Impact Evaluation Fund (SIEF). Launched in 2007 with a $14.9 million donation by Spain, and expanded by a $2.1 million donation from the United Kingdom's Department for International Development (DfID), the SIEF is the largest trust fund focused on impact evaluation ever established in the World Bank. Its main goal is to expand the evidence base on what works to improve health, education, and social protection outcomes, thereby informing development policy.

See http://www.worldbank.org/sief.

Impact Evaluation in Practice

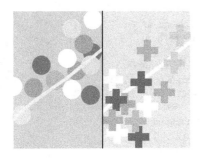

Paul J. Gertler, Sebastian Martinez,
Patrick Premand, Laura B. Rawlings,
Christel M. J. Vermeersch

THE WORLD BANK

ISBN: 978-0-8213-8541-8
eISBN: 978-0-8213-8593-7
DOI: 10.1596/978-0-8213-8541-8

Library of Congress Cataloging-in-Publication Data

Impact evaluation in practice / Paul J. Gertler ... [et al.].
    p. cm.
  Includes bibliographical references and index.
   ISBN 978-0-8213-8541-8 -- ISBN 978-0-8213-8593-7 (electronic)
   1. Economic development projects--Evaluation. 2. Evaluation research (Social action programs) I. Gertler, Paul, 1955- II. World Bank.
   HD75.9.I47 2010
   338.90072--dc22

                                                            2010034602

Cover design by Naylor Design.

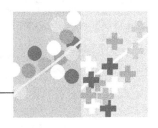

CONTENTS

Figures

Tables

PREFACE

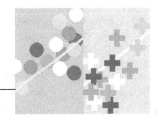

This book offers an accessible introduction to the topic of impact evaluation and its practice in development. Although the book is geared principally toward development practitioners and policy makers, we trust that it will be a valuable resource for students and others interested in impact evaluation. Prospective impact evaluations assess whether or not a program has achieved its intended results or test alternative strategies for achieving those results. We consider that more and better impact evaluations will help strengthen the evidence base for development policies and programs around the world. Our hope is that if governments and development practitioners can make policy decisions based on evidence—including evidence generated through impact evaluation—development resources will be spent more effectively to reduce poverty and improve people's lives. The three parts in this handbook provide a nontechnical introduction to impact evaluations, discussing what to evaluate and why in part 1; how to evaluate in part 2; and how to implement an evaluation in part 3. These elements are the basic tools needed to successfully carry out an impact evaluation.

The approach to impact evaluation in this book is largely intuitive, and we attempt to minimize technical notation. We provide the reader with a core set of impact evaluation tools—the concepts and methods that underpin any impact evaluation—and discuss their application to real-world development operations. The methods are drawn directly from applied research in the social sciences and share many commonalities with research methods used in the natural sciences. In this sense, impact evaluation brings the empirical research tools widely used in economics and other social sciences together with the operational and political-economy realities of policy implementation and development practice.

From a methodological standpoint, our approach to impact evaluation is largely pragmatic: we think that the most appropriate methods should be identified to fit the operational context, and not the other way around. This is best achieved at the outset of a program, through the design of prospective impact evaluations that are built into the project's implementation. We argue that gaining consensus among key stakeholders and identifying an evaluation design that fits the political and operational context are as important as the method itself. We also believe strongly that impact evaluations should be candid about their limitations and caveats. Finally, we strongly encourage policy makers and program managers to consider impact evaluations in a logical framework that clearly sets out the causal pathways by which a program works to produce outputs and influence final outcomes, and to combine impact evaluations with monitoring and complementary evaluation approaches to gain a full picture of performance.

What is perhaps most novel about this book is the approach to applying impact evaluation tools to real-world development work. Our experiences and lessons on how to do impact evaluation in practice are drawn from teaching and working with hundreds of capable government, academic, and development partners. Among all the authors, the book draws from dozens of years of experience working with impact evaluations in almost every corner of the globe.

This book builds on a core set of teaching materials developed for the "Turning Promises to Evidence" workshops organized by the office of the Chief Economist for Human Development (HDNCE), in partnership with regional units and the Development Economics Research Group (DECRG) at the World Bank. At the time of writing, the workshop had been delivered over 20 times in all regions of the world. The workshops and this handbook have been made possible thanks to generous grants from the Spanish government and the United Kingdom's Department for International Development (DfID) through contributions to the Spanish Impact Evaluation Fund (SIEF). This handbook and the accompanying presentations and lectures are available at http://www.worldbank.org/ieinpractice.

Other high-quality resources provide introductions to impact evaluation for policy, for instance, Baker 2000; Ravallion 2001, 2008, 2009; Duflo, Glennerster, and Kremer 2007; Duflo and Kremer 2008; Khandker, Koolwal, and Samad 2009; and Leeuw and Vaessen 2009. The present book differentiates itself by combining a comprehensive, nontechnical overview of quantitative impact evaluation methods with a direct link to the rules of program operations, as well as a detailed discussion of practical implementation aspects. The book also links to an impact evaluation course and supporting capacity building material.

The teaching materials on which the book is based have been through many incarnations and have been taught by a number of talented faculty, all of whom have left their mark on the methods and approach to impact evaluation. Paul Gertler and Sebastian Martinez, together with Sebastian Galiani and Sigrid Vivo, assembled a first set of teaching materials for a workshop held at the Ministry of Social Development (SEDESOL) in Mexico in 2005. Christel Vermeersch developed and refined large sections of the technical modules of the workshop and adapted a case study to the workshop setup. Laura Rawlings and Patrick Premand developed materials used in more recent versions of the workshop.

We would like to thank and acknowledge the contributions and substantive input of a number of other faculty who have co-taught the workshop, including Felipe Barrera, Sergio Bautista-Arredondo, Stefano Bertozzi, Barbara Bruns, Pedro Carneiro, Nancy Qian, Jishnu Das, Damien de Walque, David Evans, Claudio Ferraz, Jed Friedman, Emanuela Galasso, Sebastian Galiani, Gonzalo Hernández Licona, Arianna Legovini, Phillippe Leite, Mattias Lundberg, Karen Macours, Plamen Nikolov, Berk Özler, Gloria M. Rubio, and Norbert Schady. We are grateful for comments from our peer reviewers, Barbara Bruns, Arianna Legovini, Dan Levy, and Emmanuel Skoufias, as well as from Bertha Briceno, Gloria M. Rubio, and Jennifer Sturdy. We also gratefully acknowledge the efforts of a talented workshop organizing team, including Paloma Acevedo, Theresa Adobea Bampoe, Febe Mackey, Silvia Paruzzolo, Tatyana Ringland, Adam Ross, Jennifer Sturdy, and Sigrid Vivo.

The original mimeos on which parts of this book are based were written in a workshop held in Beijing, China, in July 2009. We thank all of the individuals who participated in drafting the original transcripts of the workshop, in particular Paloma Acevedo, Carlos Asenjo, Sebastian Bauhoff, Bradley Chen, Changcheng Song, Jane Zhang, and Shufang Zhang. We are also grateful to Kristine Cronin for excellent research assistance, Marco Guzman and Martin Ruegenberg for designing the illustrations, and Cindy A. Fisher, Fiona Mackintosh, and Stuart K. Tucker for editorial support during the production of the book.

We gratefully acknowledge the support for this line of work throughout the World Bank, including support and leadership from Ariel Fiszbein, Arianna Legovini, and Martin Ravallion.

Finally, we would like to thank the participants in workshops held in Mexico City, New Delhi, Cuernavaca, Ankara, Buenos Aires, Paipa, Fortaleza, Sofia, Cairo, Managua, Madrid, Washington, Manila, Pretoria, Tunis, Lima, Amman, Beijing, Sarajevo, Cape Town, San Salvador, Kathmandu, Rio de Janeiro, and Accra. Through their interest, sharp questions, and enthusiasm, we were able to learn step by step what it is that policy makers are looking for in impact evaluations. We hope this book reflects their ideas.

References

Baker, Judy. 2000. *Evaluating the Impact of Development Projects on Poverty. A Handbook for Practitioners*. Washington, DC: World Bank.

Duflo Esther, Rachel Glennerster, and Michael Kremer. 2007. "Using Randomization in Development Economics Research: A Toolkit." CEPR Discussion Paper No. 6059. Center for Economic Policy Research, London, United Kingdom.

Duflo Esther, and Michael Kremer. 2008. "Use of Randomization in the Evaluation of Development Effectiveness." In *Evaluating Development Effectiveness*, vol. 7. Washington, DC: World Bank.

Khandker, Shahidur R., Gayatri B. Koolwal, and Hussain Samad. 2009. *Handbook on Quantitative Methods of Program Evaluation*. Washington, DC: World Bank.

Leeuw, Frans, and Jos Vaessen. 2009. *Impact Evaluations and Development. NONIE Guidance on Impact Evaluation*. Washington DC: NONIE and World Bank.

Ravallion, Martin. 2001. "The Mystery of the Vanishing Benefits: Ms. Speedy Analyst's Introduction to Evaluation." *World Bank Economic Review* 15 (1): 115–40.

———. 2008. "Evaluating Anti-Poverty Programs." In *Handbook of Development Economics*, vol 4., ed. Paul Schultz and John Strauss. Amsterdam: North Holland.

———. 2009. "Evaluation in the Practice of Development." *World Bank Research Observer* 24 (1): 29–53.

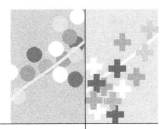

Part 1

INTRODUCTION TO IMPACT EVALUATION

In this first part of the book, we give an overview of what impact evaluation is about. In chapter 1, we discuss why impact evaluation is important and how it fits within the context of evidence-based policy making. We contrast impact evaluation with other common evaluation practices, such as monitoring and process evaluations. Finally, we introduce different modalities of impact evaluation, such as prospective and retrospective evaluation, and efficacy versus efficiency trials.

In chapter 2, we discuss how to formulate evaluation questions and hypotheses that are useful for policy. These questions and hypotheses form the basis of evaluation because they determine what it is that the evaluation will be looking for.

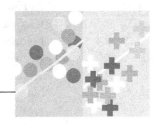

CHAPTER 1

Why Evaluate?

Development programs and policies are typically designed to change outcomes, for example, to raise incomes, to improve learning, or to reduce illness. Whether or not these changes are actually achieved is a crucial public policy question but one that is not often examined. More commonly, program managers and policy makers focus on controlling and measuring the inputs and immediate outputs of a program—how much money is spent, how many textbooks are distributed—rather than on assessing whether programs have achieved their intended goals of improving well-being.

Evidence-Based Policy Making

Impact evaluations are part of a broader agenda of *evidence-based policy making*. This growing global trend is marked by a shift in focus from inputs to outcomes and results. From the Millennium Development Goals to pay-for-performance incentives for public service providers, this global trend is reshaping how public policies are being carried out. Not only is the focus on results being used to set and track national and international targets, but results are increasingly being used by, and required of, program managers to enhance accountability, inform budget allocations, and guide policy decisions.

Monitoring and evaluation are at the heart of evidence-based policy making. They provide a core set of tools that stakeholders can use to verify and improve the quality, efficiency, and effectiveness of interventions at various stages of implementation, or in other words, to focus on results. Stakeholders who use monitoring and evaluation can be found both within governments and outside. Within a government agency or ministry, officials often need to make the case to their superiors that programs work to obtain budget allocations to continue or expand them. At the country level, sectoral ministries compete with one another to obtain funding from the ministry of finance. And finally, governments as a whole have an interest in convincing their constituents that their chosen investments have positive returns. In this sense, information and evidence become means to facilitate public awareness and promote government accountability. The information produced by monitoring and evaluation systems can be regularly shared with constituents to inform them of the performance of government programs and to build a strong foundation for transparency and accountability.

In a context in which policy makers and civil society are demanding results and accountability from public programs, impact evaluation can provide robust and credible evidence on performance and, crucially, on whether a particular program achieved its desired outcomes. At the global level, impact evaluations are also central to building knowledge about the effectiveness of development programs by illuminating what does and does not work to reduce poverty and improve welfare.

Simply put, an impact evaluation assesses the changes in the well-being of individuals that can be *attributed* to a particular project, program, or policy. This focus on attribution is the hallmark of impact evaluations. Correspondingly, the central challenge in carrying out effective impact evaluations is to identify the *causal relationship* between the project, program, or policy and the outcomes of interest.

As we will discuss below, impact evaluations generally estimate *average* impacts of a program on the welfare of beneficiaries. For example, did the introduction of a new curriculum raise test scores among students? Did a water and sanitation program increase access to safe water and improve health outcomes? Was a youth training program effective in fostering entrepreneurship and raising incomes? In addition, if the impact evaluation includes a sufficiently large sample of recipients, the results can also be compared among subgroups of recipients. For example, did the introduction of the new curriculum raise test scores among female and male students? Impact evaluations can also be used to explicitly test alternative program options. For example, an evaluation might compare the performance of a training program versus that of a promotional campaign to raise financial literacy. In each of these cases, the impact evaluation provides information on the *overall* impact of a program, as opposed to specific case studies or anecdotes, which can give only partial information and may not be representative of overall program impacts. In this sense, well-designed and well-implemented evaluations are able to provide convincing and comprehensive evidence that can be used to inform policy decisions and shape public opinion. The summary in box 1.1 illustrates

---

Box 1.1: Evaluations and Political Sustainability
The Progresa/Oportunidades Conditional Cash Transfer Program in Mexico

In the 1990s, the government of Mexico launched an innovative conditional cash transfer (CCT) program called "Progresa." Its objectives were to provide poor households with short-term income support and to create incentives to investments in children's human capital, primarily by providing cash transfers to mothers in poor households conditional on their children regularly attending school and visiting a health center.

From the beginning, the government considered that it was essential to monitor and evaluate the program. The program's officials contracted a group of researchers to design an impact evaluation and build it into the program's expansion at the same time that it was rolled out successively to the participating communities.

The 2000 presidential election led to a change of the party in power. In 2001, Progresa's external evaluators presented their findings to the newly elected administration. The results of the program were impressive: they showed that the program was well targeted to the poor and had engendered promising changes in households' human capital. Schultz (2004) found that the program significantly improved school enroll-

ment, by an average of 0.7 additional years of schooling. Gertler (2004) found that the incidence of illness in children decreased by 23 percent, while adults reported a 19 percent reduction in the number of sick or disability days. Among the nutritional outcomes, Behrman and Hoddinott (2001) found that the program reduced the probability of stunting by about 1 centimeter per year for children in the critical age range of 12 to 36 months.

These evaluation results supported a political dialogue based on evidence and contributed to the new administration's decision to continue the program. For example, the government expanded the program's reach, introducing upper-middle school scholarships and enhanced health programs for adolescents. At the same time, the results were used to modify other social assistance programs, such as the large and less well-targeted tortilla subsidy, which was scaled back.

The successful evaluation of Progresa also contributed to the rapid adoption of CCTs around the world, as well as Mexico's adoption of legislation requiring all social projects to be evaluated.

Sources: Behrman and Hoddinott 2001; Gertler 2004; Fiszbein and Schady 2009; Levy and Rodriguez 2005; Schultz 2004; Skoufias and McClafferty 2001.

how impact evaluation contributed to policy discussions around the expansion of a conditional cash transfer program in Mexico.[1] Box 1.2 illustrates how impact evaluation helped improve the allocations of the Indonesian government resources by documenting which policies were most effective in decreasing fertility rates.

Box 1.2: Evaluating to Improve Resource Allocations
Family Planning and Fertility in Indonesia

In the 1970s, Indonesia's innovative family planning efforts gained international recognition for their success in decreasing the country's fertility rates. The acclaim arose from two parallel phenomena: (1) fertility rates declined by 22 percent between 1970 and 1980, by 25 percent between 1981 and 1990, and a bit more moderately between 1991 and 1994; and (2) during the same period, the Indonesian government substantially increased resources allocated to family planning (particularly contraceptive subsidies). Given that the two things happened contemporaneously, many concluded that it was the increased investment in family planning that had led to lower fertility.

Unconvinced by the available evidence, a team of researchers tested whether family planning programs indeed lowered fertility rates. They found, contrary to what was generally believed, that family planning programs only had a moderate impact on fertility, and they argued that instead it was a change in women's status that was responsible for the decline in fertility rates. The researchers noted that before the start of the family planning program very few women of reproductive age had finished primary education. During the same period as the family planning program, however, the government undertook a large-scale education program for girls, so that by the end of the program, women entering reproductive age had benefited from that additional education. When the oil boom brought economic expansion and increased demand for labor in Indonesia, educated women's participation in the labor force increased significantly. As the value of women's time at work rose, so did the use of contraceptives. In the end, higher wages and empowerment explained 70 percent of the observed decline in fertility—more than the investment in family planning programs.

These evaluation results informed policy makers' subsequent resource allocation decisions: funding was reprogrammed away from contraception subsidies and toward programs that increased women's school enrollment. Although the ultimate goals of the two types of programs were similar, evaluation studies had shown that in the Indonesian context, lower fertility rates could be obtained more efficiently by investing in education than by investing in family planning.

Sources: Gertler and Molyneaux 1994, 2000.

What Is Impact Evaluation?

Impact evaluation figures among a broad range of complementary methods that support evidence-based policy. Although this book focuses on quantitative impact evaluation methods, we will start by placing them in the broader results context, which also includes monitoring and other types of evaluation.

Monitoring is a continuous process that tracks what is happening within a program and uses the data collected to inform program implementation and day-to-day management and decisions. Using mostly administrative data, monitoring tracks program performance against expected results, makes comparisons across programs, and analyzes trends over time. Usually, monitoring tracks inputs, activities, and outputs, though occasionally it can include outcomes, such as progress toward national development goals.

Evaluations are periodic, objective assessments of a planned, ongoing, or completed project, program, or policy. Evaluations are used to answer specific questions related to design, implementation, and results. In contrast to continuous monitoring, they are carried out at discrete points in time and often seek an outside perspective from technical experts. Their design, method, and cost vary substantially depending on the type of question the evaluation is trying to answer. Broadly speaking, evaluations can address three types of questions (Imas and Rist 2009):

- *Descriptive questions*. The evaluation seeks to determine what is taking place and describes processes, conditions, organizational relationships, and stakeholder views.

- *Normative questions*. The evaluation compares what is taking place to what should be taking place; it assesses activities and whether or not targets are accomplished. Normative questions can apply to inputs, activities, and outputs.

- *Cause-and-effect questions*. The evaluation examines outcomes and tries to assess what difference the intervention makes in outcomes.

Impact evaluations are a particular type of evaluation that seeks to answer cause-and-effect questions. Unlike general evaluations, which can answer many types of questions, impact evaluations are structured around one particular type of question: *What is the impact (or causal effect) of a program on an outcome of interest?* This basic question incorporates an important causal dimension: we are interested only in the *impact* of the program, that is, the effect on outcomes that the program directly causes. An impact evaluation looks for the changes in outcome that are *directly attributable to the program*.

The focus on causality and attribution is the hallmark of impact evaluations and determines the methodologies that can be used. To be able to estimate the causal effect or impact of a program on outcomes, any method chosen must estimate the so-called counterfactual, that is, what the outcome would have been for program participants if they had not participated in the program. In practice, impact evaluation requires that the evaluator find a comparison group to estimate what would have happened to the program participants without the program. Part 2 of the book describes the main methods that can be used to find adequate comparison groups.

The basic evaluation question—*What is the impact or causal effect of a program on an outcome of interest?*—can be applied to many contexts. For instance, what is the causal effect of scholarships on school attendance and academic achievement? What is the impact on access to health care of contracting out primary care to private providers? If dirt floors are replaced with cement floors, what will be the impact on children's health? Do improved roads increase access to labor markets and raise households' income, and if so, by how much? Does class size influence student achievement, and if it does, by how much? Are mail campaigns or training sessions more effective in increasing the use of bed nets in malarial areas?

Impact Evaluation for Policy Decisions

Impact evaluations are needed to inform policy makers on a range of decisions, from curtailing inefficient programs, to scaling up interventions that work, to adjusting program benefits, to selecting among various program alternatives. They are most effective when applied selectively to answer important policy questions, and they can be particularly effective when applied to innovative pilot programs that are testing a new, unproven, but promising approach. The Mexican Progresa/Oportunidades evaluation described in box 1.1 became so influential not only because of the innovative nature of the program, but also because its impact evaluation provided credible and strong evidence that could not be ignored in subsequent policy decisions. The program's adoption and expansion were strongly influenced by the evaluation results. Today, the Oportunidades program reaches close to one out of four Mexicans and is a centerpiece of Mexico's strategy to combat poverty.

Impact evaluations can be used to explore different types of policy questions. The basic form of impact evaluation will test the effectiveness of a given program. In other words, it will answer the question, *Is a given program effective compared to the absence of the program?* As presented in part 2, this type of impact evaluation relies on comparing a treatment group that received a project, program, or policy to a comparison group that did not in order to estimate the effectiveness of the program.

Beyond answering this basic evaluation question, evaluations can also be used to test the effectiveness of program implementation alternatives, that is, to answer the question, *When a program can be implemented in several ways, which one is the most effective?* In this type of evaluation, two or more approaches within a program can be compared with one another to generate evidence on which is the best alternative for reaching a particular goal. These program alternatives are often referred to as "treatment arms." For example, when the quantity of benefits a program should provide to be effective is unclear (20 hours of training or 80 hours?), impact evaluations can test the relative impact of the varying intensities of treatment (see box 1.3 for an example). Impact evaluations testing alternative program treatments normally include one treatment group for each of the treatment arms, as well as a "pure" comparison group that does not receive any program intervention. Impact evaluations can also be used to test innovations or implementation alternatives within a program. For example, a program may wish to test alternative outreach campaigns and select one group to receive a mailing campaign, while others received house-to-house visits, to assess which is most effective.

Box 1.3: Evaluating to Improve Program Design
Malnourishment and Cognitive Development in Colombia

In the early 1970s, the Human Ecology Research Station, in collaboration with the Colombian ministry of education, implemented a pilot program to address childhood malnutrition in Cali, Colombia, by providing health care and educational activities, as well as food and nutritional supplements. As part of the pilot, a team of evaluators was tasked to determine (1) how long such a program should last to reduce malnutrition among preschool children from low-income families and (2) whether the interventions could also lead to improvements in cognitive development.

The program was eventually made available to all eligible families, but during the pilot, the evaluators were able to compare similar groups of children who received different treatment durations. The evaluators first used a screening process to identify a target group of 333 malnourished children. These children were then classified into 20 sectors by neighborhood, and each sector was randomly assigned to one of four treatment groups. The groups differed only in the sequence in which they started the treatment and, hence, in the amount of time that they spent in the program. Group 4 started the earliest and was exposed to the treatment for the longest period, followed by groups 3, 2, and then 1. The treatment itself consisted of 6 hours of health care and

(continued)

Box 1.3 *continued*

educational activities per day, plus additional food and nutritional supplements. At regular intervals over the course of the program, the evaluators used cognitive tests to track the progress of children in all four groups.

The evaluators found that the children who were in the program for the longest time demonstrated the greatest gains in cognitive improvement. On the Stanford-Binet intelligence test, which estimates mental age minus chronological age, group 4 children averaged −5 months, and group 1 children averaged −15 months.

This example illustrates how program implementers and policy makers are able to use evaluations of multiple treatment arms to determine the most effective program alternative.

Source: McKay et al. 1978.

Deciding Whether to Evaluate

Not all programs warrant an impact evaluation. Impact evaluations can be costly, and your evaluation budget should be used strategically. If you are starting, or thinking about expanding, a new program and wondering whether to go ahead with an impact evaluation, asking a few basic questions will help with the decision.

The first question to ask would be, *What are the stakes of this program?* The answer to that question will depend on both the budget that is involved and the number of people who are, or will eventually be, affected by the program. Hence, the next questions, *Does, or will, the program require a large portion of the available budget?* and, *Does, or will, the program affect a large number of people?* If the program does not require a budget or only affects a few people, it may not be worth evaluating. For example, for a program that provides counseling to hospital patients using volunteers, the budget involved and number of people affected may not justify an impact evaluation. By contrast, a pay reform for teachers that will eventually affect all primary teachers in the country would be a program with much higher stakes.

If you determine that the stakes are high, then the next question is whether any evidence exists to show that the program works. In particular, do you know how big the program's impact would be? Is the available evidence from a similar country with similar circumstances? If no evidence is available about the potential of the type of program being contemplated, you may want to start out with a pilot that incorporates an impact evaluation. By contrast, if evidence is available from similar circumstances, the cost of an impact evaluation will probably be justified only if it can address an important and new policy question. That would be the case if your program includes some important innovations that have not yet been tested.

To justify mobilizing the technical and financial resources needed to carry out a high-quality impact evaluation, the program to be evaluated should be

- *Innovative*. It is testing a new, promising approach.

- *Replicable*. The program can be scaled up or can be applied in a different setting.

- *Strategically relevant*. The program is a flagship initiative; requires substantial resources; covers, or could be expanded to cover, a large number of people; or could generate substantial savings.

- *Untested*. Little is known about the effectiveness of the program, globally or in a particular context.

- *Influential*. The results will be used to inform key policy decisions.

Cost-Effectiveness Analysis

Once impact evaluation results are available, they can be combined with information on program costs to answer two additional questions. First, for the basic form of impact evaluation, adding cost information will allow us to perform a cost-benefit analysis, which will answer the question, *What is the cost-benefit balance for a given program?* Cost-benefit analysis estimates the total expected benefits of a program, compared to its total expected costs. It seeks to quantify all of the costs and benefits of a program in monetary terms and assesses whether benefits outweigh costs.

In an ideal world, cost-benefit analysis based on impact evaluation evidence would exist not only for a particular program, but also for a series of programs or program alternatives, so that policy makers could assess which program or alternative is most cost-effective in reaching a particular goal. When an impact evaluation is testing program alternatives, adding cost information allows us to answer the second question, *How do various program implementation alternatives compare in cost-effectiveness?* This cost-effectiveness analysis compares the relative performance of two or more programs or program alternatives in reaching a common outcome.

In a cost-benefit or cost-effectiveness analysis, impact evaluation estimates the benefit and effectiveness side, and cost analysis provides the cost information. This book focuses on impact evaluation and does not

Key Concept:
Cost-benefit analysis estimates the total expected benefits of a program, compared to its total expected costs.

Key Concept:
Cost-effectiveness analysis compares the relative performance of two or more programs or program alternatives in reaching a common outcome.

discuss in detail how to collect cost data or conduct cost-benefit analysis.[2] However, it is critically important that impact evaluation be complemented with information on the cost of the project, program, or policy being evaluated. Once impact and cost information is available for a variety of programs, cost-effectiveness analysis can identify which investments yield the highest rate of return and allow policy makers to make informed decisions on which intervention to invest in. Box 1.4 illustrates how impact evaluations can be used to identify the most cost-effective programs and improve resource allocation.

Box 1.4: Evaluating Cost-Effectiveness
Comparing Strategies to Increase School Attendance in Kenya

By evaluating a number of programs in a similar setting, it is possible to compare the relative cost-effectiveness of different approaches to improving outcomes such as school attendance. In Kenya, the nongovernmental organization International Child Support Africa (ICS Africa) implemented a series of education interventions that included treatment against intestinal worms, provision of free school uniforms, and provision of school meals. Each of the interventions was subjected to a randomized evaluation and cost-benefit analysis, and comparison among them provides interesting insights on how to increase school attendance.

A program that provided medication against intestinal worms to schoolchildren increased attendance by approximately 0.14 years per treated child, at an estimated cost of $0.49 per child. This amounts to about $3.50 per additional year of school participation, including the externalities experienced by children and adults not in the schools but in the communities that benefit from the reduced transmission of worms.

A second intervention, the Child Sponsorship Program, reduced the cost of school attendance by providing school uniforms to pupils in seven randomly selected schools. Dropout rates fell dramatically in treatment schools, and after 5 years the program was estimated to increase years in school by an average of 17 percent. However, even under the most optimistic assumptions, the cost of increasing school attendance using the school uniform program was estimated to be approximately $99 per additional year of school attendance.

Finally, a program that provided free breakfasts to children in 25 randomly selected preschools led to a 30 percent increase in attendance in treatment schools, at an estimated cost of $36 per additional year of schooling. Test scores also increased by about 0.4 standard deviations, provided the teacher was well trained prior to the program.

Although similar interventions may have different target outcomes, such as the health effects of deworming or educational achievement in addition to increased participation, comparing a number of evaluations conducted in the same context can reveal which programs achieved the desired goals at the lowest cost.

Sources: Kremer and Miguel 2004; Kremer, Moulin, and Namunyu 2003; Poverty Action Lab 2005; Vermeersch and Kremer 2005.

Prospective versus Retrospective Evaluation

Impact evaluations can be divided into two categories: prospective and retrospective. Prospective evaluations are developed at the same time as the program is being designed and are built into program implementation. Baseline data are collected prior to program implementation for both treatment and comparison groups. Retrospective evaluations assess program impact after the program has been implemented, generating treatment and comparison groups ex-post.

In general, prospective impact evaluations are more likely to produce strong and credible evaluation results, for three reasons.

First, baseline data can be collected to establish preprogram measures of outcomes of interest. Baseline data provide information on beneficiaries and comparison groups before the program is implemented and are important for measuring preintervention outcomes. Baseline data on the treatment and comparison groups should be analyzed to ensure that the groups are similar. Baselines can also be used to assess targeting effectiveness, that is, whether or not the program is going to reach its intended beneficiaries.

Key Concept:
Prospective evaluations are developed when the program is designed and are built into program implementation.

Second, defining measures of a program's success in the program's planning stage focuses the evaluation and the program on intended results. As we shall see, impact evaluations take root in a program's theory of change or results chain. The design of an impact evaluation helps to clarify program objectives, in particular because it requires establishing well-defined measures of a program's success. Policy makers should set clear goals and questions for the evaluation to ensure that the results will be highly policy relevant. Indeed, the full support of policy makers is a prerequisite for carrying out a successful evaluation; impact evaluations should not be undertaken unless policy makers are convinced of the legitimacy of the evaluation and its value for informing important policy decisions.

Third and most important, in a prospective evaluation, the treatment and comparison groups are identified before the program is implemented. As we will explain in more depth in the chapters that follow, many more options exist for carrying out valid evaluations when the evaluations are planned from the outset and informed by a project's implementation. We argue in parts 2 and 3 that a valid estimate of the counterfactual can almost always be found for any program with clear and transparent assignment rules, provided that the evaluation is designed prospectively. In short, prospective evaluations have the best chance to generate valid counterfactuals. At the design stage, alternative ways to estimate a valid counterfactual can be considered. The impact evaluation design can also be fully aligned to program operating rules, as well as to the program's rollout or expansion path.

By contrast, in retrospective evaluations, the evaluator often has such limited information that it is difficult to analyze whether the program was successfully implemented and whether its participants really benefited from it. Partly, the reason is that many programs do not collect baseline data unless the evaluation was built in from the beginning, and once the program is in place, it is too late to do so.

Retrospective evaluations using existing data are necessary to assess programs that were assigned in the past. Generally, options to obtain a valid estimate of the counterfactual are much more limited in those situations. The evaluation is dependent on clear rules of program operation regarding the assignment of benefits. It is also dependent on the availability of data with sufficient coverage of the treatment and comparison groups both before and after program implementation. As a result, the feasibility of a retrospective evaluation depends on the context and is never guaranteed. Even when feasible, retrospective evaluations often use quasi-experimental methods and rely on stronger assumptions; they thus can produce evidence that is more debatable.

Efficacy Studies and Effectiveness Studies

The main role of impact evaluation is to produce evidence on program effectiveness for the use of government officials, program managers, civil society, and other stakeholders. Impact evaluation results are particularly useful when the conclusions can be applied to the broader population of interest. The question of generalizability (known as "external validity" in the research methods literature) is key for policy makers, for it determines whether the results identified in the evaluation can be replicated for groups beyond those studied in the evaluation if the program is scaled up.

In the early days of impact evaluations of development programs, a large share of evidence was based on *efficacy studies* carried out under very specific circumstances; unfortunately, the results of those studies were often not generalizable beyond the scope of the evaluation. Efficacy studies are typically carried out in a very specific setting, with heavy technical involvement from researchers during the implementation of the program. Such efficacy studies are often undertaken for proof of concept, to test the viability of a new program. If the program does not generate anticipated impacts under these often carefully managed conditions, it is unlikely to work if rolled out under normal circumstances. Because efficacy studies are often carried out as pilots under closely managed conditions, the impacts of these often small-scale efficacy pilots may not necessarily be informative about the impact of a similar project implemented on a larger scale under normal circumstances. For instance, a pilot intervention introducing new treatment protocols may work in a hospital with excellent managers and medical staff, but the same intervention may not work in an average hospital with less-attentive managers and limited staff. In addition, cost-benefit computations will vary, as fixed costs and economies of scale may not be captured in small efficacy studies. As a result, whereas evidence from efficacy studies can be useful to test an approach, the results often have limited external validity and do not always adequately represent more general settings, which are usually the prime concern of policy makers.

By contrast, *effectiveness studies* provide evidence from interventions that take place in normal circumstances, using regular implementation channels. When effectiveness evaluations are properly designed and implemented, the results obtained will hold true not only for the evaluation sample, but also for other intended beneficiaries outside the sample. This external validity is of critical importance to policy makers because it allows them to use the results of the evaluation to inform programwide decisions that apply to intended beneficiaries beyond the evaluation sample.

Combining Sources of Information to Assess Both the "What" and the "Why"

Impact evaluations conducted in isolation from other sources of information are vulnerable both technically and in terms of their potential effectiveness. Without information on the nature and content of the program to contextualize evaluation results, policy makers are left puzzled about why certain results were or were not achieved. Whereas impact evaluations can produce reliable estimates of the causal effects of a program, they are not typically designed to provide insights into program implementation. Moreover, impact evaluations must be well aligned with a program's implementation and therefore need to be guided by information on how, when, and where the program under evaluation is being implemented.

Qualitative data, monitoring data, and process evaluations are needed to track program implementation and to examine questions of process that are critical to informing and interpreting the results from impact evaluations. In this sense, impact evaluations and other forms of evaluation are complements for one another rather than substitutes.

For example, a provincial government may decide to announce that it will pay bonuses to rural health clinics if they raise the percentage of births in the clinic attended by a health professional. If the evaluation finds that no changes occur in the percentage of births attended in the clinic, many possible explanations and corresponding needs for action may exist. First, it may be that staff in the rural clinics do not have sufficient information on the bonuses or that they do not understand the rules of the program. In that case, the provincial government may need to step up its information and education campaign to the health centers. Alternatively, if lack of equipment or electricity shortages prevent the health clinics from admitting more patients, it may be necessary to improve the support system and improve power supply. Finally, pregnant women in rural areas may not want to use clinics; they may prefer traditional birth attendants and home births for cultural reasons. In that case, it may be more efficient to tackle women's barriers to access than to give bonuses to the clinics. Thus, a good impact evaluation will allow the government to determine whether or not the rate of attended births changed as a result of the bonus program, but complementary evaluation approaches are necessary to understand whether the program was carried out as planned and where the missing links are. In this example, evaluators would want to complement their impact analysis by interviewing health clinic staff regarding their knowledge of the program, reviewing the availability of equipment in the clinics, conducting focus group discussions with pregnant women to understand their preferences and barriers to access, and examining any available data on access to health clinics in rural areas.

Using Qualitative Data

Qualitative data are a key supplement to quantitative impact evaluations because they can provide complementary perspectives on a program's performance. Evaluations that integrate qualitative and quantitative analysis are characterized as using "mixed methods" (Bamberger, Rao, and Woolcock 2010). Qualitative approaches include focus groups and interviews with selected beneficiaries and other key informants (Rao and Woolcock 2003). Although the views and opinions gathered during interviews and focus groups may not be representative of the program's beneficiaries, they are particularly useful during the three stages of an impact evaluation:

1. When designing an impact evaluation, evaluators can use focus groups and interviews with key informants to develop hypotheses as to how

and why the program would work and to clarify research questions that need to be addressed in the quantitative impact evaluation work.

2. In the intermediate stage, before quantitative impact evaluation results become available, qualitative work can help provide policy makers quick insights into what is happening in the program.

3. In the analysis stage, evaluators can apply qualitative methods to provide context and explanations for the quantitative results, to explore "outlier" cases of success and failure, and to develop systematic explanations of the program's performance as it was found in the quantitative results. In that sense, qualitative work can help explain why certain results are observed in the quantitative analysis, and it can be used to get inside the "black box" of what happened in the program (Bamberger, Rao, and Woolcock 2010).

Using Monitoring Data and Process Evaluations

Monitoring data are also a critical resource in an impact evaluation. They let the evaluator verify which participants received the program, how fast the program is expanding, how resources are being spent, and overall whether activities are being implemented as planned. This information is critical to implementing the evaluation, for example, to ensure that baseline data are collected before the program is introduced and to verify the integrity of the treatment and comparison groups. In addition, the monitoring system can provide information on the cost of implementing the program, which is also needed for cost-benefit analysis.

Finally, *process evaluations* focus on how a program is implemented and operates, assessing whether it conforms to its original design and documenting its development and operation. Process evaluations can usually be carried out relatively quickly and at a reasonable cost. In pilots and in the initial stages of a program, they can be a valuable source of information on how to improve program implementation.

Notes

1. See Fiszbein and Schady (2009) for an overview of CCT programs and the influential role played by Progresa/Oportunidades because of its impact evaluation

2. For a detailed discussion of cost-benefit analysis, see Belli et al. 2001; Boardman et al. 2001; Brent 1996; or Zerbe and Dively 1994.

References

Bamberger, Michael, Vijayendra Rao, and Michael Woolcock. 2010. "Using Mixed Methods in Monitoring and Evaluation: Experiences from International Development." Policy Research Working Paper 5245. World Bank, Washington, DC.

Behrman, Jere R., and John Hoddinott. 2001. "An Evaluation of the Impact of PROGRESA on Pre-school Child Height." FCND Briefs 104, International Food Policy Research Institute, Washington, DC.

Belli, Pedro, Jock Anderson, Howard Barnum, John Dixon, and Jee-Peng Tan. 2001. *Handbook of Economic Analysis of Investment Operations*. Washington, DC: World Bank.

Boardman, Anthony, Aidan Vining, David Greenberg, and David Weimer. 2001. *Cost-Benefit Analysis: Concepts and Practice*. New Jersey: Prentice Hall.

Brent, Robert. 1996. *Applied Cost-Benefit Analysis*. England: Edward Elgar.

Fiszbein, Ariel, and Norbert Schady. 2009. *Conditional Cash Transfer, Reducing Present and Future Poverty*. World Bank Policy Research Report. World Bank, Washington, DC.

Gertler, Paul J. 2004. "Do Conditional Cash Transfers Improve Child Health? Evidence from PROGRESA's Control Randomized Experiment." *American Economic Review* 94 (2): 336–41.

Gertler, Paul J., and John W. Molyneaux. 1994. "How Economic Development and Family Planning Programs Combined to Reduce Indonesian Fertility." *Demography* 31 (1): 33–63.

———. 2000. "The Impact of Targeted Family Planning Programs in Indonesia." *Population and Development Review* 26: 61–85.

Imas, Linda G. M., and Ray C. Rist. 2009. *The Road to Results: Designing and Conducting Effective Development Evaluations*. Washington, DC: World Bank.

Kremer, Michael, and Edward Miguel. 2004. "Worms: Identifying Impacts on Education and Health in the Presence of Treatment Externalities." *Econometrica* 72 (1): 159–217.

Kremer, Michael, Sylvie Moulin, and Robert Namunyu. 2003. "Decentralization: A Cautionary Tale." Poverty Action Lab Paper 10, Massachusetts Institute of Technology, Cambridge, MA.

Levy, Santiago, and Evelyne Rodríguez. 2005. *Sin Herencia de Pobreza: El Programa Progresa-Oportunidades de México*. Washington, DC: Inter-American Development Bank.

McKay, Harrison, Arlene McKay, Leonardo Siniestra, Hernando Gomez, and Pascuala Lloreda. 1978. "Improving Cognitive Ability in Chronically Deprived Children." *Science* 200 (21): 270–78.

Poverty Action Lab. 2005. "Primary Education for All." *Fighting Poverty: What Works?* 1 (Fall): n.p. http://www.povertyactionlab.org.

Rao, Vijayendra, and Michael Woolcock. 2003. "Integrating Qualitative and Quantitative Approaches in Program Evaluation." In *The Impact of Economic Policies on Poverty and Income Distribution: Evaluation Techniques and Tools,* ed. F. J. Bourguignon and L. Pereira da Silva, 165–90. New York: Oxford University Press.

Schultz, Paul. 2004. "School Subsidies for the Poor: Evaluating the Mexican Progresa Poverty Program." *Journal of Development Economics* 74 (1): 199–250.

Skoufias, Emmanuel, and Bonnie McClafferty. 2001. "Is *Progresa* Working? Summary of the Results of an Evaluation by IFPRI." International Food Policy Research Institute, Washington, DC.

Vermeersch, Christel, and Michael Kremer. 2005. "School Meals, Educational Achievement and School Competition: Evidence from a Randomized Evaluation." Policy Research Working Paper 3523, World Bank, Washington, DC.

Zerbe, Richard, and Dwight Dively. 1994. *Benefit Cost Analysis in Theory and Practice*. New York: Harper Collins Publishing.

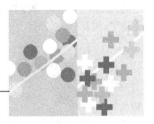

CHAPTER 2

Determining Evaluation Questions

This chapter outlines the initial steps in setting up an evaluation. The steps include establishing the type of question to be answered by the evaluation, constructing a theory of change that outlines how the project is supposed to achieve the intended results, developing a results chain, formulating hypotheses to be tested by the evaluation, and selecting performance indicators.

All of these steps contribute to determining an evaluation question and are best taken at the outset of the program, engaging a range of stakeholders from policy makers to program managers, to forge a common vision of the program's goals and how they will be achieved. This engagement builds consensus regarding the main questions to be answered and will strengthen links between the evaluation, program implementation, and policy. Applying the steps lends clarity and specificity that are useful both for developing a good impact evaluation and for designing and implementing an effective program. Each step—from the clear specification of goals and questions, to the articulation of ideas embodied in the theory of change, to the outcomes the program hopes to provide—is clearly defined and articulated within the logic model embodied in the results chain.

Types of Evaluation Questions

Any evaluation begins with the formulation of a study question that focuses the research and that is tailored to the policy interest at hand. The evaluation then consists of generating credible evidence to answer that question. As we will explain below, the basic impact evaluation question can be formulated as, *What is the impact or causal effect of the program on an outcome of interest?* In an example that we will apply throughout part 2, the study question is, *What is the effect of the Health Insurance Subsidy Program on households' out-of-pocket health expenditures?* The question can also be oriented toward testing options, such as, *Which combination of mail campaigns and family counseling works best to encourage exclusive breast feeding?* A clear evaluation question is the starting point of any effective evaluation.

Theories of Change

A theory of change is a description of how an intervention is supposed to deliver the desired results. It describes the causal logic of how and why a particular project, program, or policy will reach its intended outcomes. A theory of change is a key underpinning of any impact evaluation, given the cause-and-effect focus of the research. As one of the first steps in the evaluation design, a theory of change can help specify the research questions.

Theories of change depict a sequence of events leading to outcomes; they explore the conditions and assumptions needed for the change to take place, make explicit the causal logic behind the program, and map the program interventions along logical causal pathways. Working with the program's stakeholders to put together a theory of change can clarify and improve program design. This is especially important in programs that seek to influence behavior: theories of change can help disentangle the inputs and activities that go into providing the program interventions, the outputs that are delivered, and the outcomes that stem from expected behavioral changes among beneficiaries.

The best time to develop a theory of change for a program is at the beginning of the design process, when stakeholders can be brought together to develop a common vision for the program, its goals, and the path to achieving those goals. Stakeholders can then start program implementation from a common understanding of the program, how it works, and its objectives.

In addition, program designers should review the literature for accounts of experience with similar programs, and they should verify the contexts and assumptions behind the causal pathways in the theory of change they are outlining. In the case of the cement floors project in Mexico described in box 2.1, for example, the literature would provide valuable information on how parasites are transmitted and how parasite infestation leads to childhood diarrhea.

Box 2.1: Theory of Change
From Cement Floors to Happiness in Mexico

In their evaluation of the Piso Firme or "firm floor" project, Cattaneo et al. (2009) examined the impact of housing improvement on health and welfare. Both the project and the evaluation were motivated by a clear theory of change.

The objective of the Piso Firme project is to improve the living standards, especially the health, of vulnerable groups living in densely populated, low-income areas of Mexico. The program was first started in the northern State of Coahuila and was based on a situational assessment conducted by Governor Enrique Martínez y Martínez's campaign team.

The program's results chain is clear. Eligible neighborhoods are surveyed door-to-door, and households are offered up to 50 square meters of cement. The government purchases and delivers the cement, and the households and community volunteers supply the labor to install the floor. The output is the construction of a cement floor, which can be completed in about a day. The expected outcomes of the improved home environment include cleanliness, health, and happiness.

The rationale for this results chain is that dirt floors are a vector for parasites because they are harder to keep clean. Parasites live and breed in feces and can be ingested by humans when they are tracked into the home by animals or children or on shoes. Evidence shows that young children who live in houses with dirt floors are more likely to be infected with intestinal parasites, which can cause diarrhea and malnutrition, often leading to impaired cognitive development or even death. Cement floors interrupt the transmission of parasitic infestations. They also allow better temperature control and are more aesthetically pleasing.

Those expected outcomes informed the research questions addressed in the evaluation by Cattaneo and his colleagues. They hypothesized that replacing dirt floors with cement floors would reduce the incidence of diarrhea, malnutrition, and micronutrient deficiency. Doing that should in turn result in improved cognitive development in young children. The researchers also anticipated and tested for improvements in adult welfare, as measured by people's increased satisfaction with their housing situation and lower rates of depression and perceived stress.

Source: Catteneo et al. 2009.

The Results Chain

A theory of change can be modeled in various ways, for example using theoretical models, logic models, logical frameworks and outcome models, and results chains.[1] All of these include the basic elements of a theory of change, that is, a causal chain, outside conditions and influences, and key assumptions. In this book, we will use the results chain model because we find that it is the simplest and clearest model to outline the theory of change in the operational context of development programs.

Key Concept:

A results chain sets out the sequence of inputs, activities, and outputs that are expected to improve outcomes and final outcomes.

A results chain sets out a logical, plausible outline of how a sequence of inputs, activities, and outputs for which a project is directly responsible interacts with behavior to establish pathways through which impacts are achieved (figure 2.1). It establishes the causal logic from the initiation of the project, beginning with resources available, to the end, looking at long-term goals. A basic results chain will map the following elements:

Inputs: Resources at the disposal of the project, including staff and budget

Activities: Actions taken or work performed to convert inputs into outputs

Outputs: The tangible goods and services that the project activities produce (They are directly under the control of the implementing agency.)

Outcomes: Results likely to be achieved once the beneficiary population uses the project outputs (They are usually achieved in the short-to-medium term.)

Final outcomes: The final project goals (They can be influenced by multiple factors and are typically achieved over a longer period of time.)

The results chain has three main parts:

Implementation: Planned work delivered by the project, including inputs, activities, and outputs. These are the areas that the implementation agency can directly monitor to measure the project's performance.

Results: Intended results consist of the outcomes and final outcomes, which are not under the direct control of the project and are contingent on behavioral changes by program beneficiaries. In other words, they depend on the interactions between the supply side (implementation) and the demand side (beneficiaries). These are the areas subject to impact evaluation to measure effectiveness.

Figure 2.1 What Is a Results Chain?

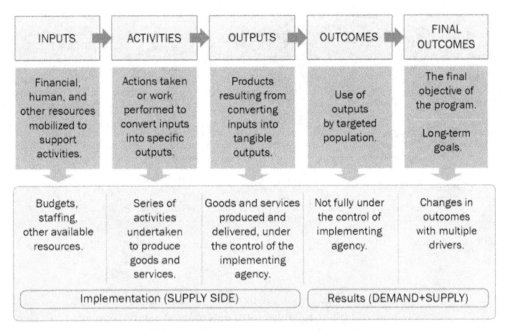

Source: Authors, drawing from multiple sources.

Assumptions and risks: These are not depicted in figure 2.1. They include any evidence from the literature on the proposed causal logic and the assumptions on which it relies, references to similar programs' performance, and a mention of risks that may affect the realization of intended results and any mitigation strategy put in place to manage those risks.

For example, imagine that the ministry of education of country A is thinking of introducing a new approach to teaching mathematics in high school. As shown in figure 2.2, the inputs to the program would include staff from the ministry, high school teachers, a budget for the new math program, and the municipal facilities where the math teachers will be trained. The program's activities consist of designing the new mathematics curriculum; developing a teacher training program; training the teachers; and commissioning, printing, and distributing new textbooks. The outputs are the number of teachers trained, the number of textbooks delivered to classrooms, and the adaptation of standardized tests to the new curriculum. The short-term outcomes consist of teachers' use of the

Figure 2.2 Results Chain for a High School Mathematics Program

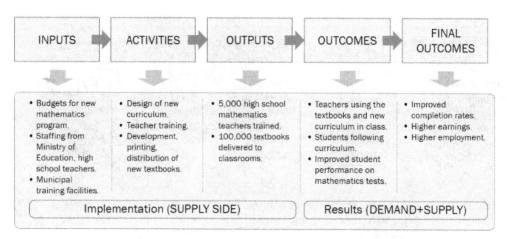

INPUTS	ACTIVITIES	OUTPUTS	OUTCOMES	FINAL OUTCOMES
• Budgets for new mathematics program. • Staffing from Ministry of Education, high school teachers. • Municipal training facilities.	• Design of new curriculum. • Teacher training. • Development, printing, distribution of new textbooks.	• 5,000 high school mathematics teachers trained. • 100,000 textbooks delivered to classrooms.	• Teachers using the textbooks and new curriculum in class. • Students following curriculum. • Improved student performance on mathematics tests.	• Improved completion rates. • Higher earnings. • Higher employment.

Implementation (SUPPLY SIDE)   Results (DEMAND+SUPPLY)

Source: Authors, drawing from multiple sources.

new methods and textbooks in their classrooms and their application of the new tests. The medium-term outcomes are improvements in student performance on the standardized mathematics tests. Final outcomes are increased high school completion rates and higher employment rates and earnings for graduates.

Results chains are useful for all projects, regardless of whether or not they will include an impact evaluation, because they allow policy makers and program managers to make program goals explicit, thus helping them to understand the causal logic and sequence of events behind a program. Results chains also facilitate discussions around monitoring and evaluation by making evident what information needs to be monitored and what outcome changes need to be included when the project is evaluated.

To compare alternative program approaches, results chains can be aggregated into results trees that represent all the viable options considered during program design or program restructuring. These results trees represent policy and operational alternatives for reaching specific objectives; they can be used in thinking through which program options could be tested and evaluated. For example, if the goal is to improve financial literacy, one may investigate options such as an advertising campaign versus classroom instruction for adults.

Hypotheses for the Evaluation

Once you have outlined the results chain, you can formulate the hypotheses that you would like to test using the impact evaluation. In the high school mathematics example, the hypotheses to be tested could be the following:

- The new curriculum is superior to the old one in imparting knowledge of mathematics.

- Trained teachers use the new curriculum in a more effective way than other teachers.

- If we train the teachers and distribute the textbooks, then the teachers will use the new textbooks and curriculum in class, and the students will follow the curriculum.

- If we train the teachers and distribute the textbooks, then the math test results will improve by 5 points on average.

- Performance in high school mathematics influences completion rates and labor market performance.

Selecting Performance Indicators

A clearly articulated results chain provides a useful map for selecting the indicators that will be measured along the chain. They will include indicators used both to monitor program implementation and to evaluate results. Again, it is useful to engage program stakeholders in selecting these indicators, to ensure that the ones selected are good measures of program performance. The acronym *SMART* is a widely used and useful rule of thumb to ensure that indicators used are

- *Specific:* to measure the information required as closely as possible

- *Measurable:* to ensure that the information can be readily obtained

- *Attributable:* to ensure that each measure is linked to the project's efforts

- *Realistic:* to ensure that the data can be obtained in a timely fashion, with reasonable frequency, and at reasonable cost

- *Targeted:* to the objective population.

When choosing indicators, remember that it is important to identify indicators all along the results chain, and not just at the level of outcomes, so that you will be able to track the causal logic of any program outcomes that are observed. Even when you implement an impact evaluation, it is still important to track implementation indicators, so you can determine whether interventions have been carried out as planned, whether they have reached their intended beneficiaries, and whether they arrived on time (see Kusek and Rist 2004 or Imas and Rist 2009 for discussion of how to select performance indicators). Without these indicators all along the results chain, the impact evaluation will produce only a "black box" that identifies whether or not the predicted results materialized; it will not be able to explain why that was the case.

Apart from selecting the indicators, it is also useful to consider the arrangements for producing the data. Table 2.1 lists the basic elements of a monitoring and evaluation (M&E) plan, covering the arrangements needed to produce each of the indicators reliably and on time.

Table 2.1 Elements of a Monitoring and Evaluation Plan

Element	Description
Expected results (outcomes and outputs)	Obtained from program design documents and results chain.
Indicators (with baselines and indicative targets)	Derived from results chain; indicators should be SMART.
Data source	Source and location from which data are to be obtained, e.g., a survey, a review, a stakeholder meeting.
Data frequency	Frequency of data availability.
Responsibilities	Who is responsible for organizing the data collection and verifying data quality and source?
Analysis and reporting	Frequency of analysis, analysis method, and responsibility for reporting.
Resources	Estimate of resources required and committed for carrying out planned M&E activities.
End use	Who will receive and review the information? What purpose does it serve?
Risks	What are the risks and assumptions in carrying out the planned M&E activities? How might they affect the planned M&E events and the quality of the data?

Source: Adapted from UNDP 2009.

Road Map to Parts 2 and 3

In this first part of the book, we discussed why an impact evaluation might be undertaken and when it is worthwhile to do so. We reviewed the various objectives that an impact evaluation can achieve and highlighted the fundamental policy questions that an evaluation can tackle. We insisted on the necessity to trace carefully the theory of change that explains the channels through which a program can influence final outcomes. Impact evaluations essentially test whether that theory of change works or does not work in practice.

In part 2 we consider *how to evaluate*, by reviewing various alternative methodologies that produce valid comparison groups and allow valid program impacts to be estimated. We begin by introducing the *counterfactual* as the crux of any impact evaluation, detailing the properties that the estimate of the counterfactual must have and providing examples of invalid or counterfeit estimates of the counterfactual. We then turn to presenting a menu of impact evaluation options that can produce valid estimates of the counterfactual. In particular, we discuss the basic intuition behind four categories of methodologies: *randomized selection methods, regression discontinuity design, difference-in-differences,* and *matching.* We discuss why and how each method can produce a valid estimate of the counterfactual, in which policy context each can be implemented, and the main limitations of each method. Throughout this part of the book, a case study—the Health Insurance Subsidy Program—is used to illustrate how the methods can be applied. In addition, we present specific examples of impact evaluations that have used each method.

Part 3 outlines the steps to implement, manage, or commission an impact evaluation. We assume at this point that the objectives of the evaluation have been defined, the theory of change formulated, and the evaluation questions specified. We review key questions that need to be answered when formulating an impact evaluation plan. We start by providing clear rules for deciding where comparison groups come from. A simple framework is set out to determine which of the impact evaluation methodologies presented in part 2 is most suitable for a given program, depending on its operational rules. We then review steps in four key phases of implementing an evaluation: putting the evaluation design into operation, choosing a sample, collecting data, and producing and disseminating findings.

Note

1. University of Wisconsin-Extension (2010) contains a detailed discussion on how to build a results chain, as well as a comprehensive list of references. Imas and Rist (2009) provide a good review of theories of change.

References

Cattaneo, Matias, Sebastian Galiani, Paul Gertler, Sebastian Martinez, and Rocio Titiunik. 2009. "Housing, Health and Happiness." *American Economic Journal: Economic Policy* 1 (1): 75–105.

Imas, Linda G. M., and Ray C. Rist. 2009. *The Road to Results: Designing and Conducting Effective Development Evaluations.* Washington, DC: World Bank.

Kusek, Jody Zall, and Ray C. Rist. 2004. *Ten Steps to a Results-Based Monitoring and Evaluation System.* Washington DC: World Bank.

UNDP (United Nations Development Programme). 2009. *Handbook on Planning, Monitoring and Evaluating for Development Results.* New York: UNDP.

University of Wisconsin-Extension. 2010. "Enhancing Program Performance with Logic Models." Online course. http://www.uwex.edu/ces/pdande/evaluation/evallogicmodel.html.

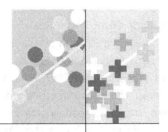

Part 2

HOW TO EVALUATE

Now that we have established the reasons for evaluating the impact of programs and policies, part 2 of this book explains what impact evaluations do, what questions they answer, what methods are available for conducting them, and the advantages and disadvantages of each. The menu of impact evaluation options discussed includes randomized selection methods, regression discontinuity design, difference-in-differences, and matching.

As we discussed in part 1, an impact evaluation seeks to establish and quantify how an intervention affects the outcomes that are of interest to analysts and policy makers. In this part, we will introduce and examine as a case study the "Health Insurance Subsidy Program" (HISP). We will answer the same evaluation question with regard to the HISP several times using the same data sources, but different, and sometimes conflicting, answers will emerge depending on what methodology is used. (The reader should assume that the data have already been properly cleaned to eliminate any data-related problems.) Your task will be to determine why the estimate of the impact of the

HISP changes with each method and which results you consider sufficiently reliable to serve as the basis for important policy recommendations.

The HISP case is an example of a government undertaking a large-scale health sector reform, with the ultimate objective of improving the health of its population. Within that general objective, the reform aims to increase access to, and improve the quality of, health services in rural areas to bring them up to the standards and coverage that prevail in urban areas. The innovative—and potentially costly—HISP is being piloted. The program subsidizes health insurance for poor rural households, covering costs related to primary health care and drugs. The central objective of HISP is to reduce the cost of health care for poor families and, ultimately, to improve health outcomes. Policy makers are considering expanding the HISP to cover the whole country. Scaling up the program would cost hundreds of millions of dollars, but policy makers are concerned that poor rural households are unable to afford basic health care without a subsidy, with detrimental consequences for their health. The key evaluation question is, *What is the effect of HISP on the out-of-pocket health care costs and the health status of poor families?* Answers to questions like this guide policy makers in deciding what policies to adopt and what programs to implement. Those policies and programs in turn can affect the welfare of millions of people around the world. This part of the book will discuss how to answer such critical evaluation questions rigorously.

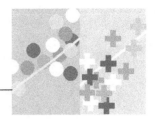

CHAPTER 3

Causal Inference and Counterfactuals

We begin by examining two concepts that are integral to the process of conducting accurate and reliable evaluations—causal inference and counterfactuals.

Causal Inference

The basic impact evaluation question essentially constitutes a *causal inference* problem. Assessing the impact of a program on a series of outcomes is equivalent to assessing the causal effect of the program on those outcomes. Most policy questions involve cause-and-effect relationships: Does teacher training *improve* students' test scores? Do conditional cash transfer programs *cause* better health outcomes in children? Do vocational training programs *increase* trainees' incomes?

Although cause-and-effect questions are common, it is not a straightforward matter to establish that a relationship is causal. In the context of a vocational training program, for example, simply observing that a trainee's income increases after he or she has completed such a program is not sufficient to establish causality. The trainee's income might have increased even if he had not taken the training course because of his own efforts, because of changing labor market conditions, or because of one of the myriad other factors that can affect income. Impact evaluations help us to overcome the challenge of establishing causality by empirically establishing to what extent a particular program—*and that program alone*—contributed to the change in an outcome. To establish causality between a program and an outcome, we use impact evaluation methods to rule out the possibility that any factors other than the program of interest explain the observed impact.

The answer to the basic impact evaluation question—*What is the impact or causal effect of a program P on an outcome of interest Y?*—is given by the basic impact evaluation formula:

$$\alpha = (Y \mid P = 1) - (Y \mid P = 0).$$

This formula says that the causal impact (α) of a program (P) on an outcome (Y) is the difference between the outcome (Y) with the program (in other words, when $P = 1$) and the same outcome (Y) without the program (that is, when $P = 0$).

For example, if P denotes a vocational training program and Y denotes income, then the causal impact of the vocational training program (α) is the difference between a person's income (Y) after participating in the vocational training program (in other words, when $P = 1$) and the same person's income (Y) at the same point in time if he or she had not participated in the program (in other words, when $P = 0$). To put it another way, we would like to measure income at the same point in time for the same unit of observation (a person, in this case), but in two different states of the world. If it were possible to do this, we would be observing how much income the same individual would have had at the same point in time both with and without the program, so that the *only* possible explanation for any difference in that person's income would be the program. By comparing the same individual with herself at the same moment, we would have managed to eliminate any outside factors that might also have explained the difference in outcomes. We could then be confident that the relationship between the vocational training program and income is causal.

The basic impact evaluation formula is valid for anything that is being analyzed—a person, a household, a community, a business, a school, a hospital, or any other unit of observation that may receive or be affected by a program. The formula is also valid for any outcome (Y) that is plausibly related to the program at hand. Once we measure the two key components of this formula—the outcome (Y) both with the program and without it—we can answer any question about the program's impact.

The Counterfactual

As discussed above, we can think of the impact (α) of a program as the difference in outcomes (Y) for the same individual with and without participation in a program. Yet we know that measuring the same person in two different states at the same time is impossible. At any given moment in time, an individual either participated in the program or did not participate. The person cannot be observed simultaneously in two different states (in other words, with and without the program). This is called "the counterfactual problem": How do we measure what would have happened if the other circumstance had prevailed? Although we can observe and measure the outcome (Y) for program participants $(Y \mid P = 1)$, there are no data to establish what their outcomes would have been in the absence of the program $(Y \mid P = 0)$. In the basic impact evaluation formula, the term $(Y \mid P = 0)$ *represents the counterfactual*. We can think of this as *what would have happened* if a participant had not participated in the program. In other words, the counterfactual is what the outcome (Y) would have been in the absence of a program (P).

For example, imagine that "Mr. Unfortunate" takes a red pill and then dies five days later. Just because Mr. Unfortunate died after taking the red pill, you cannot conclude that the red pill *caused* his death. Maybe he was very sick when he took the red pill, and it was the illness rather than the red pill that caused his death. Inferring causality will require that you rule out other potential factors that can affect the outcome under consideration. In the simple example of determining whether taking the red pill caused Mr. Unfortunate's death, an evaluator would need to establish what would have happened to Mr. Unfortunate had he *not* taken the pill. Inasmuch as Mr. Unfortunate did in fact take the red pill, it is not possible to observe directly what would have happened if he had not done so. What would have happened to him had he not taken the red pill is the counterfactual, and the evaluator's main challenge is determining what this counterfactual state of the world actually looks like (see box 3.1).

When conducting an impact evaluation, it is relatively easy to obtain the first term of the basic formula $(Y \mid P = 1)$—the outcome under treatment. We simply measure the outcome of interest for the population that participated in the program. However, the second term of the formula $(Y \mid P = 0)$ cannot be directly observed for program participants—hence, the need to fill in this missing piece of information by *estimating the counterfactual*. To do this, we typically use *comparison groups* (sometimes called "control groups"). The remainder of part 2 of this book will focus on the different methods or approaches that can be used to identify valid comparison groups that accurately reproduce or mimic the counterfactual. Identifying such comparison groups is the crux of any impact evaluation, regardless of what type of program is being evaluated. Simply put, without a valid estimate of the counterfactual, the impact of a program cannot be established.

Box 3.1: Estimating the Counterfactual
Miss Unique and the Cash Transfer Program

Miss Unique is a newborn baby girl whose mother is offered a monthly cash transfer so long as she ensures that Miss Unique receives regular health checkups at the local health center, that she is immunized, and that her growth is monitored. The government posits that the cash transfer will motivate Miss Unique's mother to seek the health services required by the program and will help Miss Unique grow strong and tall. For its impact evaluation, the government selects height as an outcome indicator for long-term health, and it measures Miss Unique's height 3 years into the cash transfer program.

Assume that you are able to measure Miss Unique's height at the age of 3. Ideally, to evaluate the impact of the program, you would want to measure Miss Unique's height at the age of 3 with her mother having received the cash transfer, and also Miss Unique's height at the age of 3 had her mother not received the cash transfer. You would then compare the two heights. If you were able to compare Miss Unique's height at the age of 3 with the program to Miss Unique's height at the age of 3 without the program, you would know that any difference in height had been caused only by the program. Because everything else about Miss Unique would be the same, there would be no other characteristics that could explain the difference in height.

Unfortunately, however, it is impossible to observe Miss Unique both with and without the cash transfer program: either her family receives the program or it does not. In other words, we do not know what the counterfactual is. Since Miss Unique's mother actually received the cash transfer program, we cannot know how tall she would have been had her mother not received the cash transfer. Finding an appropriate comparison for Miss Unique will be challenging because Miss Unique is, precisely, unique. Her exact socioeconomic background, genetic attributes, and personal characteristics cannot be found in anybody else. If we were simply to compare Miss Unique with a child who is not enrolled in the cash transfer program, say, Mr. Inimitable, the comparison may not be adequate. Miss Unique is not identical to Mr. Inimitable. Miss Unique and Mr. Inimitable may not look the same, they may not live in the same place, they may not have the same parents, and they may not have been the same height when they were born. So if we observe that Mr. Inimitable is shorter than Miss Unique at the age of 3, we cannot know whether the difference is due to the cash transfer program or to one of the many other differences between these two children.

Estimating the Counterfactual

To further illustrate the estimation of the counterfactual, we turn to a hypothetical example that, while not of any policy importance, will help us think through this key concept a bit more fully. On a conceptual level, solving the counterfactual problem requires the evaluator to identify a "perfect clone" for each program participant (figure 3.1). For example, let us say that Mr. Fulanito receives an additional $12 in his pocket money allowance, and we want to measure the impact of this treatment on his consumptions of candies. If you could identify a perfect clone for Mr. Fulanito, the evaluation would be easy: you could just compare the number of candies eaten by Mr. Fulanito (say, 6) with the number of candies eaten by his clone (say, 4). In this case, the impact of the additional pocket money would be the difference between those two numbers, or 2 candies. In practice, we know that it is impossible to identify perfect clones: even between genetically identical twins there are important differences.

Although no perfect clone exists for a single individual, statistical tools exist that can be used to generate two groups of individuals that, if their numbers are large enough, are statistically indistinguishable from each other. In practice, a key goal of an impact evaluation is to identify a group of program participants (the treatment group) and a group of nonparticipants (the comparison group) that are statistically identical in the absence of the program. If the two groups are identical, excepting only that one group participates in the program and the other does not, then we can be sure that any difference in outcomes must be due to the program.

The key challenge, then, is to identify a valid comparison group that has the same characteristics as the treatment group. Specifically, the treatment and comparison groups must be the same in at least three ways: First, the

Figure 3.1 The Perfect Clone

Impact = 6 - 4 = 2 candies

Source: Authors.

treatment group and the comparison group must be identical in the absence of the program. Although it is not necessary that every unit in the treatment group be identical to every unit in the comparison group, on average the characteristics of treatment and comparison groups should be the same. For example, the average age in the treatment group should be the same as the average age in the comparison group. Second, the treatment and comparison groups should react to the program in the same way. For example, the incomes of units in the treatment group should be as likely to benefit from training as the incomes of the comparison group. Third, the treatment and comparison groups cannot be differentially exposed to other interventions during the evaluation period. For example, if we are to isolate the impact of the additional pocket money on candy consumption, the treatment group could not also have been provided with more trips to the candy store than the controls, as that could confound the effects of the pocket money with the effect of increased access to candy.

When these three conditions are met, then only the existence of the program of interest will explain any differences in the outcome (Y) between the two groups once the program has been implemented. The reason is that the only difference between the treatment and comparison groups is that the members of the treatment group will receive the program, while the members of the comparison group will not. When the differences in outcomes can be entirely attributed to the program, the causal impact of the program has been identified. So instead of looking at the impact of additional pocket money only for Mr. Fulanito, you may be looking at the impact for a group of children (figure 3.2). If you could identify another group of children that is totally similar, except that they do not receive additional pocket money, your estimate of the impact of the program would be the difference between the two groups in average consumption of candies. Thus, if the *treated group* consumes an average of 6 candies per person, while the *comparison group* consumes an average of 4, the average impact of the additional pocket money on candy consumption would be 2.

Now that we have defined a *valid comparison group*, it is important to consider what would happen if we decided to go ahead with an evaluation without identifying such a group. Intuitively, this should now be clear: an invalid comparison group is one that differs from the treatment group in some way other than the absence of the treatment. Those additional differences can cause our impact estimate to be invalid or, in statistical terms, *biased*: it will not estimate the true impact of the program. Rather, it will estimate the effect of the program mixed with the effect of those other differences.

Key Concept:

A valid comparison group will have the same characteristics as the group of participants in the program ("treatment group"), except for the fact that the units in the comparison group do not benefit from the program.

Key Concept:

When the comparison group for an evaluation is invalid, then the estimate of the impact of the program will also be invalid: it will not estimate the true impact of the program. In statistical terms, it will be "biased."

Figure 3.2 A Valid Comparison Group

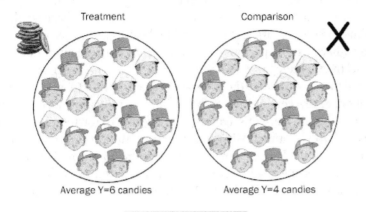

Treatment   Comparison

Average Y=6 candies   Average Y=4 candies

Impact = 6 - 4 = 2 candies

Source: Authors.

Two Types of Impact Estimates

Having estimated the impact of the program, the evaluator needs to know how to interpret the results. An evaluation always estimates the impact of a program by comparing the outcomes for the treatment group with the estimate of the counterfactual obtained from a valid comparison group, using the basic impact evaluation equation. Depending on what the treatment and the counterfactual actually represent, the interpretation of the impact of a program will vary.

The estimated impact α is called the "intention-to-treat" estimate (ITT) when the basic formula is applied to those units to whom the program has been offered, regardless of whether or not they actually enroll in it. The ITT is important for those cases in which we are trying to determine the average impact of a program on the population *targeted* by the program. By contrast, the estimated impact α is called the "treatment-on-the-treated" (TOT) when the basic impact evaluation formula is applied to those units to whom the program has been offered and who have actually enrolled. The ITT and TOT estimates will be the same when there is full compliance, that is, when all units to whom a program has been offered actually decide to enroll in it. We will return to the difference between the ITT and TOT estimates in detail in future sections, but let us begin with an example.

Consider the health insurance subsidy program, or HISP, example described in the introduction to part 2, in which any household in a treatment village can sign up for a health insurance subsidy. Even though all households in treatment villages are eligible to enroll in the program, some fraction of households, say 10 percent, may decide not to do so (perhaps because they already have insurance through their jobs, because they are healthy and do not anticipate the need for health care, or because of one of many other possible reasons). In this scenario, 90 percent of households in the treatment village decide to enroll in the program and actually receive the services that the program provides. The ITT estimate would be obtained by computing the basic impact evaluation formula for all households who were offered the program, that is, for 100 percent of the households in treatment villages. By contrast, the TOT estimate would be obtained by calculating the basic impact evaluation formula only for the subset of households who actually decided to enroll in the program, that is, for the 90 percent of households in treatment villages that enroll.

Two Counterfeit Estimates of the Counterfactual

In the remainder of part 2 of this book, we will discuss the various methods that can be used to construct valid comparison groups that will allow you to estimate the counterfactual. Before doing so, however, it is useful to discuss two common, but highly risky, methods of constructing comparison groups that can lead to inappropriate estimates of the counterfactual. These two "counterfeit" estimates of the counterfactuals are (1) *before-and-after*, or pre-post, comparisons that compare the outcomes of program participants prior to and subsequent to the introduction of a program and (2) *with-and-without* comparisons between units that choose to enroll and units that choose not to enroll.

Counterfeit Counterfactual 1: Comparing Before and After

A before-and-after comparison attempts to establish the impact of a program by tracking changes in outcomes for program participants over time. To return to the basic impact evaluation formula, the outcome for the treatment group $(Y \mid P = 1)$ is simply the postintervention outcome. However, the counterfactual $(Y \mid P = 0)$ is estimated using the preintervention outcome. In essence, this comparison assumes that if the program had never existed, the outcome (Y) for program participants would have been exactly the same as their preprogram situation. Unfortunately, in the vast majority of cases that assumption simply does not hold.

Take the evaluation of a microfinance program for poor, rural farmers. Let us say that the program provides microloans to farmers to enable them to buy fertilizer to increase their rice production. You observe that in the year before the start of the program, farmers harvested an average of 1,000 kilograms (kg) of rice per hectare. The microfinance scheme is launched, and a year later rice yields have increased to 1,100 kg per hectare. If you were trying to evaluate impact using a before-and-after comparison, you would use the preintervention outcome as a counterfactual. Applying the basic impact evaluation formula, you would conclude that the program had increased rice yields by 100 kg per hectare.

However, imagine that rainfall was normal during the year before the program was launched, but a drought occurred in the year the program started. In this context, the preintervention outcome cannot constitute an appropriate counterfactual. Figure 3.3 illustrates why. Because farmers received the program during a drought year, their average yield without the microloan scheme would have been even lower, at level D, and not level B as the before-and-after comparison assumes. In that case, the true impact of the program is larger than 100 kg. By contrast, if environmental conditions had actually improved over time, the counterfactual rice yield might have been at level C, in which case the true program impact would have been smaller than 100 kg. In other words, unless we can statistically account for

Figure 3.3 Before and After Estimates of a Microfinance Program

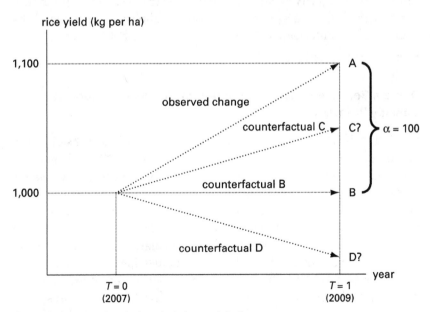

Source: Authors, based on the hypothetical example in the text.

rainfall and *every other factor* that can affect rice yields over time, we simply cannot calculate the true impact of the program by making a before-and-after comparison.

Although before-and-after comparisons may be invalid in impact evaluation, that does not mean they are not valuable for other purposes. In fact, administrative data systems for many programs typically record data about participants over time. For example, an education management information system may routinely collect data on student enrollment in the set of schools where a school meal program is operating. Those data allow program managers to observe whether the number of children enrolled in school is increasing over time. This is important and valuable information for managers who are planning and reporting about the education system. However, establishing that the school meal program has *caused* the observed change in enrollment is much more challenging because many different factors affect student enrollment over time. Thus, although monitoring changes in outcomes over time for a group of participants is extremely valuable, it does not usually allow us to determine conclusively whether—or by how much—a particular program of interest contributed to that improvement as long as other time-varying factors exist that are affecting the same outcome.

We saw in the example of the microfinance scheme and rice yields that many factors can affect rice yields over time. Likewise, many factors can affect the majority of outcomes of interest to development programs. For that reason, the preprogram outcome is almost never a good estimate of the counterfactual, and that is why we label it a "counterfeit counterfactual."

Doing a Before-and-After Evaluation of the Health Insurance Subsidy Program

Recall that the HISP is a new program in your country that subsidizes the purchase of health insurance for poor rural households and that this insurance covers expenses related to primary health care and drugs for those enrolled. The objective of the HISP is to reduce the out-of-pocket health expenditures of poor families and ultimately to improve health outcomes. Although many outcome indicators could be considered for the program evaluation, your government is particularly interested in analyzing the effects of the HISP on what poor families spend on primary care and drugs measured as a household's yearly out-of-pocket expenditures per capita (subsequently referred to simply as "health expenditures").

The HISP will represent a hefty proportion of the national budget if scaled up nationally—up to 1.5 percent of gross domestic product (GDP) by some estimates. Furthermore, substantial administrative and logistical complexities are involved in running a program of this nature. For these reasons, a decision has been made at the highest levels of government to introduce the HISP first as a pilot program and then, depending on the results of the first phase, to scale it up gradually over time. Based on the results of financial and cost-benefit analyses, the president and her cabinet have announced that for the HISP to be viable and to be extended nationally, it must reduce the average yearly per-capita health expenditures of poor rural households by at least $9 below what they would have spent in the absence of the program and it must do so within 2 years.

The HISP will be introduced in 100 rural villages during the initial pilot phase. Just before the start of the program, your government hires a survey firm to conduct a baseline survey of all 4,959 households in these villages. The survey collects detailed information on every household, including their demographic composition, assets, access to health services, and health expenditures in the past year. Shortly after the baseline survey is conducted, the HISP is introduced in the 100 pilot villages with great fanfare, including community events and other promotional campaigns to encourage eligible households to enroll.

Of the 4,959 households in the baseline sample, a total of 2,907 enroll in the HISP during the first 2 years of the program. Over the 2 years, the HISP operates successfully by most measures. Coverage rates are high, and surveys show that most enrolled households are satisfied with the program. At the end of the 2-year pilot period, a second round of evaluation data is collected on the same sample of 4,959 households.[1]

The president and the minister of health have put you in charge of overseeing the impact evaluation for the HISP and recommending whether or not to extend the program nationally. Your impact evaluation question of interest is, *By how much did the HISP lower health expenditures for poor rural households?* Remember that the stakes are high. If the HISP is found to reduce health expenditures by $9 or more, it will be extended nationally. If the program did not reach the $9 target, you will recommend against scaling up the HISP.

The first "expert" evaluation consultant you hire indicates that to estimate the impact of the HISP, you must calculate the change in health expenditures over time for the households that enrolled. The consultant argues that because the HISP covers all health costs related to primary care and medication, any decrease in expenditures over time must be largely attributable to the effect of the HISP. Using only the subset of enrolled households, therefore, you estimate their average health expenditures before the implementation of the program and 2 years later. In

Table 3.1   Case 1—HISP Impact Using Before-After (Comparison of Means)

	After	Before	Difference	t-stat
Household health expenditures	7.8	14.4	−6.6	−28.9

Source: Authors' calculations from hypothetical data set.

other words, you perform a before-and-after evaluation. The results are shown in table 3.1.

You observe that the households that enrolled in the HISP reduced their out-of-pocket health expenditures from $14.4 before the introduction of HISP, to $7.8 two years later, a reduction of $6.6 (or 45 percent) over the period. As denoted by the value of the t-statistic, the difference between health expenditures before and after the program is *statistically significant,* that is, the probability that the estimated effect is statistically equal to zero is very low.

Even though the before-and-after comparison is for the same group of households, you are concerned that some other factors may have changed over time that affected health expenditures. For example, a number of health interventions have been operating simultaneously in the villages in question. Alternatively, some changes in household expenditures may have resulted from the financial crisis that your country recently experienced. To address some of these concerns, your consultant conducts more sophisticated *regression analysis* that will control for the additional external factors. The results appear in table 3.2.

Here, the linear regression is of health expenditures on a binary (0-1) variable for whether the observation is baseline (0) or follow-up (1). The multivariate linear regression additionally *controls for,* or *holds constant,* other characteristics that are observed for the households in your sample, including indicators for wealth (assets), household composition, and so on. You note that the simple linear regression is equivalent to the simple before-and-after difference in health expenditures (a reduction of $6.59). Once you control for other factors available in your data, you find a similar result—a decrease of $6.65.

Table 3.2   Case 1—HISP Impact Using Before-After (Regression Analysis)

	Linear regression	Multivariate linear regression
Estimated impact on household health expenditures	−6.59** (0.22)	−6.65** (0.22)

Source: Authors.

Note: Standard errors are in parentheses.

** Significant at the 1 percent level.

QUESTION 1

A. Based on these results from case 1, should the HISP be scaled up nationally?

B. Does this analysis likely control for all the factors that affect health expenditures over time?

Counterfeit Counterfactual 2: Comparing Enrolled and Nonenrolled

Comparing units that receive a program to units that do not receive it ("with-and-without") constitutes another counterfeit counterfactual. Consider, for example, a vocational training program for unemployed youth. Assume that 2 years after the launching of the scheme, an evaluation attempts to estimate the impact of the program on income by comparing the average incomes of a group of youth who chose to enroll in the program versus those of a group who chose not to enroll. Assume that the results show that the youths who enrolled in the program make twice as much as those who did not enroll.

How should these results be interpreted? In this case, the counterfactual is estimated based on the incomes of individuals who decided not to enroll in the program. Yet the two groups of young people are likely to be fundamentally different. Those individuals who chose to participate may be highly motivated to improve their livelihoods and may expect a high return to training. In contrast, those who chose not to enroll may be discouraged youth who do not expect to benefit from this type of program. It is likely that these two types of young people would perform quite differently in the labor market and would have different incomes even without the vocational training program.

Therefore, the group that chose not to enroll does not provide a good estimate of the counterfactual. If a difference in incomes is observed between the two groups, we will not be able to determine whether it comes from the training program or from the underlying differences in motivation and other factors that exist between the two groups. The fact that less-motivated individuals chose not to enroll in the training program therefore leads to a bias in our assessment of the program's impact.[2] This bias is called "selection bias." In this case, if the young people who enrolled would have had higher incomes even in the absence of the program, the selection bias would be positive; in other words, we would overestimate the impact of the vocational training program on incomes.

Key Concept:
Selection bias occurs when the reasons for which an individual participates in a program are correlated with outcomes. This bias commonly occurs when the comparison group is ineligible for the program or decides not to participate in it.

Comparing Units that Chose to Enroll in the Health Insurance Subsidy Program with Those that Chose Not to Enroll

Having thought through the before-after comparison a bit further with your evaluation team, you realize that there are still many time-varying factors that can explain part of the change in health expenditures over time (in particular, the minister of finance is concerned that the recent financial crisis may have affected households' health expenditures and may explain the observed change). Another consultant suggests that it would be more appropriate to estimate the counterfactual in the postintervention period, that is, 2 years after the program started. The consultant correctly notes that of the 4,959 households in the baseline sample, only 2,907 actually enrolled in the program, and so approximately 41 percent of the households in the sample remain without the HISP coverage. The consultant argues that households within the same locality would be exposed to the same supply-side health interventions and the same local economic conditions, so that the postintervention outcomes of the nonenrolled group would help to control for many of the environmental factors that affect both enrolled and nonenrolled households.

You therefore decide to calculate average health expenditures in the postintervention period for both the households that enrolled in the program and the households that did not, producing the observations shown in table 3.3.

Using the average health expenditures of the nonenrolled households as the estimate of the counterfactual, you find that the program has reduced average health expenditures by approximately $14. When discussing this result further with the consultant, you raise the question of whether the households that chose not to enroll in the program may be systematically different from the ones that did enroll. For example, the households that signed up for the HISP may be ones that expected to have higher health expenditures, or people who were better informed about the program, or people who care more for the health of their families. Alternatively, perhaps the households that enrolled were poorer, on average, than those who did not enroll, given that the HISP is targeted to poor households. Your consultant assures you that regression analysis can control for the potential differences between the two groups. Controlling for all household characteristics that are in the data set, the consultant estimates the impact of the program as shown in table 3.4.

Table 3.3   Case 2—HISP Impact Using Enrolled-Nonenrolled (Comparison of Means)

	Enrolled	Nonenrolled	Difference	t-stat
Household health expenditures	7.8	21.8	−13.9	−39.5

Source: Authors.

Table 3.4   Case 2—HISP Impact Using Enrolled-Nonenrolled (Regression Analysis)

	Linear regression	Multivariate linear regression
Estimated impact on household health expenditures	−13.9** (0.35)	−9.4** (0.32)

Source: Authors.

Note: Standard errors are in parentheses.

** Significant at the 1 percent level.

With a simple linear regression of health expenditures on an indicator variable for whether or not a household enrolled in the program, you find an estimated impact of minus $13.90; in other words, you estimate that the program has decreased average health expenditures by $13.90. However, when all other characteristics of the sample population are held constant, you estimate that the program has reduced the expenditures of the enrolled households by $9.40 per year.

QUESTION 2

A. Based on these results from case 2, should the HISP be scaled up nationally?

B. Does this analysis likely control for all the factors that determine differences in health expenditures between the two groups?

Notes

1. Note that we are assuming zero sample attrition over 2 years, that is, no households will have left the sample. This is not a realistic assumption for most household surveys. In practice, families who move sometimes cannot be tracked to their new location, and some households break up and cease to exist altogether.

2. As another example, if youth who anticipate benefiting considerably from the training scheme are also more likely to enroll (for example, because they anticipate higher wages with training), then we will be comparing a group of individuals who anticipated higher income with a group of individuals who did not anticipate higher income.

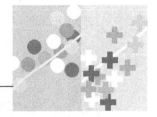

CHAPTER 4

Randomized Selection Methods

Having discussed two approaches to constructing counterfactuals that are commonly used but have a high risk of bias—before-and-after comparisons and with-and-without comparisons—we now turn to a set of methods that can be applied to estimate program impacts more accurately. As we will see, however, such estimation is not always as straightforward as it might seem at first glance. Most programs are designed and implemented in a complex and changing environment, in which many factors can influence outcomes both for program participants and for those who do not participate. Droughts, earthquakes, recessions, changes in government, and changes in international and local policies are all part of the real world, and as evaluators, we want to make sure that the estimated impact of our program remains valid despite these myriad factors.

As we will see throughout this part of the book, a program's rules for enrolling participants will be the key parameter for selecting the impact evaluation method. We believe that in most cases the evaluation methods should try to fit within the context of a program's operational rules (with a few tweaks here and there) and not the other way around. However, we also start from the premise that *all social programs should have fair and transparent rules for program assignment*. One of the fairest and most transparent rules for allocating scarce resources among equally deserving populations turns out to be giving everyone who is eligible an equal opportunity to participate in the program. One way to do that is simply to run a lottery. In this chapter, we will examine several *randomized selection methods*; these are akin to running lotteries that decide who enters a program at a given time and who does not. These randomized selection methods not only provide program administrators with a fair and transparent rule for allocating scarce resources *among equally deserving populations,* but also represent the strongest methods for evaluating the impact of a program.

Randomized selection methods can often be derived from a program's operational rules. For many programs, the population of intended participants—that is, the set of all units that the program would like to serve—is larger than the number of participants that the program can actually accommodate at a given time. For example, in a single year an education program may provide school materials and an upgraded curriculum to 500 schools out of thousands of eligible schools in the country. Or a youth employment program may have a goal of reaching 2,000 unemployed youths within its first year of operation, although there are tens of thousands of unemployed young people that the program ultimately would like to serve. For any of a variety of reasons, programs may be unable to reach the entire population of interest. Budgetary constraints may simply prevent the administrators from offering the program to all eligible units from the beginning. Even if budgets are available to cover an unlimited number of participants, capacity constraints will sometimes prevent a program from rolling out to everyone at the same time. In the youth employment training program example, the number of unemployed youth who want vocational training may be greater than the number of slots available in technical colleges during the first year of the program, and that may limit the number who can enroll.

In reality, most programs have budgetary or operational capacity constraints that prevent reaching every intended participant at the same moment. In this context, where the population of eligible participants is larger than the number of program places available, program administrators must define a rationing mechanism to allocate the program's services. In other words, someone must make a decision about who will enter the program and who will not. The program could be assigned on a first-come-first-served basis, or based on observed characteristics (for example, women and children first, or the poorest municipalities first); or selection could be based on unobserved characteristics (for example, letting individuals sign up based on their own motivation and knowledge), or even on a lottery.

Randomized Assignment of the Treatment

When a program is assigned at random over a large eligible population, we can generate a robust estimate of the counterfactual, considered the gold standard of impact evaluation. Randomized assignment of treatment essentially uses a lottery to decide who among the equally eligible population receives the program and who does not.[1] Every eligible unit of treatment (for example, an individual, household, community, school, hospital, or other) has an equal probability of selection for treatment.[2]

Before we discuss how to implement randomized assignment in practice and why it generates a strong counterfactual, let us take a few moments to consider why randomized assignment is also a fair and transparent way to assign scarce program services. Once a target population has been defined (say, households below the poverty line, or children under the age of 5, or schools in rural areas), randomized assignment is a fair allocation rule because it allows program managers to ensure that every eligible person or unit has the same chance of receiving the program and that the program is not assigned using arbitrary or subjective criteria, or even through patronage or other unfair practices. When excess demand for a program exists, randomized assignment is a rule that can be easily explained by program managers and easily understood by key constituents. When the selection process is conducted through an open and replicable process, the randomized assignment rule cannot easily be manipulated, and therefore it shields program managers from potential accusations of favoritism or corruption. Randomized assignment thus has its own merits as a rationing mechanism that go well beyond its utility as an impact evaluation tool. In fact, we have come across a number of programs that routinely use lotteries as a way to select participants from the pool of eligible individuals, primarily because of their advantages for administration and governance.[3]

Why Does Randomized Assignment Produce an Excellent Estimate of the Counterfactual?

As discussed previously, the ideal comparison group will be as similar as possible to the treatment group in all respects, except with respect to its enrollment in the program that is being evaluated. The key is that when we randomly select units to assign them to the treatment and comparison groups, that randomized assignment process in itself will produce two groups that have a high probability of being statistically identical, as long as the number of potential participants to which we apply the randomized assignment process is sufficiently large. Specifically, with a large enough number of observations, the randomized assignment process will produce groups that have statistically equivalent *averages for all their characteristics*. In turn, those averages also tend toward the average of the population from which they are drawn.[4]

Figure 4.1 illustrates why randomized assignment produces a comparison group that is statistically equivalent to the treatment group. Suppose the population of eligible units (the potential participants) consists of 1,000 people, of whom half are randomly selected and assigned to the treatment group and the other half to the comparison group. For example, one could imagine writing the names of all 1,000 people on individual pieces of paper, mixing them up in a bowl, and then asking someone to blindly draw out 500 names. If it was determined that the first 500 names would constitute the treatment group, then you would have a randomly assigned treatment group (the first 500 names drawn), and a randomly assigned comparison group (the 500 names left in the bowl).

Now assume that of the original 1,000 people, 40 percent were women. Because the names were selected at random, of the 500 names drawn from the bowl, approximately 40 percent will also be women. If among the 1,000 people, 20 percent had blue eyes, then approximately 20 percent of both the treatment and the comparison groups should have blue eyes, too. In general, if the population of eligible units is large enough, then any characteristic of the population will flow through to both the treatment group and the comparison groups. We can imagine that if observed characteristics such as sex or the color of a person's eyes flow through to both the treatment and the comparison group, then logically characteristics that are more difficult to observe (unobserved variables), such as motivation, preferences, or other difficult-to-measure personality traits, would also flow through equally to both the treatment and the comparison groups. Thus, treatment and comparison groups that are generated through randomized assignment will be similar not only in their observed characteristics but also in

Figure 4.1   Characteristics of Groups under Randomized Assignment of Treatment

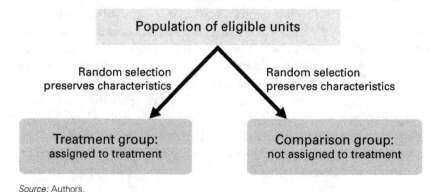

Source: Authors.

their unobserved characteristics. For example, you may not be able to observe or measure how "nice" people are, but you know that if 20 percent of the people in the population of eligible units are nice, then approximately 20 percent of the people in the treatment group will be nice, and the same will be true of the comparison group. Randomized assignment will help guarantee that, on average, the treatment and comparison groups are similar in every way, in both observed and unobserved characteristics.

When an evaluation uses randomized assignment to treatment and comparison groups, we know that theoretically the process should produce two groups that are equivalent. With baseline data on our evaluation sample, we can test this assumption empirically and verify that in fact there are no systematic differences in observed characteristics between the treatment and comparison groups before the program starts. Then, after we launch the program, if we observe differences in outcomes between the treatment and comparison groups, we will know that those differences can be explained only by the introduction of the program, since by construction the two groups were identical at baseline and are exposed to the same external environmental factors over time. In this sense, the comparison group *controls* for all factors that might also explain the outcome of interest. We can be very confident that our estimated average impact, given as the difference between the outcome under treatment (the mean outcome of the randomly assigned treatment group), and our estimate of the counterfactual (the mean outcome of the randomly assigned comparison group) constitute the true impact of the program, since by construction we have eliminated all observed and unobserved factors that might otherwise plausibly explain the difference in outcomes.

In figure 4.1 it is assumed that all units in the eligible population would be assigned to either the treatment or the comparison group. In some cases, however, it is not necessary to include all of them in the evaluation. For example, if the population of eligible units includes a million mothers, and you want to evaluate the effectiveness of cash bonuses on the probability of their vaccinating their children, it may be sufficient to take a representative sample of, say, 1,000 mothers and assign those 1,000 to either the treatment or the comparison group. Figure 4.2 illustrates this process. By the same logic explained above, taking a random sample from the population of eligible units to form the evaluation sample preserves the characteristics of the population of eligible units. The random selection of the treatment and comparison groups from the evaluation sample again preserves the characteristics.

Figure 4.2 Random Sampling and Randomized Assignment of Treatment

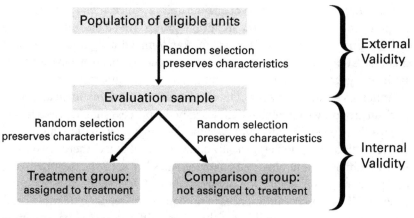

Source: Authors.

External and Internal Validity

The steps outlined above for randomized assignment of treatment will ensure both the internal and the external validity of the impact evaluation, as long as the evaluation sample is large enough (figure 4.2).

Internal validity means that the estimated impact of the program is net of all other potential confounding factors, or that the comparison group represents the true counterfactual, so that we are estimating the true impact of the program. Remember that randomized assignment produces a comparison group that is statistically equivalent to the treatment group at baseline, before the program starts. Once the program starts, the comparison group is exposed to the same set of external factors over time, the only exception being the program. Therefore, if any differences in outcomes appear between the treatment and comparison groups, they can only be due to the existence of the program in the comparison group. In other words, the internal validity of an impact evaluation is ensured through the process of *randomized assignment of treatment.*

External validity means that the impact estimated in the evaluation sample can be generalized to the population of all eligible units. For this to be possible, the evaluation sample must be representative of the population of eligible units; in practice, it means that the evaluation sample must be selected from the population by using one of several variations of *random sampling.*[5]

Note that we have brought up two different types of randomization: one for the purpose of sampling (for external validity) and one as an impact evaluation method (for internal validity). An impact evaluation can produce internally valid estimates of impact through randomized assignment of treatment; however, if the evaluation is performed on a nonrandom sample of the population, the estimated impacts may not be generalizable to the population of eligible units. Conversely, if the evaluation uses a random sample of the population of eligible units, but treatment is not assigned in a randomized way, then the sample would be representative, but the comparison group may not be valid.

When Can Randomized Assignment Be Used?

In practice, randomized assignment should be considered whenever a program is oversubscribed, that is, when the number of potential participants is larger than the number of program spaces available at a given time and the program needs to be phased in. Some circumstances also merit randomized assignment as an evaluation tool even if program resources are not limited. For example, governments may want to use randomized assignment to test new or potentially costly programs whose intended and unintended consequences are unknown. In this context, randomized assignment is justified during a pilot evaluation period to rigorously test the effects of the program before it is rolled out to a larger population.

Two scenarios commonly occur in which randomized assignment is feasible as an impact evaluation method:

1. *When the eligible population is greater than the number of program spaces available.* When the demand for a program exceeds the supply, a simple lottery can be used to select the treatment group within the eligible population. In this context, every unit in the population receives an equal chance of being selected for the program. The group that wins the lottery is the treatment group, and the rest of the population that is not offered the program is the comparison group. As long as a resource constraint exists that prevents scaling the program up to the entire population, the comparison groups can be maintained to measure the short-, medium-, and long-term impacts of the program. In this context, no ethical dilemma arises from holding a comparison group indefinitely, since a subset of the population will necessarily be left out of the program.

   As an example, suppose the ministry of education wants to provide school libraries to public schools throughout the country, but the ministry of finance budgets only enough funds to cover one-third of them. If the ministry of education wants each public school to have an equal chance of receiving a library, it would run a lottery in which each school has the same chance (1 in 3) of being selected. Schools that win the lottery receive a new library and constitute the treatment group, and the remaining two-thirds of public schools in the country are not offered the library and serve as the comparison group. Unless additional funds are allocated to the library program, a group of schools will remain that do not have funding for libraries through the program, and they can be used as a comparison group to measure the counterfactual.

2. *When a program needs to be gradually phased in until it covers the entire eligible population.* When a program is phased in, randomization of the order in which participants receive the program gives each eligible unit the same chance of receiving treatment in the first phase or in a later phase of the program. As long as the "last" group has not yet been phased into the program, it serves as a valid comparison group from which we can estimate the counterfactual for the groups that have already been phased in.

For example, suppose that the ministry of health wants to train all 15,000 nurses in the country to use a new health protocol but needs three years to train them all. In the context of an impact evaluation, the ministry could randomly select one-third of the nurses to receive training in the first year, one-third to receive training in the second year, and one-third to receive training in the third year. To evaluate the effect of the training program one year after its implementation, the group of nurses trained in year 1 would constitute the treatment group, and the group of nurses randomly assigned to training in year 3 would be the comparison group, since they would not yet have received the training.

How Do You Randomly Assign Treatment?

Now that we have discussed what randomized assignment does and why it produces a good comparison group, we will turn to the steps in successfully assigning treatment in a randomized way. Figure 4.3 illustrates this process.

Step 1 in randomized assignment is to define the units that are eligible for the program. Depending on the particular program, a unit can be a person, a health center, a school, or even an entire village or municipality. The population of eligible units consists of those for which you are interested in knowing the impact of your program. For example, if you are implementing a training program for primary school teachers in rural areas, then secondary school teachers or primary school teachers in urban areas would not belong to your population of eligible units.

Figure 4.3 Steps in Randomized Assignment to Treatment

Step 1:
Eligible units

Step 2:
Evaluation sample

Step 3:
Randomize assignment
to treatment

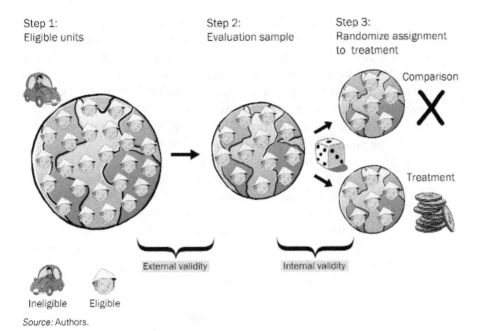

Comparison

Treatment

External validity

Internal validity

Ineligible   Eligible

Source: Authors.

Once you have determined the population of eligible units, it will be necessary to compare the size of the group with the number of observations
required for the evaluation. This number is determined through power calculations and is based on the types of questions you would like answered (see
chapter 11). If the eligible population is small, all of the eligible units may
need to be included in the evaluation. Alternatively, if there are more eligible
units than are required for the evaluation, then step 2 is to select a sample of
units from the population to be included in the evaluation sample. Note that
this second step is done mainly to limit data collection costs. If it is found that
data from existing monitoring systems can be used for the evaluation, and
that those systems cover the population of eligible units, then you will not
need to draw a separate evaluation sample. However, imagine an evaluation
in which the population of eligible units includes tens of thousands of teachers in every public school in the country, and you need to collect detailed
information on teacher pedagogical knowledge. Interviewing each and every
teacher may not be practically feasible, but you may find that it is sufficient to
take a sample of 1,000 teachers distributed over 100 schools. As long as the
sample of schools and teachers is representative of the whole population of
public school teachers, any results found in the evaluation can be generalized
to the rest of the teachers and public schools in the country. Collecting data

on this sample of 1,000 teachers will of course be much cheaper than collecting data on every teacher in all public schools in the country.

Finally, step 3 will be forming the treatment and comparison groups among the units in the evaluation sample. This requires that you first decide on a rule for how to assign participants based on random numbers. For example, if you need to assign 40 out of 100 units from the evaluation sample to the treatment group, you may decide to assign those 40 units with the highest random numbers to the treatment group and the rest to the comparison group. You then assign a random number to each unit of observation in the evaluation sample, using a spreadsheet or specialized statistical software (figure 4.4), and use your previously chosen rule to form the treatment and comparison groups. Note that it is important to decide on the rule before you run the software that gives units their random numbers; otherwise, you may be tempted to decide on a rule based on the random numbers you see, and that would invalidate the randomized assignment.

The logic behind the automated process is no different from randomized assignment based on a coin toss or picking names out of a hat: it is a mechanism that determines randomly whether each unit is in the treatment or the

Figure 4.4 Randomized Assignment to Treatment Using a Spreadsheet

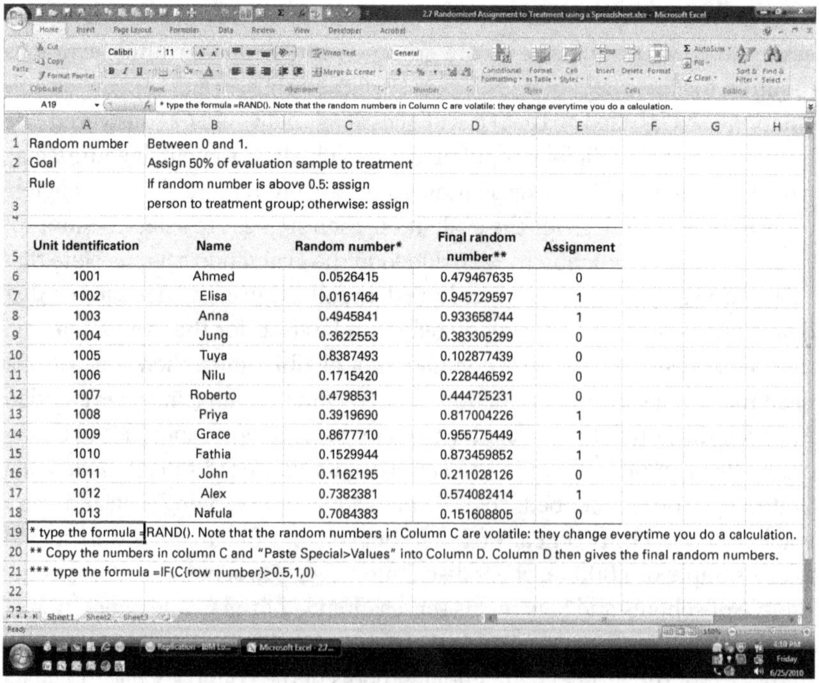

Random number	Between 0 and 1.			
Goal	Assign 50% of evaluation sample to treatment			
Rule	If random number is above 0.5: assign person to treatment group; otherwise: assign			
Unit identification	**Name**	**Random number***	**Final random number****	**Assignment**
1001	Ahmed	0.0526415	0.479467635	0
1002	Elisa	0.0161464	0.945729597	1
1003	Anna	0.4945841	0.933658744	1
1004	Jung	0.3622553	0.383305299	0
1005	Tuya	0.8387493	0.102877439	0
1006	Nilu	0.1715420	0.228446592	0
1007	Roberto	0.4798531	0.444725231	0
1008	Priya	0.3919690	0.817004226	1
1009	Grace	0.8677710	0.955775449	1
1010	Fathia	0.1529944	0.873459852	1
1011	John	0.1162195	0.211028126	0
1012	Alex	0.7382381	0.574082414	1
1013	Nafula	0.7084383	0.151608805	0

* type the formula =RAND(). Note that the random numbers in Column C are volatile: they change everytime you do a calculation.
** Copy the numbers in column C and "Paste Special>Values" into Column D. Column D then gives the final random numbers.
*** type the formula =IF(C{row number}>0.5,1,0)

Source: Authors.

comparison group. In cases where randomized assignment needs to be done in a public forum, some more "artisanal" techniques for randomized assignment might be used. The following examples assume that the unit of randomization is an individual person:

1. If you want to assign 50 percent of individuals to the treatment group and 50 percent to the comparison group, flip a coin for each person. You must decide in advance whether heads or tails on the coin will assign a person to the treatment group.

2. If you want to assign one-third of the evaluation sample to the treatment group, you can roll dice for each person. First, you must decide on a rule. For example, a thrown die that shows a 1 or a 2 could mean an assignment to the treatment group, whereas a 3, 4, 5, or 6 would mean an assignment to the comparison group. You would roll the die once for each person in the evaluation sample and assign them based on the number that comes up.

3. Write the names of all of the people on pieces of paper of identical size and shape. Fold the papers so that the names cannot be seen, and mix them thoroughly in a hat or some other container. Before you start drawing, decide on your rule, that is, how many pieces of paper you will draw and that one's name being drawn means being assigned to the treatment group. Once the rule is clear, ask someone in the crowd (someone unbiased, such as a child) to draw out as many pieces of paper as you need participants in the treatment group.

Whether you use a public lottery, a roll of dice, or computer-generated random numbers, it is important to document the process to ensure that it is transparent. That means, first, that the assignment rule has to be decided in advance and communicated to any members of the public. Second, you must stick to the rule once you draw the random numbers; and third, you must be able to show that the process was really random. In the cases of lotteries and throwing dice, you could videotape the process; computer-based assignment of random numbers requires that you provide a log of your computations, so that the process can be replicated by auditors.[6]

At What Level Do You Perform Randomized Assignment?

Randomized assignment can be done at the individual, household, community, or regional level. In general, the level at which we randomly assign units to treatment and comparison groups will be greatly affected by where and how the program is being implemented. For example, if a health program is being implemented at the health clinic level, you would first choose a random sample of health clinics and then randomly assign some of them to the treatment group and others to the comparison group.

When the level of the randomized assignment is higher, for example, at the level of regions or provinces in a country, it can become very difficult to perform an impact evaluation because the number of regions or provinces in most countries is not sufficiently large to yield balanced treatment and comparison groups. For example, if a country has only six provinces, that would permit only three treatment and three comparison provinces, numbers that are insufficient to ensure that the characteristics of the treatment and comparison groups are balanced.

But as the level of randomized assignment gets lower, for example, down to the individual or household level, the chances of spillovers and contamination increase.[7] For example, if the program consists of providing deworming medicine to households, and a household in the treatment group is located close to a household in the comparison group, then the comparison household may be positively affected by a spillover from the treatment provided to the treatment household because its chances of contracting worms from the neighbors will be reduced. Treatment and comparison households need to be located sufficiently far from each other to avoid such spillovers. Yet, as the distance between the households increases, it will become more costly both to implement the program and to administer surveys. As a rule of thumb, if spillovers can be reasonably ruled out, it is best to perform randomized assignment of the treatment at the lowest possible level of program implementation; that will ensure that the number of units in both the treatment and comparison groups is as large as possible. Spillovers are discussed in chapter 8.

Estimating Impact under Randomized Assignment

Once you have drawn a random evaluation sample and assigned treatment in a randomized fashion, it is quite easy to estimate the impact of the program. After the program has run for some time, outcomes for both the treatment and comparison units will need to be measured. The impact of the program is simply the difference between the average outcome (Y) for the treatment group and the average outcome (Y) for the comparison group. For instance, in figure 4.5, average outcome for the treatment group is 100, and average outcome for the comparison group is 80, so that the impact of the program is 20.

Figure 4.5 Estimating Impact under Randomized Assignment

	Treatment	Comparison	Impact
	Average (Y) for the treatment group = 100	Average (Y) for the comparison group = 80	Impact = ΔY = 20
Enroll if, and only if, assigned to the treatment group			

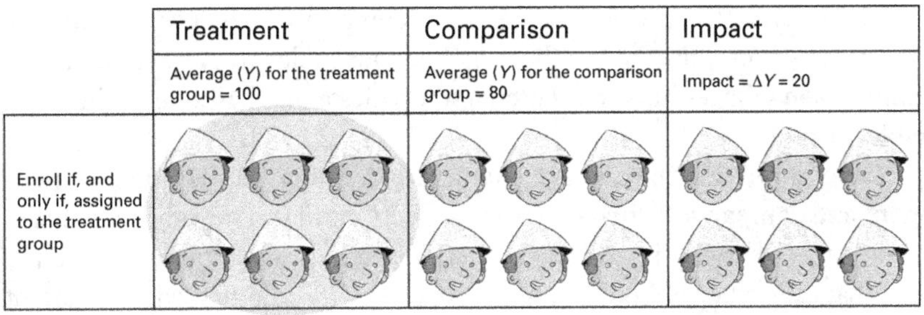

Source: Authors.

Estimating the Impact of the Health Insurance Subsidy Program under Randomized Assignment

Let us now turn back to the example of the health insurance subsidy program (HISP) and check what "randomized assignment" means in its context. Recall that you are trying to estimate the impact of the program from a pilot that involves 100 treatment villages.

Having conducted two impact assessments using potentially biased counterfactuals (and having reached conflicting policy recommendations; see chapter 3), you decide to go back to the drawing board to rethink how to obtain a more precise counterfactual. After further deliberations with your evaluation team, you are convinced that constructing a valid estimate of the counterfactual will require identifying a group of villages that are identical to the 100 treatment villages in all respects, with the only exception being that one group took part in the HISP and the other did not. Because the HISP was rolled out as a pilot, and the 100 treatment villages were selected randomly from among all of the rural villages in the country, you note that the villages should, on average, have the same characteristics as the general population of rural villages. The counterfactual can therefore be estimated in a valid way by measuring the health expenditures of eligible households in villages that did not take part in the program.

Luckily, at the time of the baseline and follow-up surveys, the survey firm collected data on an additional 100 rural villages that were not offered the program in the first round. Those 100 additional villages were also randomly chosen from the population of eligible villages, which means that they too will, on average, have the same characteristics as the general population of rural villages. Thus, the way that the two groups of villages were chosen ensures that they have identical characteristics, except that the 100 treatment villages received the HISP and the 100 comparison villages did not. Randomized assignment of the treatment has occurred.

Given randomized assignment of the treatment, you are quite confident that no external factors other than the HISP would explain any differences in outcomes between the treatment and comparison villages. To validate this assumption, you test whether eligible households in the treatment and comparison villages have similar characteristics at the baseline as shown in table 4.1.

You observe that the average characteristics of households in the treatment and comparison villages are in fact very similar. The only statistically significant difference is for the number of years of education of the spouse, and that difference is small. Note that even with a randomized experiment on a large sample, a small number of differences can be expected.[8] With the validity of the comparison group established, your estimate of the counterfactual is now the average health expenditures of eligible households in the 100 comparison villages (table 4.2).

Table 4.1 Case 3—Balance between Treatment and Comparison Villages at Baseline

Household characteristics	Treatment villages (N = 2964)	Comparison villages (N = 2664)	Difference	t-stat
Health expenditures ($ yearly per capita)	14.48	14.57	−0.09	−0.39
Head of household's age (years)	41.6	42.3	−0.7	−1.2
Spouse's age (years)	36.8	36.8	0.0	0.38
Head of household's education (years)	2.9	2.8	0.1	2.16*
Spouse's education (years)	2.7	2.6	0.1	0.006
Head of household is female = 1	0.07	0.07	−0.0	−0.66
Indigenous = 1	0.42	0.42	0.0	0.21
Number of household members	5.7	5.7	0.0	1.21
Has bathroom = 1	0.57	0.56	0.01	1.04
Hectares of land	1.67	1.71	−0.04	−1.35
Distance to hospital (km)	109	106	3	1.02

Source: Authors' calculation.

* Significant at the 5 percent level.

Table 4.2 Case 3—HISP Impact Using Randomized Assignment (Comparison of Means)

	Treatment	Comparison	Difference	t-stat
Household health expenditures baseline	14.48	14.57	−0.09	−0.39
Household health expenditures follow-up	7.8	17.9	−10.1**	−25.6

Source: Authors' calculation.

** Significant at the 1 percent level.

Table 4.3 Case 3—HISP Impact Using Randomized Assignment (Regression Analysis)

	Linear regression	Multivariate linear regression
Estimated impact on household health expenditures	−10.1** (0.39)	−10.0** (0.34)

Source: Authors' calculation.

Note: Standard errors are in parentheses.

** Significant at the 1 percent level.

Given that you now have a valid estimate of the counterfactual, you can find the impact of the HISP simply by taking the difference between the out-of-pocket health expenditures of eligible households in the treatment villages and the estimate of the counterfactual. The impact is a reduction of $10.10 over two years. Replicating this result through regression analysis yields the same result, as shown in table 4.3.

With randomized assignment, we can be confident that no factors are present that are systematically different between the treatment and comparison groups that might also explain the difference in health expenditures. Both sets of villages have been exposed to the same set of national policies and programs during the two years of treatment. Thus, the most plausible reason that poor households in treatment communities have lower expenditures than households in comparison villages is that the first group received the health insurance program and the other group did not.

QUESTION 3

A. Why is the impact estimate derived using a multivariate linear regression basically unchanged when controlling for other factors?

B. Based on the impact estimated in case 3, should the HISP be scaled up nationally?

Randomized Assignment at Work

Randomized assignment is often used in rigorous impact evaluation work, both in large-scale evaluations and in smaller ones. The evaluation of the Mexico Progresa program (Schultz 2004) is one of the most well-known, large-scale evaluations using randomized assignment (box 4.1).

Two Variations on Randomized Assignment

We now consider two variations that draw on many of the properties of randomized assignment: randomized offering of treatment and randomized promotion of treatment.

Box 4.1: Conditional Cash Transfers and Education in Mexico

The Progresa program, now called "Oportunidades," began in 1998 and provides cash transfers to poor mothers in rural Mexico conditional on their children's enrollment in school, with their attendance confirmed by the teacher. This large-scale social program was one of the first to be designed with a rigorous evaluation in mind, and randomized assignment was used to help identify the effect of conditional cash transfers on a number of outcomes, in particular school enrollment.

The grants, for children in grades 3 through 9, amount to about 50 percent to 75 percent of the private cost of schooling and are guaranteed for three years. The communities and households eligible for the program were determined based on a poverty index created from census data and baseline data collection. Because of a need to phase in the large-scale social program, about two-thirds of the localities (314 out of 495) were randomly selected to receive the program in the first two years, and the remaining 181 served as a control group before entering the program in the third year.

Based on the randomized assignment, Schultz (2004) found an average increase in enrollment of 3.4 percent for all students in grades 1–8, with the largest increase among girls who had completed grade 6, at 14.8 percent.[a] The likely reason is that girls tend to drop out of school at greater rates as they get older, and so they were given a slightly larger transfer to stay in school past the primary grade levels. These short-run impacts were then extrapolated to predict the longer-term impact of the Progresa program on lifetime schooling and earnings.

Source: Schultz 2004.

a. To be precise, Schultz combined randomized assignment with difference-in-difference methods. Chapter 8 discusses the benefits of combining various impact evaluation methodologies.

Randomized Offering: When Not Everyone Complies with Their Assignment

In the earlier, discussion of randomized assignment, we have assumed that the program administrator has the power to assign units to treatment and comparison groups, with those assigned to the treatment taking the program and those assigned to the comparison group not taking the program. In other words, units that were assigned to the treatment and comparison groups *complied with* their assignment. Full compliance is more frequently attained in laboratory settings or medical trials, where the researcher can carefully make sure, first, that all subjects in the treatment group take the pill, and second, that none of the subjects in the comparison group take it.[9]

In real-life social programs, full compliance with a program's selection criteria (and hence, adherence to treatment or comparison status) is optimal, and policy makers and impact evaluators alike strive to come as close to that ideal as possible. In practice, however, strict 100 percent compliance to treatment and comparison assignments may not occur, despite the best efforts of the program implementer and the impact evaluator. Just because a teacher is assigned to the treatment group and is offered training does not mean that she or he will actually show up on the first day of the course. Similarly, a teacher who is assigned to the comparison group may find a way to attend the course anyway. Under these circumstances, a straight comparison of the group originally assigned to treatment with the group originally assigned to comparison will yield the *"intention-to-treat" estimate (ITT)*. The reason is that we will be comparing those whom we intended to treat (those assigned to the treatment group) with those whom we intended not to treat (those assigned to the comparison group). By itself, this is a very interesting and relevant measure of impact, since most policy makers and program managers can only offer a program and cannot force the program on their target population.

But at the same time, we may also be interested in estimating the impact of the program on those who actually take up or accept the treatment. Doing that requires correcting for the fact that some of the units assigned to the treatment group did not actually receive the treatment, or that some of the units assigned to the comparison group actually did receive it. In other words, we want to estimate the impact of the program on those to whom treatment was offered *and* who actually enrolled. This is the *"treatment-on-the-treated" estimate (TOT)*.

Randomized Offering of a Program and Final Take-Up

Imagine that you are evaluating the impact of a job training program on individuals' wages. The program is randomly assigned at the individual level, and the treatment group is offered the program while the comparison group is not. Most likely, you will find three types of individuals in the population:

- *Enroll-if-offered*. These are the individuals who comply with their assignment. If they are assigned to the treatment group (offered the program), they take it up, or enroll; if they are assigned to the comparison group (not offered the program), they do not enroll.

- *Never*. These are the individuals that never enroll in or take up the program, even if they are assigned to the treatment group. They are noncompliers in the treatment group.

- *Always*. These are the individuals who will find a way to enroll in the program or take it up, even if they are assigned to the comparison group. They are noncompliers in the comparison group.

In the context of the job training program, the *Never* group might be unmotivated people who, even if offered a place in the course, do not show up. The *Always* group, in contrast, are so motivated that they find a way to enter the program even if they were originally assigned to the comparison group. The *Enroll-if-offered* group are those who would enroll in the course if it is offered (the treatment group) but do not seek to enroll if they are assigned to the comparison group.

Figure 4.6 presents the randomized offering of the program and the final enrollment, or take-up, when *Enroll-if-offered, Never,* and *Always* groups are present. We assume that the population of units has 80 percent *Enroll-if-offered,* 10 percent *Never,* and 10 percent *Always.* If we take a random sample of the population for the evaluation sample, then the evaluation sample will also have approximately 80 percent *Enroll-if-offered,* 10 percent *Never,* and 10 percent *Always.* Then if we randomly divide the evaluation sample into a treatment group and a comparison group, we should again have approximately 80 percent *Enroll-if-offered,* 10 percent *Never,* and 10 percent *Always* in both groups. In the group that is offered treatment, the *Enroll-if-offered* and *Always* individuals will enroll, and only the *Never* people will stay away. In the group that is not offered treatment, the *Always* will enroll, while the *Enroll-if-offered* and *Never* groups will stay out.

Estimating Impact under Randomized Offering

Having established the difference between offering a program and actual enrollment or take-up, we turn to a technique that can be used to estimate the impact of treatment on the treated, that is, the impact of the program on

Impact Evaluation in Practice

Figure 4.6 Randomized Offering of a Program

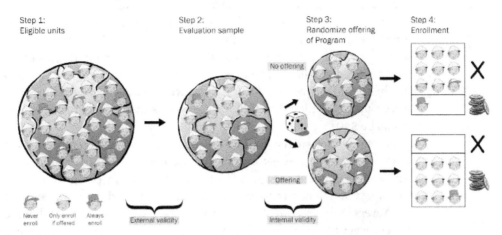

Step 1:
Eligible units

Step 2:
Evaluation sample

Step 3:
Randomize offering
of Program

Step 4:
Enrollment

No offering

Offering

Never
enroll

Only enroll
if offered

Always
enroll

External validity

Internal validity

Source: Authors.

Figure 4.7 Estimating the Impact of Treatment on the Treated under Randomized Offering

	Group offered treatment	Group not offered treatment	Impact
	% enrolled = 90% Average Y for those offered treatment = 110	% enrolled = 10% Average Y for those not offered treatment = 70	Δ% enrolled = 80% ΔY = ITT = 40 ToT = 40/80% = 50
Never enroll			—
Only enroll if offered the program			
Always enroll			—

Source: Authors.

Note: ITT is the "intention-to-treat" estimate obtained by comparing outcomes for those to whom treatment was offered with those to whom treatment was not offered (irrespective of actual enrollment). TOT is the "treatment-on-the-treated" estimate, i.e., the impact of the program estimated on those who were offered treatment and who actually enroll. Characters on shaded background are those that actually enroll.

Randomized Selection Methods

those who were offered treatment *and* who actually enroll. This estimation is done in two steps, which are illustrated in figure 4.7.[10]

First, we estimate the impact of intention to treat. Remember that this is just the straight difference in the outcome indicator (Y) for the group to whom we offered treatment and the same indicator for the group to whom we did not offer treatment. For example, if the average income (Y) for the treatment group is $110, and the average income for the comparison group is $70, then the intention-to-treat estimate of the impact (ITT) would be $40.

Second, we need to recover the treatment-on-the-treated estimate (TOT) from the intention-to-treat estimate. To do that, we will need to identify where the $40 difference came from. Let us proceed by elimination. First, we know that the difference cannot be caused by any differences between the *Nevers* in the treatment and comparison groups. The reason is that the *Nevers* never enroll in the program, so that for them, it makes no difference whether they are in the treatment group or in the comparison group. Second, we know that the $40 difference cannot be caused by differences between the *Always* people in the treatment and comparison groups because the *Always* people always enroll in the program. For them, too, it makes no difference whether they are in the treatment group or the comparison group. Thus, the difference in outcomes between the two groups must necessarily come from the effect of the program on the only group affected by their assignment to treatment or comparison, that is, the *Enroll-if-offered* group. So if we can identify the *Enroll-if-offered* in both groups, it will be easy to estimate the impact of the program on them.

In reality, although we know that these three types of individuals exist in the population, we cannot uniquely separate out individuals by whether they are *Enroll-if-offered, Never,* or *Always.* In the group that was offered treatment, we can identify the *Nevers* (because they have not enrolled), but we cannot differentiate between the *Always* and the *Enroll-if-offered* (because both are enrolled). In the group that was not offered treatment, we can identify the *Always* group (because they enroll in the program), but we cannot differentiate between the *Nevers* and the *Enroll-if-offered.*

However, once we observe that 90 percent of units in the group offered treatment enroll, we can deduce that 10 percent of the units in our population must be *Nevers* (that is the fraction of individuals in the group offered treatment that did not enroll). In addition, if we observe that 10 percent of units in the group not offered treatment enroll, we know that 10 percent are *Always* (again, the fraction of individuals in our group that was not offered treatment who did enroll). This leaves 80 percent of the units in the *Enroll-if-offered* group. We know that the entire impact of $40 came from a difference in enrollment for the 80 percent of the units in our sample who are

Enroll-if-offered. Now if 80 percent of the units are responsible for an average impact of $40 for the entire group offered treatment, then the impact on those 80 percent of *Enroll-if-offered* must be 40/0.8, or $50. Put another way, the impact of the program for the *Enroll-if-offered* is $50, but when this impact is spread across the entire group offered treatment, the average effect is watered down by the 20 percent that was noncompliant with the original randomized assignment.

Remember that one of the basic issues with self-selection into programs is that you cannot always know why some people choose to participate and others do not. When we randomly assign units to the program, but actual participation is voluntary or a way may exist for units in the comparison group to get into the program, then we have a similar problem: we will not always understand the behavioral processes that determine whether an individual behaves like a *Never*, an *Always*, or an *Enroll-if-offered* in our example above. However, provided that the non-compliance is not too large, the initial randomized assignment still provides a powerful tool for estimating impact. The downside of randomized assignment with imperfect compliance is that this impact estimate is no longer valid for the entire population. Instead, it applies only to a specific subgroup within our target population, the *Enroll-if-offered*.

Randomized offering of a program has two important characteristics that allow us to estimate impact even without full compliance (see box 4.2):[11]

1. It can serve as a predictor of actual enrollment in the program if most people behave as *Enroll-if-offered*, enrolling in the program when offered treatment and not enrolling when not offered treatment.

2. Since the two groups (offered and not offered treatment) are generated through a random selection process, the characteristics of individuals in the two groups are not correlated with anything else, such as ability or motivation, that may also affect the outcomes (Y).

Randomized Promotion or Encouragement Design

In the previous section, we saw how to estimate impact based on randomized assignment of treatment, even when compliance with the originally assigned treatment and comparison groups is incomplete. Next we propose a very similar approach that can be applied to evaluate programs that have universal eligibility or open enrollment or in which the program administrator cannot control who participates and who does not.

Governments commonly implement programs for which it is difficult either to exclude any potential participants or to force them to participate. Many programs allow potential participants to choose to enroll and are

Box 4.2: Randomized Offering of School Vouchers in Colombia

The Program for Extending the Coverage of Secondary School (Programa de Ampliación de Cobertura de la Educación Secundaria [PACES]), in Colombia, provided more than 125,000 students with vouchers covering slightly over half the cost of attending private secondary school. Because of the limited PACES budget, the vouchers were allocated via a lottery. Angrist et al. (2002) took advantage of this randomly assigned treatment to determine the effect of the voucher program on educational and social outcomes.

They found that lottery winners were 10 percent more likely to complete the 8th grade and scored, on average, 0.2 standard deviations higher on standardized tests three years after the initial lottery. They also found that the educational effects were greater for girls than boys. The researchers then looked at the impact of the program on several noneducational outcomes and found that lottery winners were less likely to be married and worked about 1.2 fewer hours per week.

There was some noncompliance with the randomized design, in that about 90 percent of the lottery winners had actually used the voucher or another form of scholarship and 24 percent of the lottery losers had actually received scholarships. Angrist and colleagues therefore also used intent-to-treat, or a student's lottery win or loss status, as an instrumental variable for the treatment-on-the-treated, or actual scholarship receipt. Finally, the researchers were able to calculate a cost-benefit analysis to better understand the impact of the voucher program on both household and government expenditures. They concluded that the total social costs of the program are small and are outweighed by the expected returns to participants and their families, thus suggesting that demand-side programs such as PACES can be a cost-effective way to increase educational attainment.

Source: Angrist et al. 2002.

not, therefore, able to exclude potential participants who want to enroll. In addition, some programs have a budget that is big enough to supply the program to the entire eligible population immediately, so that randomly choosing treatment and comparison groups and excluding potential participants for the sake of an evaluation would not be ethical. We therefore need an alternative way to evaluate the impact of these kinds of programs—those with voluntary enrollment and those with universal coverage.

Voluntary enrollment programs typically allow individuals who are interested in the program to approach on their own to enroll and participate. Imagine again the job training program discussed earlier, but this time randomized assignment is not possible, and any individual who wishes to enroll in the program is free to do so. Very much in line with our previous example, we will expect to encounter three types of people: compliers, a *Never* group, and an *Always* group. As in the previous case, *Always* people will always enroll in the program and *Never* people will never enroll. But how about the compliers? In this context, any individual who would like to enroll in the program is free to do so. And what about individuals who may be very interested in enrolling but who, for a variety of reasons, may not have sufficient information or the right incentive to enroll? The compliers in this context will be precisely that group. The compliers here are those who *enroll-if-promoted*: they are a group of individuals who only enroll in the program if given an additional incentive, or promotion, that motivates them to enroll. Without this additional stimulus, the *Enroll-if-promoted* would simply remain out of the program.

Again coming back to the job training example, if the agency that organizes the training is well funded and has sufficient capacity to train everyone who wants to be trained, then the job training program will be open to every unemployed person who wants to participate. It is unlikely, however, that every unemployed person will actually want to participate or will even know of the existence of the program. Some unemployed people may be reluctant to enroll because they know very little about the content of the training and find it hard to obtain additional information. Now assume that the job training agency hires a community outreach worker to go around town to enlist unemployed persons into the job training program. Carrying a list of unemployed people, she knocks on their doors, describes the training program, and offers to help the person to enroll in the program on the spot. Of course, she cannot force anyone to participate. In addition, the unemployed persons whom the outreach worker does not visit can also enroll, although they will have to go to the agency themselves to do so. So we now have two groups of unemployed people—those who were visited by the outreach worker and those who were not visited. If the outreach effort is effective, the enrollment rate among unemployed people who were visited should be higher than the rate among unemployed people who were not visited.

Now let us think about how we can evaluate this job training program. As we know, we cannot just compare those unemployed people who enroll with those who do not enroll. The reason is that the unemployed who enroll are probably very different from those who do not enroll in both observed and nonobserved ways: they may be more educated (this can be observed easily), and they are probably more motivated and eager to find a job (this is hard to observe and measure).

However, we do have some additional variation that we can exploit to find a valid comparison group. Let us consider for a moment whether we can compare the group that was visited by the outreach worker with the group that was not visited. Both groups contain very motivated persons

(*Always*) who will enroll whether or not the outreach worker knocks on their door. Both groups also contain unmotivated persons (*Never*) who will not enroll in the program despite the efforts of the outreach worker. And finally, some people (*Enroll-if-promoted*) will enroll in the training if the outreach worker visits them but will not enroll if the worker does not come knocking.

If the outreach worker randomly selected the people on her list to visit, we would be able to use the treatment-on-the-treated method discussed earlier. The only difference would be that, instead of randomly *offering* the program, we would be randomly *promoting* it. As long as *Enroll-if-promoted* people (who enroll when we reach out to them but do not enroll when we do not reach out to them) appear, we would have a variation between the group *with* the promotion or outreach and the group *without* the promotion or outreach that would allow us to identify the impact of the training on the *Enroll-if-promoted*. Instead of complying with the offer of the treatment, the *Enroll-if-promoted* are now complying with the promotion.

We want the outreach strategy to be effective and to increase enrollment substantially among the *Enroll-if-promoted* group. At the same time, we do not want the promotion activities to be so widespread and effective that they influence the outcome of interest. For example, if the outreach workers offered large amounts of money to unemployed people to get them to enroll, it would be hard to tell whether any later changes in income were caused by the training or by the outreach or promotion itself.

Randomized promotion is a creative strategy that generates the equivalent of a comparison group for the purposes of impact evaluation. It can be used when it is feasible to organize a promotion campaign aimed at a random sample of the population of interest. Readers with a background in econometrics may again recognize the terminology introduced in the previous section: the randomized promotion is an instrumental variable that allows us to create variation between units and exploit that variation to create a valid comparison group.

You Said "Promotion"?

Randomized promotion seeks to increase the take-up of a voluntary program in a subsample of the population. It can take several forms. For instance, we may choose to initiate an information campaign to reach those individuals who had not enrolled because they did not know or fully understand the content of the program. Alternatively, we may choose to provide incentives to sign up, such as offering small gifts or prizes or making transportation or other help available.

A number of conditions must be met for the randomized promotion methodology to produce a valid impact evaluation.

1. The promoted and nonpromoted groups must be comparable. The characteristics of the two groups must be similar. This is achieved by randomly assigning the outreach or promotion activities among the units in the evaluation sample.

2. The promotion campaign must increase enrollment by those in the promoted group substantially above the rate of the nonpromoted group. This can be verified by checking that enrollment rates are higher in the group that receives the promotion than in the group that does not.

3. It is important that the promotion itself does not directly affect the outcomes of interest, so that we can tell that changes in the outcomes of interest are caused by the program itself and not by the promotion.

The Randomized Promotion Process

The process of randomized promotion is presented in figure 4.8. As in the previous methods, we begin with the population of eligible units for the program. In contrast with randomized assignment, we can no longer randomly choose who will receive the program and who will not receive the program because the program is fully voluntary. However, within the population of eligible units, there will be three types of units:

- *Always*—those who will always want to enroll in the program

- *Enroll-if-promoted*—those who will sign up for the program only when given additional promotion

- *Never*—those who never want to sign up for the program, whether or not we offer them promotion

Again, note that being an *Always*, an *Enroll-if-promoted*, or a *Never* is an intrinsic characteristic of units that cannot be measured by the program evaluator because it is related to factors such as intrinsic motivation and intelligence.

Once the eligible population is defined, the next step is to randomly select a sample from the population to be part of the evaluation. These are the units on whom we will collect data. In some cases—for example, when we have data for the entire population of eligible units—we may decide to include this entire population in the evaluation sample.

Figure 4.8 Randomized Promotion

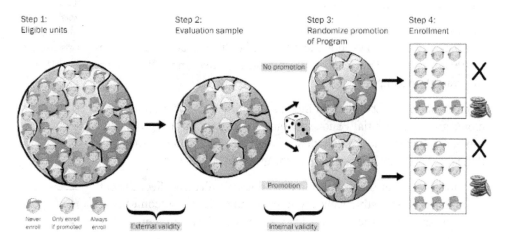

| Step 1: Eligible units | Step 2: Evaluation sample | Step 3: Randomize promotion of Program | Step 4: Enrollment |

Source: Authors.

Once the evaluation sample is defined, randomized promotion randomly assigns the evaluation sample into a promoted group and a nonpromoted group. Since we are randomly choosing the members of both the promoted group and the nonpromoted group, both groups will share the characteristics of the overall evaluation sample, and those will be equivalent to the characteristics of the population of eligible units. Therefore, the promoted group and the nonpromoted group will have similar characteristics.

After the promotion campaign is over, we can observe the enrollment rates in the promoted and nonpromoted groups. In the nonpromoted group, only the *Always* will enroll. Although we thus will be able to know which units are *Always* in the nonpromoted group, we will not be able to distinguish between the *Never* and *Enroll-if-promoted* in that group. By contrast, in the promoted group both the *Enroll-if-promoted* and the *Always* will enroll, whereas the *Never* will not enroll. So in the promoted group we will be able to identify the *Never* group, but we will not be able to distinguish between the *Enroll-if-promoted* and the *Always*.

Estimating Impact under Randomized Promotion

Estimating the impact of a program using randomized promotion is a special case of the treatment-on-the-treated method (figure 4.9). Imagine that the promotion campaign raises enrollment from 30 percent in the nonpromoted group (3 *Always*) to 80 percent in the promoted group (3 *Always* and 5 *Enroll-if-promoted*). Assume that average outcome for all individuals in

Figure 4.9 Estimating Impact under Randomized Promotion

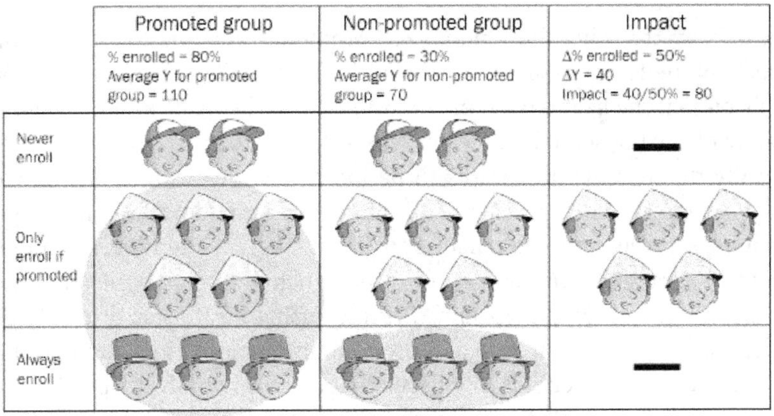

	Promoted group	Non-promoted group	Impact
	% enrolled = 80% Average Y for promoted group = 110	% enrolled = 30% Average Y for non-promoted group = 70	Δ% enrolled = 50% ΔY = 40 Impact = 40/50% = 80
Never enroll			▬
Only enroll if promoted			
Always enroll			▬

Source: Authors.

Note: Characters on shaded background are those that enroll.

the nonpromoted group (10 individuals) is 70, and that average outcome for all individuals in the promoted group (10 individuals) is 110. Then what would the impact of the program be?

First, we can compute the straight difference between the promoted and the nonpromoted groups, which is 40. We also know that none of this difference of 40 comes from the *Nevers* because they do not enroll in either group. We also know that none of this difference of 40 comes from the *Enroll-if-promoted* because they enroll in both groups.

The second step is to recover the impact that the program has had on the *Enroll-if-promoted*. We know the entire average effect of 40 can be attributed to the *Enroll-if-promoted*, who make up only 50 percent of the population. To assess the average effect of the program on a complier, we divide 40 by the percentage of *Enroll-if-promoted* in the population. Although we cannot directly identify the *Enroll-if-promoted*, we are able to deduce what must be their *percentage* of the population: it is the difference in the enrollment rates of the promoted and the nonpromoted groups (50 percent or 0.5). Therefore, the average impact of the program on a complier is 40/0.5 = 80

Given that the promotion is assigned randomly, the promoted and non-promoted groups have equal characteristics, on average. Thus, the differences that we observe in average outcomes between the two groups must be caused by the fact that in the promoted group the *Enroll-if-promoted* enroll, while in the nonpromoted group they do not.[12]

Using Randomized Promotion to Estimate the Impact of the Health Insurance Subsidy Program

Let us now try using the randomized promotion method to evaluate the impact of the HISP. Assume that the ministry of health makes an executive decision that the health insurance subsidy should be made available immediately to any household that wants to enroll. However, you know that realistically this national scale-up will be incremental over time, and so you reach an agreement to accelerate enrollment in a random subset of villages through a promotion campaign. You undertake an intensive promotion effort in a random subsample of villages, including communication and social marketing campaigns aimed at increasing awareness of the HISP. After two years of promotion and program implementation, you find that 49.2 percent of households in villages that were randomly assigned to the promotion have enrolled in the program, while only 8.4 percent of households in nonpromoted villages have enrolled (table 4.4).

Because the promoted and nonpromoted villages were assigned at random, you know that the average characteristics of the two groups should be the same in the absence of the program. You can verify that assumption by comparing the baseline health expenditures (as well as any other characteristics) of the two populations. After two years of program implementation, you observe that the average health expenditure in the promoted villages is $14.9 compared with $18.8 in nonpromoted areas (a difference of minus $3.9). However, because the only difference between the promoted and nonpromoted villages is that promoted villages have greater enrollment in the program (thanks to the promotion), this difference of $3.9 in health expenditures must be due to the 40.4 percent of households that enrolled in the promoted villages because of the promotion. Therefore, we need to adjust

Table 4.4   Case 4—HISP Impact Using Randomized Promotion (Comparison of Means)

	Promoted villages	Nonpromoted villages	Difference	t-stat
Household health expenditures baseline	17.1	17.2	−0.1	−0.47
Household health expenditures follow-up	14.9	18.8	−3.9	−18.3
Enrollment in HISP	49.2%	8.4%	40.4%	

Source: Authors' calculation.

** Significant at the 1 percent level.

Table 4.5 Case 4—HISP Impact Using Randomized Promotion (Regression Analysis)

	Linear regression	Multivariate linear regression
Estimated impact on household health expenditures	−9.4** (0.51)	−9.7** (0.45)

Source: Authors' calculation.

Note: Standard errors are in parentheses.

** Significant at the 1 percent level.

the difference in health expenditures to be able to find the impact of the program on the *Enroll-if-promoted.* To do this, we divide the straight difference between the promoted groups by the percentage of *Enroll-if-promoted:* −3.9/0.404 = −$9.65. Your colleague, who took an econometrics class, then estimates the impact of the program through two-stage least squares and finds the results shown in table 4.5. This estimated impact is valid for those households that enrolled in the program because of the promotion but who otherwise would not have done so, in other words, for the *Enroll-if-promoted.* To extrapolate this result for the full population, we must assume that all other households would have reacted in a similar way had they enrolled in the program.

QUESTION 4
A. What are the basic assumptions required to accept the result from case 4?
B. Based on the result from case 4, should the HISP be scaled up nationally?

Randomized Promotion at Work

The randomized promotion method can be used in various settings. Gertler, Martinez, and Vivo (2008) used it to evaluate a maternal and child health insurance program in Argentina. Following the 2001 economic crisis, the government of Argentina observed that the population's health indicators had started deteriorating and, in particular, that infant mortality was increasing. It decided to introduce a national insurance scheme for mothers and their children, which was to be scaled up to the entire country within a year. Still, government officials wanted to evaluate the impact of the program to make sure that it was really improving the health status of the population. How could a comparison group be found if every mother and child in the country was entitled to enroll in the insurance scheme if they so desired? Data for the first provinces implementing the intervention showed that only

40 percent to 50 percent of households were actually enrolling in the program. So the government launched an intensive promotion campaign seeking to inform households about the program. However, the promotion campaign was implemented only in a random sample of villages, not in the entire country.

Other examples include assistance from nongovernmental organizations in a community-based school management evaluation, in Nepal, and the Bolivian Social Investment Fund (detailed in box 4.3).

Limitations of the Randomized Promotion Method

Randomized promotion is a useful strategy for evaluating the impact of voluntary programs and programs with universal eligibility, particularly because it does not require the exclusion of any eligible units. Nevertheless, the approach has some noteworthy limitations compared to randomized assignment of the treatment.

First, the promotion strategy must be effective. If the promotion campaign does not increase enrollment, then no difference between the pro-

---

Box 4.3: Promoting Education Infrastructure Investments in Bolivia

In 1991, Bolivia institutionalized and scaled up a successful Social Investment Fund (SIF) which provided financing to rural communities to carry out small-scale investments in education, health, and water infrastructure. The World Bank, which was helping to finance SIF, was able to build an impact evaluation into the program design.

As part of the impact evaluation of the education component, communities in the Chaco region were randomly selected for active promotion of the SIF intervention and received additional visits and encouragement to apply from program staff. The program was open to all eligible communities in the region and was demand driven in that communities had to apply for funds for a specific project. Not all communities took up the program, but take-up was higher among promoted communities.

Newman et al. (2002) used the randomized promotion as an instrumental variable. They found that the education investments succeeded in improving measures of school infrastructure quality such as electricity, sanitation facilities, textbooks per student, and student-teacher ratios. However they detected little impact on educational outcomes, except for a decrease of about 2.5 percent in the dropout rate. As a result of these findings, the ministry of education and the SIF now focus more attention and resources on the "software" of education, funding physical infrastructure improvements only when they form part of an integrated intervention.

Source: Newman et al. 2002.

Impact Evaluation in Practice

moted and the nonpromoted groups will appear, and there will be nothing to compare. It is thus crucial to pilot the promotion campaign extensively to make sure that it will be effective. On the positive side, the design of the promotion campaign can help program managers by teaching them how to increase enrollment.

Second, the methodology estimates the impact of the program only for a subset of the population of eligible units. Specifically, the program's average impact is computed from the group of individuals who sign up for the program only when encouraged to do so. However, individuals in this group may have very different characteristics than those individuals who always or never enroll, and therefore the average treatment effect for the entire population may be different from the average treatment effect estimated for individuals who participate only when encouraged.

Notes

1. Randomized assignment of treatment is also commonly referred to as "randomized control trials," "randomized evaluations," "experimental evaluations," and "social experiments," among other terms.

2. Note that this probability does not necessarily mean a 50-50 chance of winning the lottery. In fact, most randomized assignment evaluations will give each eligible unit a probability of selection that is determined so that the number of winners (treatments) equals the total available number of benefits. For example, if a program has enough funding to serve only 1,000 communities, out of a population of 10,000 eligible communities, then each community will be given a chance of 1 in 10 of being selected for treatment. Statistical power (a concept discussed in more detail in chapter 11) will be maximized when the evaluation sample is divided equally between the treatment and control groups. In the example here, for a total sample size of 2,000 communities, statistical power will be maximized by sampling all 1,000 treatment communities and a subsample of 1,000 control communities, rather than by taking a simple random sample of 20 percent of the original 10,000 eligible communities (which would produce an evaluation sample of roughly 200 treatment communities and 1,800 control communities).

3. For example, housing programs that provide subsidized homes routinely use lotteries to select program participants.

4. This property comes from the Law of Large Numbers.

5. An evaluation sample can be stratified by population subtypes and can also be clustered by sampling units. The sample size will depend on the particular type of random sampling used (see part 3).

6. Most software programs allow you to set a "seed number" to make the results of the randomized assignment fully transparent and replicable.

7. We will discuss concepts such as spillovers or contamination in more detail in chapter 8.

8. For statistical reasons, not all observed characteristics have to be similar in the treatment and comparison groups for randomization to be successful. As a rule of thumb, randomization will be considered successful if about 95 percent of the observed characteristics are similar. By "similar," we mean that we cannot reject the null hypothesis that the means are different between the two groups when using a 95 percent confidence interval. Even when the characteristics of the two groups are truly equal, one can expect that about 5 percent of the characteristics will show up with a statistically significant difference.

9. Note that in the medical sciences, patients in the comparison group typically receive a placebo, that is, something like a sugar pill that should have no effect on the intended outcome. That is done to additionally control for the "placebo effect," meaning the potential changes in behavior and outcomes from receiving a treatment, even if the treatment itself is ineffective.

10. These two steps correspond to the econometric technique of two-stage-least-squares, which produces a local average treatment effect.

11. Readers with a background in econometrics may recognize the concept: in statistical terms, the randomized offering of the program is used as an instrumental variable for actual enrollment. The two characteristics listed are exactly what would be required from a good instrumental variable:

    • The instrumental variable must be correlated with program participation.
    • The instrumental variable may not be correlated with outcomes (Y) (except through program participation) or with unobserved variables.

12. Again, readers familiar with econometrics may recognize that the impact is estimated by using "randomized assignment to the promoted and nonpromoted groups" as an instrumental variable for actual enrollment in the program.

References

Angrist, Joshua, Eric Bettinger, Erik Bloom, Elizabeth King, and Michael Kremer. 2002. "Vouchers for Private Schooling in Colombia: Evidence from a Randomized Natural Experiment." *American Economic Review* 92 (5): 1535–58.

Gertler, Paul, Sebastian Martinez, and Sigrid Vivo. 2008. "Child-Mother Provincial Investment Project *Plan Nacer*." University of California Berkeley and World Bank, Washington, DC.

Newman, John, Menno Pradhan, Laura B. Rawlings, Geert Ridder, Ramiro Coa, and Jose Luis Evia. 2002. "An Impact Evaluation of Education, Health, and Water Supply Investments by the Bolivian Social Investment Fund." *World Bank Economic Review* 16 (2): 241–74.

Schultz, Paul. 2004. "School Subsidies for the Poor: Evaluating the Mexican Progresa Poverty Program." *Journal of Development Economics* 74 (1): 199–250.

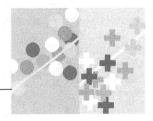

CHAPTER 5

Regression Discontinuity Design

Social programs often use an index to decide who is eligible to enroll in the program and who is not. For example, antipoverty programs are typically targeted to poor households, which are identified by a poverty score or index. The poverty score can be based on a proxy means formula that measures a set of basic household assets. Households with low scores are classified as poor, and households with higher scores are considered relatively well-off. The program authorities typically determine a threshold or cutoff score, below which households are deemed poor and are eligible for the program. Examples include the Mexico Progresa program (Buddelmeyer and Skoufias 2004) and Colombia's system for selecting beneficiaries of social spending, the so-called SISBEN (Barrera-Osorio, Linden, and Usquiola 2007).

Pension programs are another example of a type of program that targets units based on an eligibility index, albeit one of a different kind. Age constitutes a continuous index, and the retirement age constitutes the cutoff that determines eligibility. In other words, only people above a certain age are eligible to receive the pension. A third example of a continuous eligibility index would be test scores. Many countries award scholarships or prizes to the top performers on a standardized test, whose results are ranked from the lowest to the highest performer. If the number of scholarships is limited, then only students who score above a certain threshold score (such as the top 15 percent of students) will be eligible for the scholarship.

The regression discontinuity design (RDD) is an impact evaluation method that can be used for programs that have a continuous eligibility index with a clearly defined cutoff score to determine who is eligible and who is not. To apply a regression discontinuity design, two main conditions are needed:

1. A continuous eligibility index, in other words, a continuous measure on which the population of interest can be ranked, such as a poverty index, a test score, or age.

2. A clearly defined cutoff score, that is, a point on the index above or below which the population is classified as eligible for the program. For example, households with a poverty index score less than 50 out of 100 might be classified as poor, individuals age 67 and older might be classified as pensioners, and students with a test score of 90 or more out of 100 might be eligible for a scholarship. The cutoff scores in these examples are 50, 67, and 90, respectively.

Case 1: Subsidies for Fertilizer in Rice Production

Consider an agriculture program that subsidizes rice farmers' purchase of fertilizer with the objective of improving total yields. The program targets small and medium-size farms, which it classifies as farms with fewer than 50 acres of total land. Before the program starts, we might expect the relationship between farm size and total rice production to be as shown in figure 5.1, in that smaller farms have lower total outputs than larger farms. The eligibility score in this case is the number of acres of the farm, and the cutoff is 50 acres. Under program eligibility rules, farms below the 50-acre cutoff are eligible to receive fertilizer subsidies, and farms with 50 or more acres are not. In this case, we might expect to see a number of farms with 48, 49, or even 49.9 acres that participate in the program. Another group of farms with 50, 50.1, and 50.2 acres will not participate in the program because they fell just to the wrong side of the cutoff. The group of farms with 49.9 acres is likely to be very similar to the group of farms with 50.1 acres in all respects, except that one group received the fertilizer subsidy and the other group did not. As we move further away from the eligibility cutoff, eligible and ineligible units will become more different by construction, but we have a measure of how different they are based on the eligibility criteria and therefore we can control for those differences.

Once the program rolls out and subsidizes the cost of fertilizer for small and medium farms, the program evaluators could use a regression discon-

Figure 5.1 Rice Yield

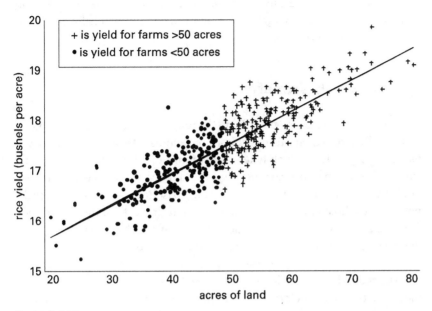

Source: Authors.

tinuity method to evaluate its impact. The regression discontinuity measures the difference in postintervention outcomes, such as total rice yields, between the units near the eligibility cutoff, which in our example is a farm size of 50 acres. The farms that were just too large to enroll in the program constitute the comparison group and generate an estimate of the counterfactual outcome for those farms in the treatment group that were just small enough to enroll. Given that these two groups of farms were very similar at baseline and are exposed to the same set of external factors over time (such as weather, price shocks, local and national agricultural policies, and so on), the only plausible reason for different outcomes in the postintervention period must be the program itself.

The regression discontinuity method allows us to successfully estimate the impact of a program without excluding any eligible population. However, note that the estimated impact is only valid in the neighborhood around the eligibility cutoff score. In our example, we have a valid estimate of the impact of the fertilizer subsidy program for the larger of the medium-size farms, that is, those with just under 50 acres of land. The impact evaluation will not necessarily be able to directly identify the impact of the program on small farms, say, those with 1 or 2 acres of land, where the effects of a fertilizer subsidy may differ in important ways from the effects observed on medium-size farms with 48 or 49 acres.

No comparison group exists for the small farms, since all of them are eligible to enroll in the program. The only valid comparison is for the farms near the cutoff score of 50.

Case 2: Cash Transfers

Assume that we are trying to evaluate the impact of a cash transfer program on the daily food expenditures of poor households. Also assume that we can use a poverty index,[1] which takes observations of a household's assets and summarizes them into a score between 0 and 100 that is used to rank households from the poorest to the richest. At the baseline, you would expect the poorer households to spend less on food, on average, than the richer ones. Figure 5.2 presents a possible relationship between the poverty index and daily household expenditures (the outcome) on food.

Now assume that the program targets only poor households, which are determined to be those with a score below 50. In other words, the poverty index can be used to determine eligibility: treatment will be offered only to households with a score of 50 or less. Households with a score above 50 are

Figure 5.2 Household Expenditures in Relation to Poverty (Preintervention)

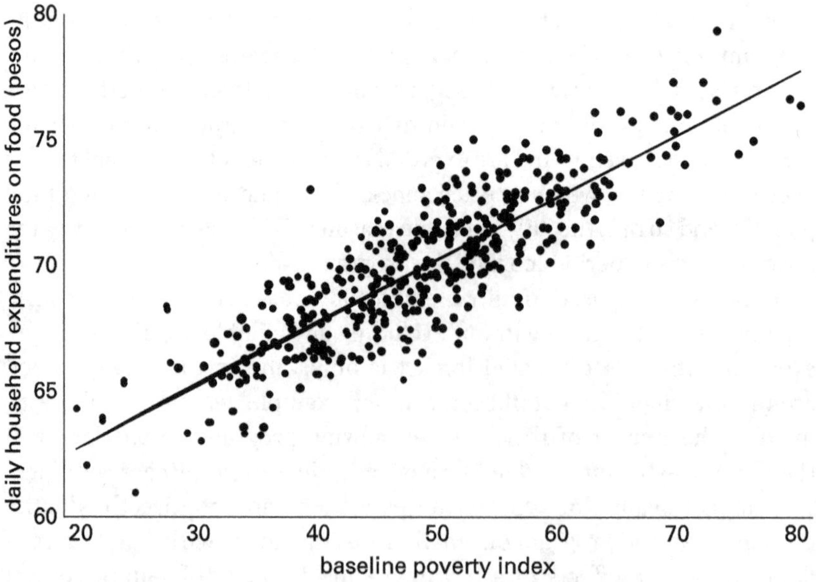

Source: Authors.

Figure 5.3 A Discontinuity in Eligibility for the Cash Transfer Program

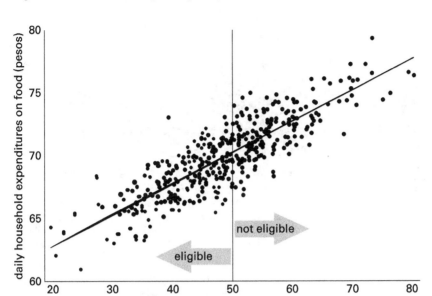

Source: Authors.

ineligible. In this example, the continuous eligibility index is simply the poverty index, and the cutoff score is 50. The continuous relationship between the eligibility index and the outcome variable (daily food expenditures) is illustrated in figure 5.3. Households just below the cutoff score are eligible for the program, while those just above the cutoff score are ineligible, even though the two types of households are very similar.

The RDD strategy exploits the discontinuity around the cutoff score to estimate the counterfactual. Intuitively, eligible households with scores just below the cutoff (50 and just below) will be very similar to households with a score just above the cutoff (for example, those scoring 51). On the continuous poverty index, the program has decided on one particular point (50) at which there is a sudden change, or discontinuity, in eligibility for the program. Since the households just above the cutoff score of 50 are similar to the ones that are just below it, except that they do not receive the cash transfers, the households just above can be used as a comparison group for the households just below. In other words, households ineligible for the program but close enough to the cutoff will be used as a comparison group to estimate the counterfactual (what would have happened to the group of eligible households in the absence of the program).

Figure 5.4 Household Expenditures in Relation to Poverty (Postintervention)

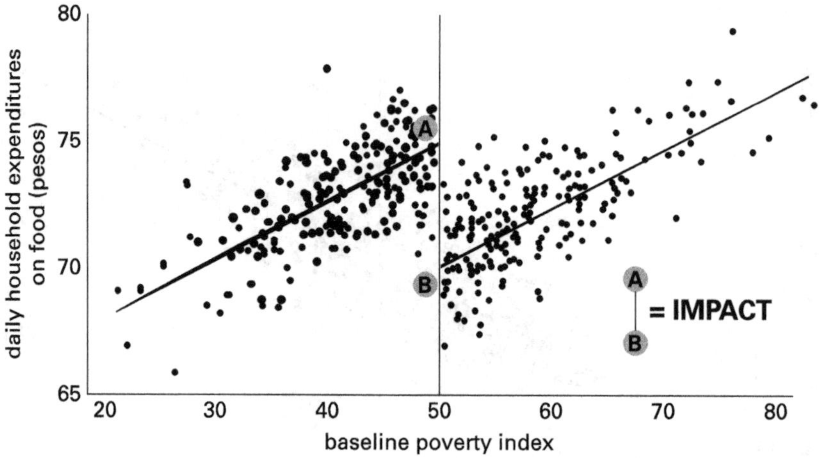

Source: Authors.

Figure 5.4 presents a possible postintervention situation conveying the intuition behind the RDD identification strategy. Average outcomes for (eligible) households with baseline poverty scores below the cutoff score are now higher than average outcomes for (ineligible) households with baseline scores just above the cutoff. Given the continuous relationship between scores on the poverty index and daily expenditures on food before the program, the only plausible explanation for the discontinuity that we observe postintervention must be the existence of the cash transfer program. In other words, since households in the vicinity (right and left) of the cutoff score had similar baseline characteristics, the difference in average food expenditures between the two groups is a valid estimate of the program's impact.

Using the Regression Discontinuity Design Method to Evaluate the Health Insurance Subsidy Program

Let us apply RDD to our health insurance subsidy program (HISP). After doing some more investigation into the design of the HISP, you find that in practice the authorities targeted the program to low-income households using the national poverty line. The poverty line is based on a poverty index that assigns each household in the country a score between 20 and 100 based on its assets, housing conditions, and sociodemographic struc-

Figure 5.5 Poverty Index and Health Expenditures at the Health Insurance Subsidy Program Baseline

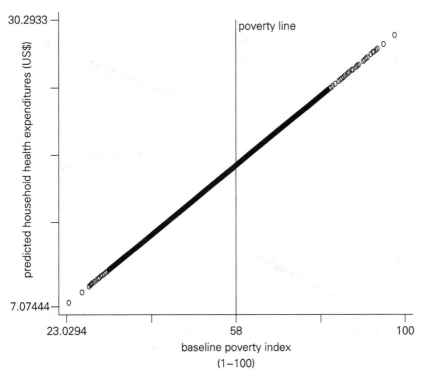

Source: Authors.

ture. The poverty line has been officially set at 58. This means that all households with a score of less than 58 are classified as poor, and all households with a score of more than 58 are considered to be nonpoor. Even in the treatment villages, only poor households were eligible to enroll in the HISP; nonetheless, your sample includes data on both poor and nonpoor households in the treatment villages.

Using the households in your sample of treatment villages, a colleague helps you run a multivariate regression and plot the relationship between the poverty index and predicted household health expenditures before HISP started (figure 5.5). The figure shows clearly that as a household's score on the poverty index rises, the regression predicts a higher level of health expenditures, reflecting the fact that wealthier households tended to have higher expenditures on, and consumption of, drugs and primary health services. Note that the relationship between the poverty index and health expenditures is continuous, that is, there is no evidence of a change in the relationship around the poverty line.

Figure 5.6 Poverty Index and Health Expenditures – Health Insurance Subsidy Program Two Years Later

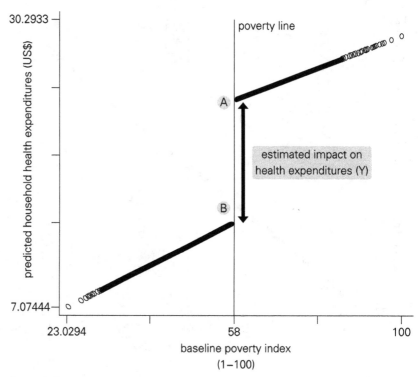

Source: Authors.

Two years after the start of the pilot, you observe that only households with a score below 58 (that is, to the left of the poverty line) have been allowed to enroll in the HISP. Using follow-up data, you again plot the relationship between the scores on the poverty index and predicted health expenditures and find the relation illustrated in figure 5.6. This time, the relationship between the poverty index and the predicted health expendi-

Table 5.1 Case 5—HISP Impact Using Regression Discontinuity Design (Regression Analysis)

	Multivariate linear regression
Estimated impact on household health expenditures	−9.05** (0.43)

Source: Authors.

Note: Standard errors are in parentheses.

** Significant at the 1 percent level.

tures is no longer continuous—there is a clear break, or "discontinuity," at the poverty line.

The discontinuity reflects a decrease in health expenditures for those households eligible to receive the program. Given that households on both sides of the cutoff score of 58 are very similar, the only plausible explanation for the different level of health expenditures is that one group of households was eligible to enroll in the program and the other was not. You estimate this difference through a regression with the findings shown in table 5.1.

QUESTION 5

A. Is the result shown in table 5.1 valid for all eligible households?

B. Compared with the impact estimated with randomized assignment, what does this result say about those households with a poverty index of just under 58?

C. Based on this result from case 5, should the HISP be scaled up nationally?

The RDD Method at Work

Regression discontinuity design has been used in various contexts. Lemieux and Milligan (2005) analyzed the effects of social assistance on labor supply in Quebec. Martinez (2004) studied the effect of old age

---

Box 5.1: Social Assistance and Labor Supply in Canada

One of the classic studies using the RDD method took advantage of a sharp discontinuity in a social assistance program in Quebec, Canada, to understand the effects of the program on labor market outcomes. The welfare program, funded through the Canadian Assistance Plan, provides help to the unemployed. For many years, the program offered significantly lower payments to individuals under the age of 30 with no children, compared to individuals older than 30—$185 a month versus $507.

To rigorously evaluate this program, Lemieux and Milligan (2005) limited the sample to men without children and without a high school diploma and gathered data from the Canadian Census and the Labor Force Survey. To justify using the RDD approach, they showed that men close to the discontinuity (between the ages of 25 and 39) are very similar on observable characteristics.

Comparing men on both sides of the eligibility threshold, the authors found that access to greater social assistance benefits actually reduced employment by about 4.5 percent for men in this age range without children.

Source: Lemieux and Milligan 2005.

---

pensions on consumption in Bolivia. Filmer and Schady (2009) assessed the impact of a program that provided scholarships to poor students to encourage school enrollment and increase test scores in Cambodia. Buddelmeyer and Skoufias (2004) examined the performance of regression discontinuity relative to the randomized experiment in the case of Progresa and found that the impacts estimated using the two methods are similar for a large majority of the outcomes analyzed. A few of these examples are described in detail in boxes 5.1, 5.2, and 5.3.

Box 5.2: School Fees and Enrollment Rates in Colombia

In Colombia, Barrera-Osorio, Linden, and Urquiola (2007) used regression discontinuity design to evaluate the impact of a school fee reduction program (Gratuitad) on school enrollment rates in the city of Bogota. That program is targeted based on an index called the SISBEN, which is a continuous poverty index whose value is determined by household characteristics, such as location, the building materials of the home, the services that are available there, demographics, health, education, income, and the occupations of household members. The government established two cutoff scores along the SISBEN index: children of households with scores below cutoff score no. 1 are eligible for free education from grades 1 to 11; children of households with scores between cutoff scores no. 1 and no. 2 are eligible for a 50 percent subsidy on fees for grades 10 and 11; and children from households with scores above cutoff score no. 2 are not eligible for free education or subsidies.

The authors used regression discontinuity design for four reasons. First, household characteristics such as income or the education level of the household head are continu-

ous along the SISBEN score at the baseline; in other words, there are no "jumps" in characteristics along the SISBEN score. Second, households on both sides of the cutoff scores have similar characteristics, suggesting that the design had produced credible comparison groups. Third, a large sample of households was available. Finally, the government kept the formula used to calculate the SISBEN index secret, so that households would not be able to manipulate their scores.

Using the RDD method, the researchers found that the program had a significant positive impact on school enrollment rates. Specifically, enrollment was three percentage points higher for primary school students from households below cutoff score no. 1 and 6 percent higher for high school students from households between cutoff scores no. 1 and no. 2. This study provides evidence on the benefits of reducing the direct costs of schooling, particularly for at-risk students. However, its authors also call for further research on price elasticities to better inform the design of subsidy programs such as this one.

Source: Barrera-Osorio, Linden, and Urquiola 2007.

Box 5.3: Social Safety Nets Based on a Poverty Index in Jamaica

The RDD method was also used to evaluate the impact of a social safety net initiative in Jamaica. In 2001, the government of Jamaica initiated the Programme of Advancement through Health and Education (PATH) to increase investments in human capital and improve the targeting of welfare benefits to the poor. The program provided health and education grants to children in eligible poor households, conditional on school attendance and regular health care visits. The average monthly benefit for each child was about $6.50 in addition to government waiver of certain health and education fees.

Because eligibility for the program was determined by a scoring formula, Levy and Ohls (2007) were able to compare households just below the eligibility threshold to households just above (between 2 and 15 points from the cutoff). The researchers justify using the RDD method with baseline data showing that the treatment and comparison households had similar levels of poverty, measured by proxy means scores,

and similar levels of motivation, in that all of the households in the sample had applied to the program. The researchers also used the program eligibility score in the regression analysis to help control for any differences between the two groups.

Levy and Ohls (2007) found that the PATH program increased school attendance for children ages 6 to 17 by an average of 0.5 days per month, which is significant given an already fairly high attendance rate of 85 percent. Also, health care visits by children ages 0 to 6 increased by approximately 38 percent. While the researchers were unable to find any longer-term impacts on school achievement or health care status, they concluded that the magnitude of the impacts they did find was broadly consistent with conditional cash transfer programs implemented in other countries. A final interesting aspect of this evaluation is that it gathered both quantitative and qualitative data, using information systems, interviews, focus groups, and household surveys.

Source: Levy and Ohls 2007.

Limitations and Interpretation of the Regression Discontinuity Design Method

Regression discontinuity design estimates *local* average impacts around the eligibility cutoff at the point where treatment and comparison units are most similar. As we get closer to the cutoff, the units that are to the left and right of it will look more similar. In fact, when we get extremely close to the cutoff score, the units on the left and right of the line will be so similar that our comparison will be as good as if we had chosen the treatment and comparison groups using randomized assignment of the treatment.

Because the RDD method estimates the impact of the program around the cutoff score, or *locally*, the estimate cannot necessarily be generalized to units whose scores are further away from the cutoff score, this is, where eligible and ineligible individuals may not be as similar. The fact that the RDD method will not be able to compute an average treatment effect for all program participants can be seen as both a strength and a limitation of the method, depending on the evaluation question of interest. If the evaluation primarily seeks to answer the question, Should the program exist or not?, then the average treatment effect for the entire eligible population may be the most relevant parameter, and clearly the RDD will fall short of being perfect. However, if the policy question of interest is, Should the program be cut or expanded at the margin?, then the RDD produces precisely the local estimate of interest to inform this important policy decision.

The fact that the RDD method produces local average treatment effects also raises challenges in terms of the statistical power of the analysis. Since effects are estimated only around the cutoff score, fewer observations can be used than in other methods that would include all units. Relatively large evaluation samples are required to obtain sufficient statistical power when applying RDD. In practice, we determine a bandwidth around the cutoff score that will be included in the estimation by considering the balance in observed characteristics of the population above and below the cutoff. We can then do the estimation again using different bandwidths to check whether the estimates are sensitive to the chosen bandwidth. As a general rule, the wider the bandwidth, the greater the statistical power of the analysis, since more observations are included. However, moving further from the cutoff may also require additional functional form assumptions to obtain a credible estimate of impact.

An additional caveat when using the RDD method is that the specification may be sensitive to the functional form used in modeling the relationship between the eligibility score and the outcome of interest. In the example of the cash transfer program, we assumed that the baseline relation between the poverty index of households and their daily expenditures on food was simple and linear. In reality, the relation between the eligibility index and the outcome of interest (Y) at the baseline could be much more complex and could involve nonlinear relationships and interactions between variables. If we do not account for these complex relationships in the estimation, they might be mistaken for a discontinuity in the postintervention outcomes. In practice, we can estimate program impact using various functional forms (linear, quadratic, cubic, etc.) to assess whether, in fact, the impact estimates are sensitive to functional form.

Even with these limitations, regression discontinuity design yields unbiased estimates of the impact in the vicinity of the eligibility cutoff. The regression discontinuity strategy takes advantage of the program assignment rules, using continuous eligibility indexes, which are already common in many social programs. When index-based targeting rules are applied, it is not necessary to exclude a group of eligible households or individuals from receiving the treatment for the sake of the evaluation because regression discontinuity design can be used instead.

Note

1. This is sometimes called a "proxy-means test" because it takes the household's assets as a proxy or estimator for its means or purchasing power.

References

Barrera-Osorio, Felipe, Leigh Linden, and Miguel Urquiola. 2007. "The Effects of User Fee Reductions on Enrollment: Evidence from a Quasi-Experiment." Columbia University and World Bank, Washington, DC.

Buddelmeyer, Hielke, and Emmanuel Skoufias. 2004. "An Evaluation of the Performance of Regression Discontinuity Design on PROGRESA." World Bank Policy Research Working Paper 3386, IZA Discussion Paper 827, World Bank, Washington, DC.

Filmer, Deon, and Norbert Schady. 2009. "School Enrollment, Selection and Test Scores." World Bank Policy Research Working Paper 4998, World Bank, Washington, DC.

Lemieux, Thomas, and Kevin Milligan. 2005. "Incentive Effects of Social Assistance: A Regression Discontinuity Approach." NBER Working Paper 10541, National Bureau of Economic Research, Cambridge, MA.

Levy, Dan, and Jim Ohls. 2007. "Evaluation of Jamaica's PATH Program: Final Report." Mathematica Policy Research, Inc., Ref. 8966-090, Washington, DC.

Martinez, S. 2004. "Pensions, Poverty and Household Investments in Bolivia." University of California, Berkeley, CA.

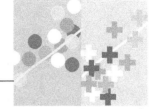

CHAPTER 6

Difference-in-Differences

The three impact evaluation methods discussed up to this point—*randomized assignment, randomized promotion,* and *regression discontinuity design* (RDD)—all produce estimates of the counterfactual through explicit program assignment rules that the evaluator knows and understands. We have discussed why these methods offer credible estimates of the counterfactual with relatively few assumptions and conditions. The next two types of methods—*difference-in-differences* (DD) and *matching methods*—offer the evaluator an additional set of tools that can be applied in situations in which the program assignment rules are less clear or in which none of the three methods previously described is feasible. As we will see, both DD and matching methods can be powerful statistical tools; many times they will be used together or in conjunction with other impact evaluation methods.

Both difference-in-differences and matching are commonly used; however, both also typically require stronger assumptions than randomized selection methods. We also stress at the outset that both of these methods absolutely require the existence of baseline data.[1]

The difference-in-differences method does what its name suggests. It compares the *changes* in outcomes over time between a population that is enrolled in a program (the treatment group) and a population that is not (the comparison group). Take, for example, a road construction program that cannot be randomly assigned and is not assigned based on an index with a clearly defined cutoff that would permit an RDD. One of the program's objectives is to improve access to labor markets, with one of the outcome

Key Concept:

Difference-in-differences estimates the counterfactual for the change in outcome for the treatment group by calculating the change in outcome for the comparison group. This method allows us to take into account any differences between the treatment and comparison groups that are constant over time.

indicators being employment. As we saw in chapter 3, simply observing the before-and-after change in employment rates for areas affected by the program will not give us the program's causal impact because many other factors are also likely to influence employment over time. At the same time, comparing areas that received and did not receive the roads program will be problematic if unobserved reasons exist for why some areas received the program and others did not (the selection bias problem discussed in the enrolled–versus–not-enrolled scenario).

However, what if we combined the two methods and compared the before-and-after changes in outcomes for a group that enrolled in the program to the before-and-after changes for a group that did not enroll in the program? The difference in the before-and-after outcomes for the enrolled group—the first difference—*controls* for factors that are constant over time in that group, since we are comparing the same group to itself. But we are still left with the outside time-varying factors. One way to capture those time-varying factors is to measure the before-and-after change in outcomes for a group that did *not* enroll in the program but was exposed to the same set of environmental conditions—the second difference. If we "clean" the first difference of other time-varying factors that affect the outcome of interest by subtracting the second difference, then we have eliminated the main source of bias that worried us in the simple before-and-after comparisons. The difference-in-differences approach thus combines the two counterfeit counterfactuals (before-and-after comparisons and comparisons between those who choose to enroll and those who choose not to enroll) to produce a better estimate of the counterfactual. In our roads case, the DD method might compare the change in employment before and after the program is implemented for individuals living in areas affected by the road construction program to changes in employment in areas where the roads program was not implemented.

It is important to note that the counterfactual being estimated here is the *change* in outcomes for the comparison group. The treatment and comparison groups do not necessarily need to have the same preintervention conditions. But for DD to be valid, the comparison group must accurately represent the change in outcomes that would have been experienced by the treatment group in the absence of treatment. To apply difference-in-differences, all that is necessary is to measure outcomes in the group that receives the program (the treatment group) and the group that does not (the comparison group) both before and after the program. The method does not require us to specify the rules by which the treatment is assigned.

Figure 6.1 illustrates the difference-in-differences method. A treatment group is enrolled in a program, and a comparison group is not enrolled. The

Figure 6.1 Difference-in-Differences

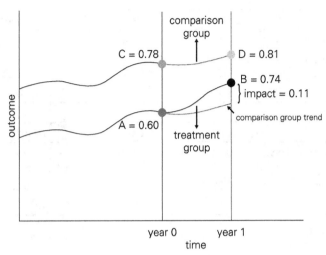

Source: Authors.

before-and-after outcome variables for the treatment group are *A* and *B*, respectively, while the outcome for the comparison group goes from *C*, before the program, to *D* after the program has been implemented.

You will remember our two counterfeit counterfactuals—the difference in outcomes before and after the intervention for the treatment group *(B – A)* and the difference in outcomes[2] after the intervention between the treatment and comparison groups *(B – D)*. In difference-in-differences, the estimate of the counterfactual is obtained by computing the change in outcomes for the comparison group *(D – C)*. This counterfactual change is then subtracted from the change in outcomes for the treatment group *(B - A)*.

In summary, the impact of the program is simply computed as the difference between two differences:

DD impact = *(B – A) – (D – C) = (B – E) =* (0.74 – 0.60) – (0.81 – 0.78) = 0.11.

The relationships presented in figure 6.1 can also be presented in a simple table. Table 6.1 disentangles the components of the difference-in-differences estimates. The first row contains outcomes for the treatment group before *(A)* and after *(B)* the intervention. The before-and-after comparison for the treatment group is the first difference *(B – A)*. The second row contains outcomes for the comparison group before the intervention *(C)* and after the intervention *(D)*, so the second (counterfactual) difference is *(D – C)*.

Table 6.1 The Difference-in-Differences Method

	After	Before	Difference
Treatment/enrolled	B	A	B – A
Comparison/ nonenrolled	D	C	D – C
Difference	B – D	A – C	DD = (B – A) – (D – C)

	After	Before	Difference
Treatment enrolled	0.74	0.60	0.14
Comparison/ nonenrolled	0.81	0.78	0.03
Difference	–0.07	–0.18	DD = 0.14 – 0.03 = 0.11

Source: Authors.

The difference-in-differences method computes the impact estimate as follows:

1. We calculate the difference in the outcome (*Y*) between the before and after situations for the treatment group (*B – A*).

2. We calculate the difference in the outcome (*Y*) between the before and after situations for the comparison group (*D – C*).

3. Then we calculate the difference between the difference in outcomes for the treatment group (*B – A*) and the difference for the comparison group (*D – C*), or DD = (*B – A*) – (*D – C*). This "difference-in-differences" is our impact estimate.

How Is the Difference-in-Differences Method Helpful?

To understand how difference-in-differences is helpful, let us start with our second counterfeit counterfactual, which compared units that were enrolled in a program with those that were not enrolled in the program. Remember that the primary concern with this was that the two sets of units may have had different characteristics and that it may be those characteristics rather than the program that explain the difference in outcomes between the two groups. The *unobserved* differences in characteristics were particularly worrying: by definition, it is impossible for us to include unobserved differences in characteristics in the analysis.

The difference-in-differences method helps resolve this problem to the extent that many characteristics of units or individuals can reasonably be assumed to be constant over time (or *time-invariant*). Think, for example, of *observed* characteristics, such as a person's year of birth, a region's location close to the ocean, a town's level of economic development, or a father's level of education. Most of these types of variables, although plausibly related to outcomes, will probably not change over the course of an evaluation. Using the same reasoning, we might conclude that many *unobserved* characteristics of individuals are also more or less constant over time. Consider, for example, a person's intelligence or such personality traits as motivation, optimism, self-discipline, or family health history. It is plausible that many of these intrinsic characteristics of a person would not change over time.

When the same individual is observed before and after a program and we compute a simple difference in outcome for that individual, we cancel out the effect of all of the characteristics that are unique to that individual and that do not change over time. Interestingly, we are canceling out (or controlling for) not only the effect of *observed* time-invariant characteristics but also the effect of *unobserved* time-invariant characteristics such as those mentioned above.

The "Equal Trends" Assumption in Difference-in-Differences

Although difference-in-differences allows us to take care of differences between the treatment and the comparison group that are constant over time, it will not help us eliminate the differences between the treatment and comparison groups that change over time. In the roads example above, if treatment areas also benefit from the construction of a new seaport at the same time as the road construction, we will not be able to account for the seaport construction by using a difference-in-differences approach. For the method to provide a valid estimate of the counterfactual, we must assume that no such time-varying differences exist between the treatment and comparison groups.

Another way to think about this is that in the absence of the program, the differences in outcomes between the treatment and comparison groups would need to move in tandem. That is, without treatment, outcomes would need to increase or decrease at the same rate in both groups; we require that outcomes display *equal trends in the absence of treatment*.

Unfortunately, there is no way for us to prove that the differences between the treatment and comparison groups would have moved in tandem in the absence of the program. The reason is that we cannot observe what would have happened to the treatment group in the absence of the treatment—in other words, we cannot observe the counterfactual!

Thus, when we use the difference-in-differences method, we must *assume* that, in the absence of the program, the outcome in the treatment group would have moved in tandem with the outcome in the comparison group. Figure 6.2 illustrates a violation of this fundamental assumption, which is needed for the difference-in-differences method to produce credible impact estimates. If outcome trends are different for the treatment and comparison groups, then the estimated treatment effect obtained by difference-in-difference methods would be invalid, or biased. The reason is that the trend for the comparison group is not a valid estimate of the counterfactual trend that would have prevailed for the treatment group in the absence of the program. As we see in figure 6.2, outcomes for the comparison group grow faster than outcomes for the treatment group in the absence of the program, so using the trend for the comparison group as a counterfactual for the trend for the treatment group leads to an underestimation of the program's impact.

Testing the Validity of the "Equal Trends" Assumption in Difference-in-Differences

The validity of the underlying assumption of equal trends can be assessed even though it cannot be proved. A good validity check is to compare

Figure 6.2 Difference-in-Differences when Outcome Trends Differ

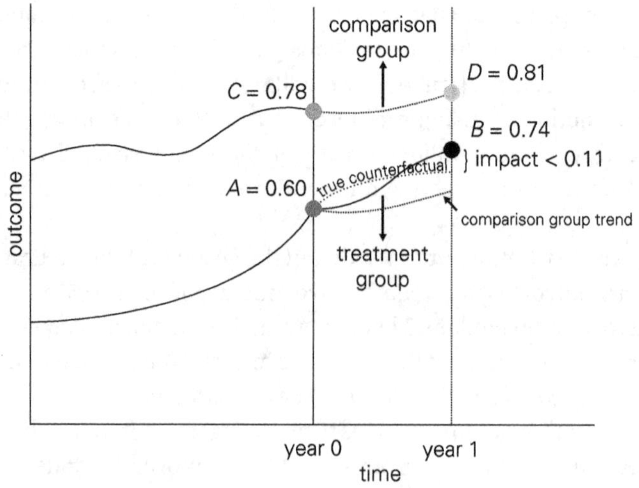

Source: Authors.

changes in outcomes for the treatment and comparison groups *before* the program is implemented. If the outcomes moved in tandem before the program started, we gain confidence that outcomes would have continued to move in tandem in the postintervention period. To check for equality of preintervention trends, we need at least two serial observations on the treatment and comparison groups before the start of the program. This means that the evaluation would require three serial observations—two preintervention observations to assess the preprogram trends and at least one postintervention observation to assess impact with the difference-in-differences formula.

A second way to test the assumption of equal trends would be to perform what is known as a "placebo" test. For this test, you perform an additional difference-in-differences estimation using a "fake" treatment group, that is, a group that you know was not affected by the program. Say, for example, that you estimate how additional tutoring for grade 7 students affects their probability of attending school, and you choose grade 8 students as the comparison group. To test whether seventh and eighth graders have the same trends in terms of school attendance, you could test whether eighth graders and sixth graders have the same trends. You know that sixth graders are not affected by the program, so if you perform a difference-in-differences estimation using grade 8 students as the comparison group and grade 6 students as the fake treatment group, you *have to* find a zero impact. If you do not, then the impact that you find must come from some underlying difference in trends between sixth graders and eighth graders. This, in turn, casts doubt on whether seventh graders and eighth graders can be assumed to have parallel trends in the absence of the program.

A placebo test can be performed not only with a fake treatment group but also with a fake outcome. In the tutoring example, you may want to test the validity of using the grade 8 students as a comparison group by estimating the impact of the tutoring on an outcome that you know is not affected by it, such as the number of siblings that the students have. If your difference-in-differences estimation finds an "impact" of the tutoring on the number of siblings that the students have, then you know that your comparison group must be flawed.

A fourth way to test the assumption of parallel trends would be to perform the difference-in-differences estimation using different comparison groups. In the tutoring example, you would first do the estimation using grade 8 students as the comparison group, and then do a second estimation using grade 6 students as the comparison group. If both groups are valid comparison groups, you would find that the estimated impact is approximately the same in both calculations.

Using Difference-in-Differences to Evaluate the Health Insurance Subsidy Program

Difference-in-differences can be used to evaluate our health insurance subsidy program (HISP). In this scenario, you have two rounds of data on two groups of households, one group that enrolled in the program and another that did not. Remembering the case of the selected enrolled and nonenrolled groups, you realize that you cannot simply compare the average health expenditures of the two groups because of selection bias. Because you have data for two periods for each household in the sample, you can use those data to solve some of these challenges by comparing the change in expenditures for the two groups, assuming that the change in the health expenditures of the nonenrolled group reflects what would have happened to the expenditures of the enrolled group in the absence of the program (see table 6.2). Note that it does not matter which way you calculate the double difference.

Next, you estimate the effect using regression analysis (table 6.3). Using a simple linear regression, you find that the program reduced household health expenditures by $7.8. You then refine your analysis by using multivariate linear regression to take into account a host of other factors, and you find the same reduction in household health expenditures.

QUESTION 6

A. What are the basic assumptions required to accept this result from case 6?

B. Based on the result from case 6, should the HISP be scaled up nationally?

Table 6.2   Case 6—HISP Impact Using Difference-in-Differences (Comparison of Means)

	After (follow-up)	Before (baseline)	Difference
Enrolled	7.8	14.4	−6.6
Nonenrolled	21.8	20.6	1.2
Difference			DD = −6.6 − 1.2 = −7.8

Source: Authors.

Table 6.3   Case 6—HISP Impact Using Difference-in-Differences (Regression Analysis)

	Linear regression	Multivariate linear regression
Estimated impact on household health expenditures	−7.8** (0.33)	−7.8** (0.33)

Source: Authors.

Note: Standard errors are in parentheses.

** Significant at the 1 percent level.

The Difference-in-Differences Method at Work

Despite its limitations, the difference-in-differences method remains one of the most frequently used impact evaluation methodologies, and many examples appear in the literature. For example, Duflo (2001) analyzed the schooling and labor market impacts of school construction in Indonesia. DiTella and Schargrodsky (2005) examined whether an increase in police forces reduces crime. Another key example from the literature is described in box 6.1.

Box 6.1: Water Privatization and Infant Mortality in Argentina

Galiani, Gertler, and Schargrodsky (2005) used the difference-in-differences method to address an important policy question: whether privatizing the provision of water services can improve health outcomes and help alleviate poverty. During the 1990s, Argentina initiated one of the largest privatization campaigns ever, transferring local water companies to regulated private companies covering about 30 percent of the country's municipalities and 60 percent of the population. The privatization process took place over a decade, with the largest number of privatizations occurring after 1995.

Galiani, Gertler, and Schargrodsky (2005) took advantage of that variation in ownership status over time to determine the impact of privatization on under-age-5 mortality. Before 1995, the rates of child mortality were declining at about the same pace throughout Argentina; after 1995, mortality rates declined faster in municipalities that had privatized their water services. The researchers argue that, in this context, the identification assumptions behind difference-in-differences are likely to hold true. First, they show that the decision to privatize was uncorrelated with economic shocks or historical levels of child mortality. Second, they show that no differences in child mortality trends are observed between the comparison and treatment municipalities before the privatization movement began.

They checked the strength of their findings by decomposing the effect of privatization on child mortality by cause of death and found that the privatization of water services is correlated with reductions in deaths from infectious and parasitic diseases but not from causes unrelated to water conditions, such as accidents or congenital diseases. In the end, the evaluation determined that child mortality fell about 8 percent in areas that privatized and that the effect was largest, about 26 percent, in the poorest areas, where the expansion of the water network was the greatest. This study shed light on a number of important policy debates surrounding the privatization of public services. The researchers concluded that in Argentina, the regulated private sector proved more successful than the public sector in improving indicators of access, service, and most significantly, child mortality.

Source: Galiani, Gertler, and Schargrodsky 2005.

Limitations of the Difference-in-Differences Method

Difference-in-differences is generally less robust than the randomized selection methods (randomized assignment, randomized offering, and randomized promotion). Even when trends are parallel before the start of the intervention, bias in the estimation may still appear. The reason is that DD attributes to the intervention *any differences in trends* between the treatment and comparison groups that occur *from the time intervention begins*. If any other factors are present that affect the difference in trends between the two groups, the estimation will be invalid or biased.

Let us say that you are trying to estimate the impact on rice production of subsidizing fertilizer and are doing this by measuring the rice production of subsidized (treatment) farmers and unsubsidized (comparison) farmers before and after the distribution of the subsidies. If in year 1 the subsidized farmers are affected by drought, whereas the unsubsidized farmers are not, then the difference-in-differences estimate will produce an invalid estimate of the impact of subsidizing fertilizer. In general, any factor that affects only the treatment group, and does so at the same time that the group receives the treatment, has the potential to invalidate or bias the estimate of the impact of the program. Difference-in-differences *assumes* that no such factor is present.

Notes

1. Although randomized assignment, randomized promotion, and regression discontinuity design theoretically do not require baseline data, in practice having a baseline is very useful for confirming that the characteristics of the treatment and comparison groups are balanced. For this reason, we recommend including a baseline as part of the evaluation. In addition to verifying balance, a number of other good reasons argue for collecting baseline data, even when the method does not absolutely require them. First, having preintervention (exogenous) population characteristics can enable the evaluator to determine whether the program has a different impact on different groups of the eligible population (so-called heterogeneity analysis). Second, the baseline data can also be used to perform analysis that can guide policy even before the intervention starts, and collecting the baseline data can serve as a massive pilot for the postintervention data collection. Third, baseline data can serve as an "insurance policy" in case randomized assignment is not implemented; as a second option, the evaluator could use a combination of matching and differences-in-differences. Finally, baseline data can add statistical power to the analysis when the number of units in the treatment and comparison groups is limited.

2. All differences between points should be read as vertical differences in outcomes on the vertical axis.

References

DiTella, Rafael, and Ernesto Schargrodsky. 2005. "Do Police Reduce Crime? Estimates Using the Allocation of Police Forces after a Terrorist Attack." *American Economic Review* 94 (1): 115–33.

Duflo, Esther. 2001. "Schooling and Labor Market Consequences of School Construction in Indonesia: Evidence from an Unusual Policy Experiment." *American Economic Review* 91 (4): 795–813.

Galiani, Sebastian, Paul Gertler, and Ernesto Schargrodsky. 2005. "Water for Life: The Impact of the Privatization of Water Services on Child Mortality." *Journal of Political Economy* 113 (1): 83–120.

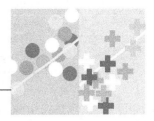

CHAPTER 7

Matching

The method described in this chapter consists of a set of statistical techniques that we will refer to collectively as "matching." Matching methods can be applied in the context of almost any program assignment rules, so long as a group exists that has not participated in the program. Matching methods typically rely on observed characteristics to construct a comparison group, and so the methods require the strong assumption of no unobserved differences in the treatment and comparison populations that are also associated with the outcomes of interest. Because of that strong assumption, matching methods are typically most useful in combination with one of the other methodologies that we have discussed.

Matching essentially uses statistical techniques to construct an artificial comparison group by identifying for every possible observation under treatment a nontreatment observation (or set of nontreatment observations) that has the most similar characteristics possible. Consider a case in which you are attempting to evaluate the impact of a program and have a data set that contains both households that enrolled in the program and households that did not enroll, for example, the Demographic and Health Survey. The program that you are trying to evaluate does not have any clear assignment rules (such as randomized assignment or an eligibility index) that explain why some households enrolled in the program and others did not. In such a context, matching methods will enable you to identify the set of nonenrolled households that look most similar to the treatment households, based on the characteristics that you have available in your data set. These "matched"

Key Concept:

Matching uses large data sets and heavy statistical techniques to construct the best possible artificial comparison group for a given treatment group.

nonenrolled households then become the comparison group that you use to estimate the counterfactual.

Finding a good match for each program participant requires approximating as closely as possible the variables or *determinants* that explain that individual's decision to enroll in the program. Unfortunately, this is easier said than done. If the list of relevant observed characteristics is very large, or if each characteristic takes on many values, it may be hard to identify a match for each of the units in the treatment group. As you increase the number of characteristics or dimensions against which you want to match units that enrolled in the program, you may run into what is called "the curse of dimensionality." For example, if you use only three important characteristics to identify the matched comparison group, such as age, gender, and region of birth, you will probably find matches for all program enrollees in the pool of nonenrollees, but you run the risk of leaving out other potentially important characteristics. However, if you increase the list of variables, say, to include number of children, number of years of education, age of the mother, age of the father, and so forth, your database may not contain a good match for most of the program enrollees, unless it contains a very large number of observations. Figure 7.1 illustrates matching based on four characteristics: age, gender, months unemployed, and secondary school diploma.

Fortunately, the curse of dimensionality can be quite easily solved using a method called "propensity score matching" (Rosenbaum and Rubin 1983). In this approach, we no longer need to try to match each enrolled unit to a nonenrolled unit that has exactly the same value for all observed control characteristics. Instead, for each unit in the treatment group and in the pool of nonenrollees we compute the probability that a unit will enroll in the

Figure 7.1 Exact Matching on Four Characteristics

Treated units					Untreated units			
Age	Gender	Months unemployed	Secondary diploma		Age	Gender	Months unemployed	Secondary diploma
19	1	3	0		24	1	8	1
35	1	12	1		38	0	2	0
41	0	17	1		58	1	7	1
23	1	6	0		21	0	2	1
55	0	21	1		34	1	20	0
27	0	4	1		41	0	17	1
24	1	8	1		46	0	9	0
46	0	3	0		41	0	11	1
33	0	12	1		19	1	3	0
40	1	2	0		27	0	4	0

Source: Authors, drawing from multiple sources.

program based on the observed values of its characteristics, the so-called propensity score. This score is a single number ranging from 0 to 1 that summarizes all of the observed characteristics of the units as they influence the likelihood of enrolling in the program.

Once the propensity score has been computed for all units, then units in the treatment group can be matched with units in the pool of nonenrollees that have the closest propensity score.[1] These "closest units" become the comparison group and are used to produce an estimate of the counterfactual. The propensity score matching method tries to mimic the randomized assignment to treatment and comparison groups by choosing for the comparison group those units that have similar propensities to the units in the treatment group. Since propensity score matching is not a real randomized assignment method, but tries to imitate one, it belongs to the category of quasi-experimental methods.

The difference in outcomes (Y) between the treatment or enrolled units and their matched comparison units produces the estimated impact of the program. In summary, the program's impact is estimated by comparing the average outcomes of a treatment or enrolled group and the average outcome among a statistically matched subgroup of units, the match being based on observed characteristics available in the data at hand.

For propensity score matching to produce externally valid estimates of a program's impact, all treatment or enrolled units need to be successfully matched to a nonenrolled unit.[2] It may happen that for some enrolled units, no units in the pool of nonenrollees have similar propensity scores. In technical terms, there may be a "lack of common support," or lack of overlap, between the propensity scores of the treatment or enrolled group and those of the pool of nonenrollees.

Figure 7.2 provides an example of lack of common support. The likelihood that each unit in the sample enrolls in the program is first estimated based on the observed characteristics of the unit. Based on that, each unit is assigned a propensity score, in other words, the estimated probability of the unit's participating in the program. The figure shows the distribution of propensity scores separately for enrollees and nonenrollees. Crucially, these distributions do not overlap perfectly. In the middle of the distribution, matches are relatively easy to find because enrollees and nonenrollees have similar characteristics. However, units with predicted propensity scores close to 1 cannot be matched to any nonenrollees with similar propensity scores. Intuitively, units who are highly likely to enroll in the program are so dissimilar to nonenrolling units that we cannot find a good match for them. A lack of common support thus appears at the extremes, or tails, of the distribution of propensity scores.

Figure 7.2   Propensity Score Matching and Common Support

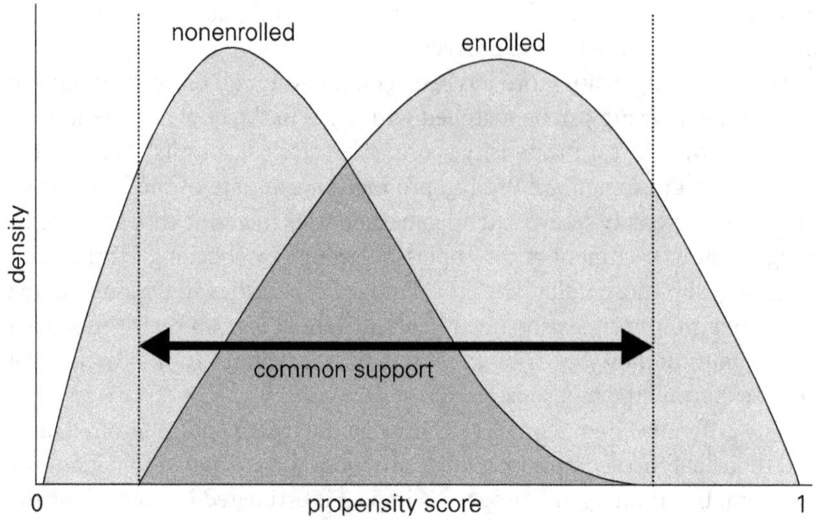

Source: Authors, drawing from multiple sources.

Jalan and Ravallion (2003a) summarize the steps to be taken when applying propensity score matching.[3] First, you will need representative and highly comparable surveys to identify the units that enrolled in the program and those that did not. Second, you must pool the two samples and estimate the probability that each individual enrolls in the program, based on individual characteristics observed in the survey. This step yields the propensity score. Third, you restrict the sample to units for which common support appears in the propensity score distribution. Fourth, for each enrolled unit, you locate a subgroup of nonenrolled units that have similar propensity scores. Fifth, you compare the outcomes for the treatment or enrolled units and their matched comparison or nonenrolled units. The difference in average outcomes for these two subgroups is the measure of the impact that can be attributed to the program for that particular treated observation. Sixth, the mean of these individual impacts yields the estimated average treatment effect.

Overall, it is important to remember two crucial issues about matching. First, matching must be done using baseline characteristics. Second, the matching method is only as good as the characteristics that are used for matching, so that having a large number of background characteristics is crucial.

Using Matching Techniques to Select Participant and Nonparticipant Households in the Health Insurance Subsidy Program

Having learned about matching techniques, you may wonder whether you could improve on the previous estimates of the impact of the Health Insurance Subsidy Program (HISP). You decide to use some matching techniques to select a group of enrolled and nonenrolled households that look similar based on observed characteristics. First, you estimate the probability that a unit will enroll in the program based on the observed values of characteristics (the "explanatory variables"), such as the age of the household head and of the spouse, their level of education, whether the head of the household is a female, whether the household is indigenous, and so on. As shown in table 7.1, the likelihood that a household is enrolled in the program is smaller if the household is older, more educated, female headed, or owns a bathroom or larger amounts of land. By contrast, being indigenous, having more household members, and having a dirt floor all increase the likelihood that a

Table 7.1 Estimating the Propensity Score Based on Observed Characteristics

Dependent Variable: *Enrolled = 1*	
Explanatory variables / characteristics	**Coefficient**
Head of household's age (years)	−0.022**
Spouse's age (years)	−0.017**
Head of household's education (years)	−0.059**
Spouse's education (years)	−0.030**
Head of household is female = 1	−0.067
Indigenous = 1	0.345**
Number of household members	0.216**
Dirt floor = 1	0.676**
Bathroom = 1	−0.197**
Hectares of land	−0.042**
Distance to hospital (km)	0.001*
Constant	0.664**

Source: Authors.

Note: Probit regression. The dependent variable is 1 if the household enrolled in HISP, and 0 otherwise. The coefficients represent the contribution of each listed explanatory variable / characteristic to the probability that a household enrolled in HISP.

* Significant at the 5 percent level; ** Significant at the 1 percent level.

Table 7.2 Case 7—HISP Impact Using Matching (Comparison of Means)

	Enrolled	Matched comparison	Difference	t-stat
Household health expenditures	7.8	16.1	−8.3	−13.1

Source: Authors.

Table 7.3 Case 7—HISP Impact Using Matching (Regression Analysis)

	Multivariate linear regression
Estimated impact on household health expenditures	−8.3** (0.63)

Source: Authors.

Note: Standard errors are in parentheses.

** Significant at the 1 percent level.

household is enrolled in the program. So overall, it seems that poorer and less-educated households are more likely to be enrolled, which is good news for a program that targets poor people.

Now that you have estimated the probability that each household is enrolled in the program (the propensity score), you restrict the sample to those households in the enrolled and nonenrolled groups for which you can find a match in the other group. For each enrolled household, you locate a subgroup of nonenrolled households that have similar propensity scores. Table 7.2 compares the average outcomes for the enrolled households and their matched comparison or nonenrolled households.

To obtain the estimated impact using the matching method, you need first to compute the impact for each treated household individually (using each household's matched comparison households), and then average those individual impacts. Table 7.3 shows that the impact estimated from applying this procedure is a reduction of $8.3 in household health expenditures.

QUESTION 7

A. What are the basic assumptions required to accept this result from case 7?

B. Compare the result from case 7 with the result from case 3. Why do you think the results are so different?

C. Based on the result from case 7, should the HISP be scaled up nationally?

The Matching Method at Work

Although the matching technique requires a significant amount of data and has other statistical limitations, it is a relatively versatile method that has been used to evaluate development programs in a number of settings. Two illustrative cases are detailed in boxes 7.1 and 7.2.

Limitations of the Matching Method

Although matching procedures can be applied in many settings, regardless of a program's assignment rules, they have several serious shortcomings.

Box 7.1: Workfare Program and Incomes in Argentina

Jalan and Ravallion (2003a) used propensity score matching techniques to evaluate the impact of the Argentinean workfare program A Trabajar on income. In response to the 1996–97 macroeconomic crisis in Argentina, the government introduced A Trabajar rapidly, without using any randomized selection techniques or collecting any baseline data. For these reasons, the researchers chose to use matching techniques to evaluate the impact of the program. In this kind of context, using matching techniques also makes it possible to analyze how income gains vary among households across the preintervention income distribution.

In mid-1997 a survey was administered to both participants and nonparticipants. To estimate the impact of the program by propensity score matching, Jalan and Ravallion considered a large set of about 200 background characteristics (at both the household and community levels) that were measured in the survey. For instance, estimating the propensity score equation showed that

program participants were poorer and were more likely to be married, male household heads, and active in neighborhood associations.

After computing the estimated propensity scores, the authors restricted their analysis to units whose propensity scores fell in the area of common support, where the propensity scores of participants and nonparticipants overlap. By matching participants to their nearest nonparticipant neighbors in the area of common support, and by averaging the differences in income between all of these matched groups, they estimated that the program resulted in an average income gain equivalent to about half of the workfare program wage. The researchers checked the robustness of results to various matching procedures. They stress that their estimates might be biased because of some unobserved characteristics. Indeed, when using matching methods we can never rule out bias caused by unobserved variables, and that is their most serious limitation.

Source: Jalan and Ravallion 2003a.

Box 7.2: Piped Water and Child Health in India

Jalan and Ravallion (2003b) used matching methods to look at the effect of having piped water on the prevalence and duration of diarrhea among children under age 5 in rural India. In particular, the researchers evaluated a policy intervention to expand access to piped water to understand how gains may vary depending on household circumstances such as income and education level. This impact is difficult to detect because it may also depend on privately provided health inputs from parents that also affect the incidence of diarrhea, such as boiling water, providing good nutrition, or using oral rehydration salts when a child is sick.

The researchers used data from a large survey conducted in 1993–94 by India's National Council of Applied Economic Research that contained data on the health and education status of 33,000 rural households from 16 states in India. This rich body of data allowed the researchers to use propensity score matching at both the individual and the village level, balancing the treatment and comparison groups by their predicted probability of receiving piped water through the national campaign.

The evaluation found that having piped water reduced diarrheal disease—its prevalence would be 21 percent higher and duration 29 percent longer without piped water. However, these impacts are not seen by the low-income groups unless the woman in the household has more than a primary school education. In fact, Jalan and Ravallion found that the health impacts of piped water are larger and more significant in households with better-educated women. They concluded that their study illustrates the need to combine infrastructure investments, such as piped water, with other programs to improve education and reduce poverty.

Source: Jalan and Ravallion 2003b.

First, they require extensive data sets on large samples of units, and even when those are available, a lack of common support between the treatment or enrolled group and the pool of nonparticipants may appear. Second, matching can only be performed based on observed characteristics; by definition, we cannot incorporate unobserved characteristics in the calculation of the propensity score. So for the matching procedure to identify a valid comparison group, we must be sure that no systematic differences in unobserved characteristics between the treatment units and the matched comparison units exist[4] that could influence the outcome (*Y*). Since we cannot *prove* that no such unobserved characteristics that affect both participation and outcomes exist, we have to *assume* that none exist. This is usually a very strong assumption. Although matching helps to control for *observed* background characteristics, we can never rule out bias that stems from *unobserved* characteristics. In summary, the assumption that no selection bias has occurred stemming from unobserved characteristics is very strong, and most problematic, it cannot be tested.

Matching is generally less robust than the other evaluation methods we have discussed. For instance, randomized selection methods do not require the untestable assumption that there are no unobserved variables that explain both participation in the program and outcomes. They also do not require such large samples or as extensive background characteristics as propensity score matching.

In practice, matching methods are typically used when randomized selection, regression discontinuity design, and difference-in-differences options are not possible. Many authors use so-called ex-post matching when no baseline data are available on the outcome of interest or on background characteristics. They use a survey that was collected after the start of the program (that is, ex-post) to infer what people's background characteristics were at baseline (for example, age, marital status), and then match the treated group to a comparison group using those inferred characteristics. Of course, this is risky: they may inadvertently match based on characteristics that were also affected by the program, and in that case, the estimation result would be invalid or biased.

By contrast, when baseline data are available, matching based on baseline background characteristics can be very useful when it is combined with other techniques, for instance, difference-in-differences, which accounts for time-invariant, unobserved heterogeneity. Matching is also more useful when the program assignment rule is known, in which case matching can be performed on that rule (see chapter 8).

By now, it is probably clear to readers that impact evaluations are best designed before a program begins to be implemented. Once the program has started, if one has no way to influence how it is allocated and no baseline data have been collected, very few, or no, solid options for the evaluation will be available.

Notes

1. In practice, many definitions of what constitutes the "closest" or "nearest" propensity score are used to perform matching. The nearest controls can be defined based on a stratification of the propensity score—the identification of the treatment unit's nearest neighbors, based on distance, within a given radius—or using kernel techniques. It is considered good practice to check the robustness of matching results by using various matching algorithms.

2. The discussion on matching in this book focuses on one-to-one matching. Various other types of matching, such as one-to-many matching or

replacement/nonreplacement matching, will not be discussed. In all cases, however, the conceptual framework described here would still apply.

3. Rosenbaum 2002 presents a detailed review of matching.

4. For readers with a background in econometrics, this means that participation is independent of outcomes, given the background characteristics used to do the matching.

References

Jalan, Jyotsna, and Martin Ravallion. 2003a. "Estimating the Benefit Incidence of an Antipoverty Program by Propensity-Score Matching." *Journal of Business & Economic Statistics* 21 (1): 19–30.

———. 2003b. "Does Piped Water Reduce Diarrhea for Children in Rural India?" *Journal of Econometrics* 112 (1): 153–73.

Rosenbaum, Paul. 2002. *Observational Studies.* 2nd ed. Springer Series in Statistics. New York: Springer-Verlag.

Rosenbaum, Paul, and Donald Rubin. 1983. "The Central Role of the Propensity Score in Observational Studies of Causal Effects." *Biometrika* 70 (1): 41–55.

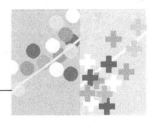

CHAPTER 8

Combining Methods

We have seen that most impact evaluation methods only produce valid estimates of the counterfactual under specific assumptions. The main risk in applying any method is that its underlying assumptions do not hold true, resulting in biased estimates of the program's impact. This section reviews these methodological issues and discusses strategies to reduce the risk of bias. And since the risk of bias stems primarily from deviations from the underlying assumptions, we will focus on how you can go about verifying those assumptions.

In the cases of a number of evaluation methods, the validity of the assumptions on which they rely can be verified. For other methods, you cannot verify validity outright, but you can still use various so-called falsification tests to improve confidence about whether the assumptions behind the methods hold. Falsification tests are like stress tests: failing them is a strong sign that the assumptions behind the method do not hold in that particular context. Nevertheless, passing them provides only tentative support for the assumptions: you can never be fully sure that they hold. Box 8.1 presents a checklist of verification and falsification tests that can be used to assess whether a method is appropriate in the context of your evaluation. The checklist contains practical questions that can be answered by analyzing baseline data.

Box 8.1: Checklist of Verification and Falsification Tests

Randomized Assignment

Randomized assignment is the most robust method for estimating counterfactuals; it is considered the gold standard of impact evaluation. Some basic tests should still be considered to assess the validity of this evaluation strategy in a given context.

- Are the baseline characteristics balanced? Compare the baseline characteristics of the treatment group and the comparison group.[a]

- Has any noncompliance with the assignment occurred? Check whether all eligible units have received the treatment and that no ineligible units have received the treatment. If noncompliance appears, use the randomized offering method.

- Are the numbers of units in the treatment and comparison groups sufficiently large? If not, you may want to combine randomized assignment with difference-in-differences.

Randomized Offering

Noncompliance in randomized assignment amounts to randomized offering.

- Are the baseline characteristics balanced? Compare the baseline characteristics of the units being offered the program and the units not being offered the program.

Randomized Promotion

Randomized promotion leads to valid estimates of the counterfactual if the promotion campaign substantially increases take-up of the program without directly affecting the outcomes of interest.

- Are the baseline characteristics balanced between the units who received the promotion campaign and those who did not? Compare the baseline characteristics of the two groups.

- Does the promotion campaign substantially affect the take-up of the program? It should. Compare the program take-up rates in the promoted and the nonpromoted samples.

- Does the promotion campaign directly affect outcomes? It should not. This cannot usually be directly tested, and so we need to rely on theory and common sense to guide us.

Regression Discontinuity Design (RDD)

Regression discontinuity design requires that the eligibility index be continuous around the cutoff score and that units be comparable in the vicinity of the cutoff score.

- Is the index continuous around the cutoff score at the time of the baseline?

- Has any noncompliance with the cutoff for treatment appeared? Test whether all eligible units and no ineligible units have received the treatment. If you find noncompliance, you will need to combine RDD with more advanced techniques to correct for this "fuzzy discontinuity."[b]

Difference-in-Differences (DD)

Difference-in-differences assumes that outcome trends are similar in the comparison and treatment groups before the intervention and that the only factors explaining changes in outcomes between the two groups are constant over time.

- Would outcomes have moved in tandem in the treatment and comparison groups in the absence of the program? This can

(continued)

Impact Evaluation in Practice

Box 8.1 *continued*

be assessed by using several falsification tests, such as the following: (1) Are the outcomes in the treatment and comparison groups moving in tandem before the intervention? If two rounds of data are available before the start of the program, test to see if any difference in trends appears between the two groups. (2) How about fake outcomes that should not be affected by the program? Are they moving in tandem before and after the start of the intervention in the treatment and comparison groups?

- Perform the difference-in-differences analysis using several plausible comparison groups. Do you obtain similar estimates of the impact of the program?

- Perform the difference-in-differences analysis using your chosen treatment and comparison groups and a fake outcome that should not be affected by the program. You should find zero impact of the program on that outcome.

- Perform the difference-in-differences analysis using your chosen outcome variable with two groups that you know were not affected by the program. You should find zero impact of the program.

Matching

Matching relies on the assumption that enrolled and nonenrolled units are similar in terms of any unobserved variables that could affect both the probability of participating in the program and the outcome (Y).

- Is program participation determined by variables that cannot be observed? This cannot be directly tested, so we need to rely on theory and common sense.

- Are the observed characteristics well balanced between matched subgroups? Compare the observed characteristics of each treatment and its matched comparison group of units.

- Can a matched comparison unit be found for each treatment unit? Check whether sufficient common support exists in the distribution of the propensity scores. Small areas of common support indicate that enrolled and nonenrolled persons are very different, and that casts doubt as to whether matching is a credible method.

Source: Authors.

a. As mentioned earlier, for statistical reasons, not all observed characteristics have to be similar in the treatment and comparison groups for randomization to be successful. Even when the characteristics of the two groups are truly equal, one can expect that 5 percent of the characteristics will show up with a statistically significant difference when we use a 95 percent confidence level for the test.

b. Although we will not elaborate on this technique here, readers may wish to know that one would combine RDD with an instrumental variables approach. One would use the location left or right of the cutoff point as an instrumental variable for actual program take-up in the first stage of a two-stage least squares estimation.

Combining Methods

Even though all evaluation methods have risks for bias, the risk can sometimes be reduced by using a combination of methods. By combining methods, we can often offset the limitations of a single method and thus increase the robustness of the estimated counterfactual.

Matched difference-in-differences (matched DD) is one example of combining methods. As discussed previously, simple propensity score matching cannot account for unobserved characteristics that might explain why a group chooses to enroll in a program and that might also affect outcomes. By contrast, matching combined with difference-in-differences at least takes care of any unobserved characteristics that are constant across time between the two groups. It is implemented as follows:

- First, perform matching based on observed baseline characteristics (as discussed in chapter 7).

- Second, apply the difference-in-differences method to estimate a counterfactual for the change in outcomes in each subgroup of matched units.

- Finally, average out those double differences across matched subgroups.

Box 8.2 provides an example of an evaluation that used the matched difference-in-differences method in practice.

Difference-in-differences regression discontinuity design (DD RDD) is a second example of combining methods. Remember that simple RDD assumes that units on both sides of the eligibility threshold are very similar. Insofar as some differences remain between the units on either side of the threshold, adding difference-in-differences allows us to control for differences in unobserved characteristics that do not vary over time. You can implement DD RDD by taking double-difference in outcomes for units on both sides of the eligibility cutoff.

Imperfect Compliance

Imperfect compliance is a discrepancy between intended treatment status and actual treatment status. We have discussed it in reference to randomized assignment, but in reality imperfect compliance is a potential problem in most impact evaluation methods. Before you are able to interpret the impact estimates produced by any method, you need to know whether imperfect compliance occurred in the program.

Imperfect compliance has two manifestations: (1) some intended treatment units may not receive treatment, and (2) some intended comparison units may receive treatment. Imperfect compliance can occur in a variety of ways:

- Not all intended program participants actually participate in the program. Sometimes units that are offered a program choose not to participate.

- Some intended participants are not offered the program through administrative or implementation errors.

Box 8.2: Matched Difference-in-Differences
Cement Floors, Child Health, and Maternal Happiness in Mexico

The Piso Firme program in Mexico offers households with dirt floors up to 50 square meters of concrete flooring. Piso Firme began as a local program in the state of Coahuila but then was adopted nationally. Cattaneo et al. (2009) took advantage of the geographic variation to evaluate the impact of this large-scale housing improvement effort on health and welfare outcomes.

The researchers used the difference-in-differences method in conjunction with matching to compare households in Coahuila to similar families in the neighboring state of Durango, which at the time of the survey had not yet implemented the program. To improve comparability between the treatment and comparison groups, the researchers limited their sample to households in the neighboring cities that lie just on either side of the border between the two states. They sampled from the blocks in the two cities that had the most similar preintervention characteristics based on a 2002 census.

Using the offer of a cement floor as an instrumental variable for actually having cement floors, the researchers recovered the treatment-on-the-treated from the intent-to-treat and found that the program led to an 18.2 percent reduction in the presence of parasites, a 12.4 percent reduction in the prevalence of diarrhea, and a 19.4 percent reduction in the prevalence of anemia. Fur-

thermore, they were able to use variability in the amount of total floor space actually covered by cement to predict that a complete replacement of dirt floors with cement floors in a household would lead to a 78 percent reduction in parasitic infestations, a 49 percent reduction in diarrhea, an 81 percent reduction in anemia, and a 36 percent to 96 percent improvement in cognitive development. The authors also collected data on adult welfare and found that cement floors make mothers happier, with a 59 percent increase in self-reported satisfaction with housing, a 69 percent increase in self-reported satisfaction with quality of life, a 52 percent reduction on a depression assessment scale, and a 45 percent reduction on a perceived stress assessment scale.

Cattaneo et al. (2009) concluded by illustrating that Piso Firme has a larger absolute impact on child cognitive development at a lower cost than Mexico's large-scale conditional cash transfer program, Oportunidades/Progresa, as well as comparable programs in nutritional supplementation and early childhood cognitive stimulation. The cement floors also prevented more parasitic infections than the common deworming treatment. The authors state that programs to replace dirt floors with cement floors are likely to improve child health cost-effectively in similar contexts.

Source: Cattaneo et al. 2009.

- Some units of the comparison group are mistakenly offered the program and enroll in it.

- Some units of the comparison group manage to participate in the program even though it is not offered to them. This is sometimes called "contamination" of the comparison group. If contamination affects a large portion of the comparison group, unbiased estimates of the counterfactual cannot be obtained.

- The program is assigned based on a continuous prioritization score, but the eligibility cutoff is not strictly enforced.

- Selective migration takes place based on treatment status. For example, we may use the difference-in-differences method to compare outcomes for treated and nontreated municipalities, but individuals may choose to move to another municipality if they do not like the treatment status of their municipality.

In general, in the presence of imperfect compliance, standard impact evaluation methods produce intention-to-treat estimates. However, treatment-on-the-treated estimates can be recovered from the intention-to-treat estimates using the instrumental variable approach.

In chapter 4 we presented the basic intuition for dealing with imperfect compliance in the context of randomized assignment. Using an adjustment for the percentage of compliers in the evaluation sample, we were able to recover the impact of treatment on the treated from the intention-to-treat estimate. This "fix" can be extended to other methods through application of the more general instrumental variable approach. The instrumental variable is a variable that helps you clear up, or correct, the bias that may stem from imperfect compliance. In the case of randomized offering, we use a 0/1 (or "dummy") variable that that takes value 1 if the unit was originally assigned to the treatment group, and 0 if the unit was originally assigned to the comparison group. During the analysis stage, the instrumental variable is often used in the context of a *two-stage regression* that allows you to identify the impact of the treatment on the compliers.

The logic of the instrumental variable approach can be extended in the context of other evaluation methods:

- In the context of regression discontinuity design, the instrumental variable you would use is a 0/1 variable that indicates whether a unit is located on the ineligible side or the eligible side of the cutoff score.

- In the context of difference-in-differences and selective migration, a possible instrumental variable for the location of the individual after the start of the program would be the location of the individual before the announcement of the program.

Despite the possibility of "fixing" imperfect compliance using instrumental variables, two points are important to remember:

1. From a technical point of view, it is not desirable to have a large portion of the comparison group enroll in the program. Evaluators and policy makers involved in the impact evaluation must work together to keep this fraction to a minimum.

2. The instrumental variable method is valid only under certain circumstances; it is definitely not a universal solution.

Spillovers

Even when the comparison group is not directly provided with the program, it may indirectly be affected by spillovers from the treatment group. An interesting example of this is discussed by Kremer and Miguel (2004), who examined the impact of administering deworming medicine to children in Kenyan schools (box 8.3). Intestinal worms are parasites that can be transmitted from one person to another through contact with contaminated fecal matter. When a child receives deworming medicine, her "worm load" will decrease, but so will the worm load of persons living in the same environment, as they will no longer come in contact with the child's worms. Thus, in the Kenya example, when the medicine was administered to the children in one school, it benefited not only those children (direct benefit) but also those in neighboring schools (indirect benefit).

As depicted in figure 8.1, deworming in group A schools also diminishes the number of worms that affect nonprogram schools in group B, which are located close to group A schools. However, nonprogram schools farther away from group A schools—the so-called group C schools—do not experience such spillover effects because the medicine administered in group A does not kill any of the worms that affect group C. Kremer and Miguel (2004) found that deworming significantly reduced school absenteeism not only in program schools (by comparing group A with group C) but also in nearby nonprogram schools (by comparing group B with group C).

Because spillovers occur, it is important that the evaluator verify that they do not affect the entire comparison group. As long as enough comparison units remain that are not affected by spillovers (group C in the deworming example), you will be able to estimate the impact of the program by comparing outcomes for the treatment units with outcomes for

Box 8.3: Working with Spillovers
Deworming, Externalities, and Education in Kenya

The Primary School Deworming Project in Busia, Kenya, was carried out by the Dutch nonprofit International Child Support Africa, in cooperation with the ministry of health, and was designed to test a variety of aspects of worm treatment and prevention. The project involved 75 schools with a total enrollment of more than 30,000 students between the ages of 6 and 18. The schools were treated with worm medication in accordance with World Health Organization recommendations and also received worm prevention education in the form of health lectures, wall charts, and teacher training.

Due to administrative and financial constraints, the rollout was phased in alphabetically, with the first group of 25 schools starting in 1998, the second group in 1999, and the third group in 2001. By randomizing at the level of school, Kremer and Miguel (2004) were able both to estimate the impact of deworming on a school and to identify spillovers across schools using exogenous variation in the closeness of control schools to treatment schools. Although compliance to the randomized design was relatively high (with 75 percent of those assigned to the treatment receiving worm medication, and only a small percentage of the comparison group units receiving treatment), the researchers were also able to take advantage of noncompliance to determine within-

school health externalities, or spillovers. Kremer and Miguel (2004) found that the within-school externality effect was a 12 percentage point reduction in the proportion of moderate-to-heavy worm infections, while the additional direct effect of actually taking the worm medication was about 14 percentage points more. Also, in terms of cross-school externalities, the presence of each additional thousand students attending a treatment school was associated with 26 percentage points fewer moderate-to-heavy infections. These health effects also led to an increase in school participation of at least seven percentage points and reduced absenteeism by at least one-quarter. No significant impact on test scores was found.

Because the cost of worm treatment is so low and the health and education effects relatively high, the researchers concluded that deworming is a relatively cost-efficient way to improve participation rates in schools. The study also illustrates that tropical diseases such as worms may play a significant role in educational outcomes and strengthens claims that Africa's high disease burden may be contributing to its low income. Thus, the study's authors argue that it makes a strong case for public subsidies to disease treatments with similar spillover benefits in developing countries.

Source: Kremer and Miguel 2004.

the "pure" comparison units. On the downside, the evaluation will not be able to generalize the estimated treatment effects to the entire population. If, at the design stage, you expect that a program will have spillover effects, you can adapt the evaluation design to produce better results. First, the design needs to identify a pure comparison group, so that it will be possi-

Figure 8.1   Spillovers

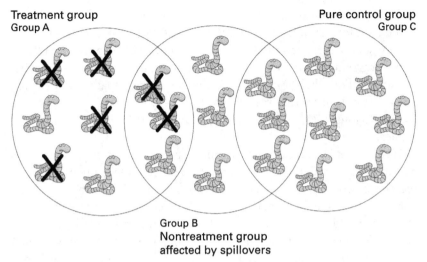

Source: Authors.

ble to generalize the estimated program impact. Second, the design should also make it possible to estimate the magnitude of spillover effects by identifying a comparison group that is likely to receive spillovers. In fact, spillovers themselves are often of policy interest because they constitute indirect program impacts.

Figure 8.1 illustrates how it is possible to estimate both a program's impact and any spillover effects. Group A receives the medication. The effect of the medication spills over to group B. Group C is farther away and, thus, receives no spillover effects of the medication. This design can be obtained by randomly assigning treatment between two nearby units and a similar unit farther away. In this simple framework, the impact of the program can be estimated by comparing outcomes for group A to outcomes for group C, and spillover effects can be estimated by comparing outcomes for group B with those for group C.

Additional Considerations

In addition to imperfect compliance and spillovers, other factors also need to be considered when an impact evaluation is being designed. These factors are common to most of the methodologies that we have discussed, and they tend to be harder to mitigate.[1]

When planning an evaluation, you should determine the right time to collect data. If a program takes time to have an impact on outcomes, then collecting data too soon will result in no impact of the program being found (see, for example, King and Behrman 2009). Conversely, if the follow-up survey is fielded too late, you will not be able capture the effects of the program in time to inform policy makers. In cases where you wish to estimate both the short-term and the long-term impact of a program, several rounds of postintervention or follow-up data will need to be collected. Chapter 10 will offer further guidance on the best evaluation time frames.

If you are estimating a program's impact on an entire group, your results may mask some differences in responses to the treatment among different recipients. Most impact evaluation methods assume that a program affects outcomes in a simple, linear way for all of the units in the population. However, problems can arise when the size of the response depends in a nonlinear way on the size of the intervention, or when a group with high treatment intensity is compared with a group with low treatment intensity. If you think that different subpopulations may have experienced the impact of a program very differently, then you may want to consider having separate samples for each subpopulation. Say, for example, that you are interested in knowing the impact of a school meal program on girls, but only 10 percent of the students are girls. In that case, even a "large" random sample of students may not contain a sufficient number of girls to allow you to estimate the impact of the program on girls. For your evaluation's sample design, you would want to stratify the sample on gender and include a sufficiently large number of girls to allow you to detect a given effect size.

When conducting an impact evaluation, you may also induce unintended behavioral responses from the population that you are studying, and that may limit the external validity of the evaluation results. For instance, the "Hawthorne effect" occurs when the mere fact that you are observing units makes them behave differently (Levitt and List 2009). The "John Henry effect" happens when comparison units work harder to compensate for not being offered a treatment. Anticipation can lead to another type of unintended behavioral effect. In a randomized rollout, units in the comparison group may expect to receive the program in the future and begin changing their behavior before the program actually appears. If you have reason to believe that these unintended behavioral responses may be present, then building in additional comparison groups that are completely unaffected by the intervention is sometimes an option, one that in fact allows you to explicitly test for such responses.

A Backup Plan for Your Evaluation

Sometimes, even with the best impact evaluation design and the best intentions, things do not go exactly as planned. In the recent experience of a job training program, the implementation agency planned to randomly select participants from the pool of applicants, based on presumed oversubscription to the program. Because of high unemployment among the target population, it was anticipated that the pool of applicants for the job training program would be much larger than the number of places available. Unfortunately, advertisement for the program was not as effective as expected, and in the end, the number of applicants was just below the number of training slots available. Without oversubscription from which to draw a comparison group, and with no backup plan in place, the initial attempt to evaluate the program had to be dropped entirely. This kind of situation is common, as are unanticipated changes in the operational or political context of a program. Therefore, it is useful to have a backup plan in case the first choice of methodology does not work out. Part 3 of this book discusses operational and political aspects of the evaluation in more detail.

Planning for using several impact evaluation methods is also good practice from the methodological point of view. If you have doubts about whether one of your methods may have remaining bias, you will be able to check the results against the other method. When a program is implemented in a randomized rollout (see chapter 10), the comparison group will eventually be incorporated into the program. That limits the time during which the comparison group is available for the evaluation. If, however, in addition to the randomized assignment design, a randomized promotion design is also implemented, then a comparison group will be available for the entire period of the program. Before the incorporation of the final group of the rollout, two alternative comparison groups will exist (from the randomized assignment and the randomized promotion), though in the longer term only the randomized promotion comparison group will remain.

Note

1. In chapter 3 other sources of limited external validity related to sampling biases and biases resulting from differentiated attrition in treatment and comparison groups are discussed.

References

Cattaneo, Matias, Sebastian Galiani, Paul Gertler, Sebastian Martinez, and Rocio Titiunik. 2009. "Housing, Health and Happiness." *American Economic Journal: Economic Policy* 1 (1): 75–105.

King, Elizabeth M., and Jere R. Behrman. 2009. "Timing and Duration of Exposure in Evaluations of Social Programs." *World Bank Research Observer* 24 (1): 55–82.

Kremer, Michael, and Edward Miguel. 2004. "Worms: Identifying Impacts on Education and Health in the Presence of Treatment Externalities." *Econometrica* 72 (1): 159–217.

Levitt, Steven D., and John A. List. 2009. "Was There Really a Hawthorne Effect at the Hawthorne Plant? An Analysis of the Original Illumination Experiments." NBER Working Paper 15016. National Bureau of Economic Research, Cambridge, MA.

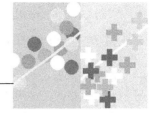

CHAPTER 9

Evaluating Multifaceted Programs

Up to now, we have discussed programs that include only one kind of treatment. In reality, many highly relevant policy questions arise in the context of multifaceted programs, that is, programs that combine several treatment options.[1] Policy makers may be interested in knowing not only whether or not a program works, but also whether the program works better than another or at lower cost. For example, if we want to increase school attendance, is it more effective to implement demand-side interventions (such as cash transfers to families) or supply-side interventions (such as greater incentives for teachers)? And if we introduce the two interventions together, do they work better than each of them alone? In other words, are they complementary? Alternatively, if program cost-effectiveness is a priority, you may well wonder what is the optimal level of services that the program should deliver. For instance, what is the optimal duration of a vocational training program? Does a 6-month program have a greater effect on trainees' finding jobs than a 3-month program? If so, is the difference large enough to justify the additional resources needed for a 6-month program?

Beyond simply estimating the impact of an intervention on an outcome of interest, impact evaluations can help to answer broader questions such as these:

- *What is the impact of one treatment compared with that of another treatment?* For example, what is the impact on children's cognitive development of a program providing parenting training as opposed to a nutrition intervention?

- *Is the joint impact of a first treatment and a second treatment larger than the sum of the two individual impacts?* For example, is the total impact of the parenting intervention and the nutrition intervention greater than, less than, or equal to the sum of the effects of the two individual interventions?

- *What is the additional impact of a higher-intensity treatment compared to a lower-intensity treatment?* For example, what is the effect on stunted children's cognitive development if a social worker visits them at home every two weeks, as compared to visiting them only once a month?

This chapter provides examples of how to design impact evaluations for two types of multifaceted programs: ones with multiple levels of the same treatment and ones with multiple treatments. First, we discuss how to design an impact evaluation for a program with various service levels, and then we turn to how to disentangle the various kinds of impact of a program with multiple treatments. The discussion assumes that we are using the randomized assignment mechanism, but it can be generalized to other methods.

Evaluating Programs with Different Treatment Levels

It is relatively easy to design an impact evaluation for a program with varying treatment levels. Imagine that you are trying to evaluate the impact of a program that has two levels of treatment: high (for example, biweekly visits) and low (say, monthly visits). You want to evaluate the impact of both options, and you also want to know how much the additional visits affect outcomes. To do this, you can run a lottery to decide who receives the high level of treatment, who receives the low level of treatment, and who is assigned to the comparison group. Figure 9.1 illustrates this process.

As in standard randomized assignment, step 1 is to define the population of eligible units for your program. Step 2 is to select a random sample of units to be included in the evaluation, the so-called evaluation sample. Once you have the evaluation sample, in step 3 you then randomly assign units to the group receiving high-level treatment, the group receiving low-level treatment, or the comparison group. As a result of randomized assignment to multiple treatment levels, you will have created three distinct groups:

Figure 9.1 Steps in Randomized Assignment of Two Levels of Treatment

Step 1:
Eligible units

Step 2:
Evaluation sample

Step 3:
Randomize assignment to
high and low levels of treatment

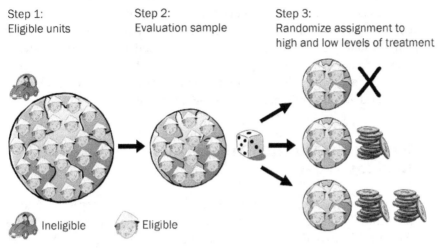

Ineligible   Eligible

Source: Authors.

- Group A constitutes the comparison group.

- Group B receives the low level of treatment.

- Group C receives the high level of treatment.

When correctly implemented, randomized assignment ensures that the three groups are similar. Therefore, you can estimate the impact of the high-level treatment by comparing the average outcome for group C with the average outcome for group A. You can also estimate the impact of the low-level treatment by comparing the average outcome for group B with that for group A. Finally, you can assess whether the high-level treatment has a larger impact than the low-level treatment by comparing the average outcomes for groups B and C.

Estimating the impact of a program with more than two treatment levels will follow the same logic. If there are three levels of treatment, the randomization process will create three different treatment groups, plus a comparison group. In general, with *n* different treatment levels, there will be *n* treatment groups, plus a comparison group.

When randomized assignment is not feasible, other evaluation methods have to be used. Fortunately, all the evaluation methods described thus far are capable of analyzing the relative impact of different treatment levels. For example, suppose you are interested in evaluating the impact of varying the amount of money offered to students in a scholarship program that seeks to increase secondary school enrollment. A $60 scholarship is given to the 25 students with the highest test scores in each school at the end of primary school, and a $45 scholarship is given to the 25 students with the next-highest test scores. The lower-ranked students in the schools do not receive any scholarship. In this context, a regression discontinuity design can be used to compare the test scores of students not only around the $45 threshold but also around to the $60 threshold. Filmer and Schady (2009) presented the results from such an evaluation in Cambodia, in which they found no evidence that the $60 scholarship increased enrollment more than the $45 scholarship.

Evaluating Multiple Treatments with Crossover Designs

In addition to comparing various levels of treatment, you may want to compare entirely different treatment options. In fact, policy makers usually prefer to be able to compare the relative merits of different interventions, rather than know the impact of only a single intervention.

Imagine that you want to evaluate the impact on school enrollment of a program with two different interventions, conditional cash transfers to the students' families and free bus transportation to school. You may want to know the impact of each intervention separately, and you may also want to know whether the combination of the two is better than just the sum of the individual effects. Seen from the participants' point of view, the program is available in three different forms: conditional cash transfers only, free bus transportation only, or a combination of conditional cash transfers and free bus transportation.

Randomized assignment for a program with two interventions is very much like the process for a program with a single intervention. The main difference is the need to conduct several independent lotteries instead of one. This produces a *crossover design*, sometimes also called a cross-cutting design. Figure 9.2 illustrates this process. As before, step 1 is to define the population of units eligible for the program. Step 2 is to select a random sample of eligible units from the population to form the evaluation sample. Once you obtain the evaluation sample, step 3 is to randomly assign units from the evaluation sample to a treatment group and a control group. In step 4, you use a second lottery to randomly assign a subset of the treatment group to receive the second intervention. Finally, in step 5 you conduct another lottery to assign a subset of the initial control group to receive the second intervention, while the other subset will remain as a "pure" control.

As a result of the randomized assignment to the two treatments, you will have created four groups, as illustrated in figure 9.3:

Figure 9.2   Steps in Randomized Assignment of Two Interventions

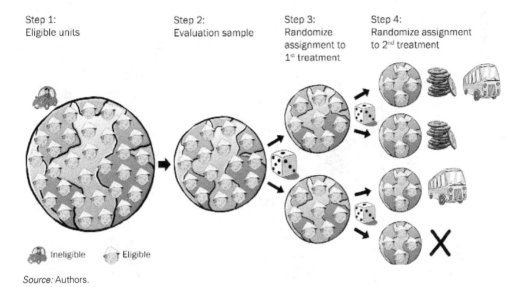

Source: Authors.

- Group A receives both interventions (cash transfers and bus transportation).

- Group B receives intervention 1 but not intervention 2 (cash transfers only).

- Group C does not receive intervention 2 but receives intervention 1 (bus transportation only).

- Group D receives neither intervention 1 nor intervention 2 and constitutes the pure comparison group.

When correctly implemented, randomized assignment ensures that the four groups are similar. You can therefore estimate the impact of the first intervention by comparing the outcome for group B with the outcome for the pure comparison group, group D. You can also estimate the impact of the second intervention by comparing the outcome for group C to the outcome for the pure comparison group. In addition, this design also makes it possible to compare the incremental impact of receiving the second intervention when a unit already receives the first one. Comparing the outcomes of group A and group B will yield the impact of the second intervention for those units that have already received the first intervention, and comparing the outcomes of group A and group C will yield the impact of the first intervention for those units that have already received the second intervention.

Figure 9.3 Treatment and Comparison Groups for a Program with Two Interventions

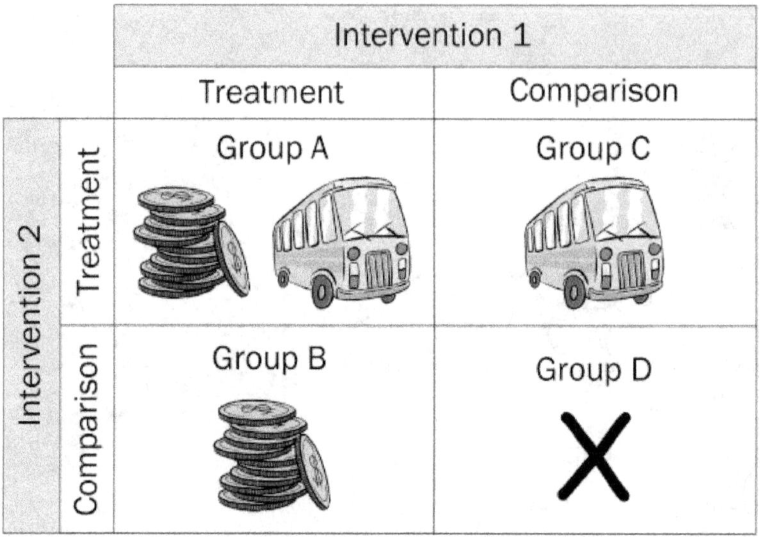

		Intervention 1	
		Treatment	Comparison
Intervention 2	Treatment	Group A	Group C
	Comparison	Group B	Group D ✗

Source: Authors.

The foregoing description has used the example of randomized assignment to explain how an impact evaluation can be designed for a program with two different interventions. When a program comprises more than two interventions, one can increase the number of lotteries and continue to subdivide the evaluation to construct groups that receive the various combinations of interventions. Designs with multiple treatments and multiple treatment levels can also be implemented. Even if the number of groups increases, the basic theory behind the design remains the same as described earlier.

However, evaluating more than one or two interventions will create practical challenges both for the evaluation and for program operation, as the complexity of the design will increase exponentially with the number of treatment arms. For the evaluation of one intervention, only two groups are needed: one treatment group and one comparison group. For the evaluation of two interventions, four groups are needed: three treatment groups and one comparison group. If you were to evaluate three interventions, including all possible combinations among the three interventions, you would need $2 \times 2 \times 2 = 8$ groups in the evaluation. In general, for an evaluation that is to include all possible combinations among n interventions, one would need 2^n groups. In addition, to be able to distinguish dif-

Box 9.1: Testing Program Alternatives for HIV/AIDS Prevention in Kenya

Duflo et al. (2006) used a crosscutting design to evaluate the impact of a number of HIV/AIDS prevention programs in two rural districts of western Kenya. The study was based on a sample of 328 schools, which were divided into six groups, as shown in the accompanying table summarizing the program design. Each group received a different, randomly assigned combination of three treatments. The treatments included providing a teacher training program to improve capacity to teach the national HIV/AIDS education curriculum, encouraging schools to hold debates on the role of condoms and essay contests on prevention, and reducing the cost of education by providing students with free school uniforms (see table).

Summary of Program Design

Group	Number of schools	National program	Teacher training reinforcement	Condom debate and essay (spring 2005)	Reducing the cost of education (spring 2003 and fall 2004)
1	88	Yes			
2	41	Yes	Yes		
3	42	Yes	Yes	Yes	
4	83				Yes
5	40	Yes	Yes		Yes
6	40	Yes	Yes	Yes	Yes

The researchers found that after two years, the teacher training program had had little impact on students' knowledge, self-reported sexual activity, condom use, or teen childbearing, though it did improve the teaching of the national curriculum. The debates and essay competition increased self-reported knowledge and use of condoms without increasing self-reported sexual activity. Finally, reducing the cost of education by providing school uniforms reduced both dropout rates and teen childbearing. Thus, the researchers concluded that providing school uniforms proved more successful in reducing teenage childbearing than training teachers in the national HIV/AIDS curriculum.

Source: Duflo et al. 2006.

Box 9.2: Testing Program Alternatives for Monitoring Corruption in Indonesia

In Indonesia, Olken (2007) used an innovative crosscutting design to test different methods for controlling corruption, from a top-down enforcement approach to more grassroots community monitoring. He used a randomized assignment methodology in more than 600 villages that were building roads as part of a nationwide infrastructure improvement project.

One of the multiple treatments included randomly selecting some villages to be informed that their construction project would be audited by a government agent. Then, to test community participation in monitoring, the researchers implemented two interventions. They passed out invitations to community accountability meetings, and they provided comment forms that could be submitted anonymously. To measure the levels of corruption, an independent team of engineers and surveyors took core samples of the new roads, estimated the cost of the materials used, and then compared their calculations to the reported budgets.

Olken found that increasing government audits (from about a 4 percent chance of being audited to a 100 percent chance) reduced missing expenditures by about 8 percentage points (from 24 percent). Increasing community participation in monitoring had an impact on missing labor but not on missing expenditures. The comment forms were effective only when they were distributed to children at school to give to their families and not when handed out by the village leaders.

Source: Olken 2007.

ferences in outcomes among the different groups, each group must contain a sufficient number of units of observation to ensure sufficient statistical power. In fact, detecting differences between different intervention arms may require larger samples than when comparing a treatment to a pure control. If the two treatment arms are successful in causing changes in the desired outcomes, larger samples will be required to detect the potentially minor differences between the two groups.

Finally, crossover designs can also be put in place in evaluation designs that combine various evaluation methods (boxes 9.1 and 9.2). The operational rules that guide the assignment of each treatment will determine which combination of methods has to be used. For instance, it may be that the first treatment is allocated based on an eligibility score, but the second one is allocated in a randomized fashion. In that case, the design can use a regression discontinuity design for the first intervention and a randomized assignment method for the second intervention.

Note

1. See Banerjee and Duflo (2009) for a longer discussion.

References

Banerjee, Abhijit, and Esther Duflo. 2009. "The Experimental Approach to Development Economics." NBER Working Paper 14467, National Bureau of Economic Research, Cambridge, MA.

Duflo, Esther, Pascaline Dupas, Michael Kremer, and Sameul Sinei. 2006. "Education and HIV/AIDS Prevention: Evidence from a Randomized Evaluation in Western Kenya." World Bank Policy Research Working Paper 402. World Bank, Washington, DC.

Filmer, Deon, and Norbert Schady. 2009. "School Enrollment, Selection and Test Scores." World Bank Policy Research Working Paper 4998, World Bank, Washington, DC.

Olken, Benjamin. 2007. "Monitoring Corruption: Evidence from a Field Experiment in Indonesia." *Journal of Political Economy* 115 (2): 200–49.

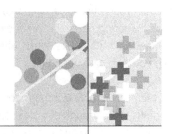

Part 3

HOW TO IMPLEMENT AN IMPACT EVALUATION

In part 1 of this book, we discussed why an impact evaluation would be undertaken and when it is worthwhile to do so. In principle, evaluations should be designed to address questions that need to be answered for policy-making purposes, for example, for budget negotiations or for decisions about whether to expand a nutrition program, increase scholarship benefits, or roll out a hospital reform. The evaluation objectives and questions should flow directly from the policy questions. Once it is clear what policy needs to be evaluated and what policy questions the evaluation must address, you will need to develop a theory of change such as a results chain for your program, which will then allow you to choose appropriate indicators. In part 2 of this book, we described a series of methods that can be used to evaluate the impact of programs and discussed their advantages and disadvantages, with examples for each method.

This third part of the book focuses on the operational steps in managing or commissioning an impact evaluation. These steps constitute the building blocks of an impact evaluation that will answer the policy questions that have been formulated and estimate the causal impact of the program. We have grouped the operational steps of an impact evaluation into four broad phases: *operationalizing the evaluation design, choosing a sample, collecting data,* and *producing and disseminating findings.* The figure on the next page illustrates their sequence, and chapters 10 through 13 deal with each of the four phases.

In chapter 10, we discuss the key components of operationalizing the design for the evaluation. That is, you will examine the program's implementation plans and choose an appropriate evaluation design. Before you can move on to implementing the evaluation, you must confirm that your proposed evaluation design is ethical. Once that is clear, you will assemble a team for the evaluation, construct a budget, and identify funding.

In chapter 11, we discuss how to sample respondents for the surveys and how many survey respondents are required.

In chapter 12, we review the steps in collecting data. Bearing in mind the policy questions you wish to answer, as well as your evaluation design, you must determine what data can be extracted from existing sources and decide what kind of data need to be collected. You must oversee the development of an appropriate questionnaire for the data that are to be collected. Once that is done, help must be hired from a firm or government agency that specializes in data collection. That entity will recruit and train field staff and pilot test the questionnaire. After making the necessary adjustments, the firm or agency will be able to go ahead with fieldwork. Finally, the data that are collected must be digitized or processed and validated before they can be used.

In chapter 13, we deal with the final stages of the evaluation. We describe what products an evaluation will deliver and what the evaluation reports should contain, and we provide some guidelines on how to disseminate findings among policy makers and other stakeholders.

Figure P3.1 Roadmap for Implementing an Impact Evaluation

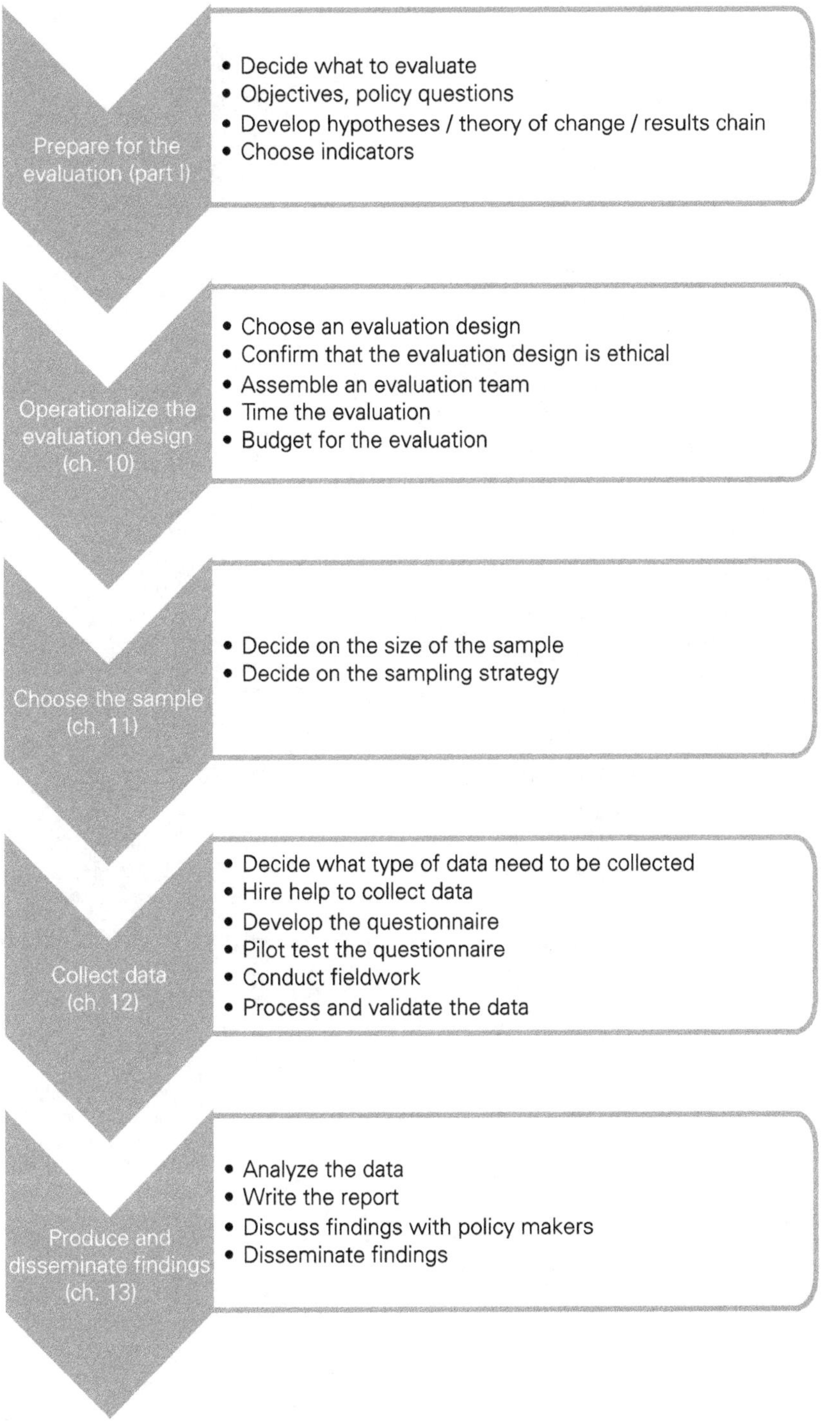

Prepare for the evaluation (part I)
- Decide what to evaluate
- Objectives, policy questions
- Develop hypotheses / theory of change / results chain
- Choose indicators

Operationalize the evaluation design (ch. 10)
- Choose an evaluation design
- Confirm that the evaluation design is ethical
- Assemble an evaluation team
- Time the evaluation
- Budget for the evaluation

Choose the sample (ch. 11)
- Decide on the size of the sample
- Decide on the sampling strategy

Collect data (ch. 12)
- Decide what type of data need to be collected
- Hire help to collect data
- Develop the questionnaire
- Pilot test the questionnaire
- Conduct fieldwork
- Process and validate the data

Produce and disseminate findings (ch. 13)
- Analyze the data
- Write the report
- Discuss findings with policy makers
- Disseminate findings

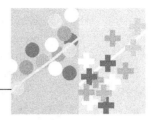

CHAPTER 10

Operationalizing the Impact Evaluation Design

In part 2, we described various alternative methodologies that produce valid comparison groups. Based on those comparison groups, the causal impact of a program can be estimated. We now turn to the practical aspects of choosing which method to use for your own program. We will show that the program's operational rules provide clear guidance on how to generate comparison groups and, thus, on which method is most appropriate for your policy context.

Choosing an Impact Evaluation Method

The key to estimating a causal impact is finding a valid comparison group. In part 2, we discussed a number of valid comparison groups, including those generated from randomized assignment, randomized promotion, regression discontinuity, difference-in-differences, and matching. In this chapter, we consider the question of which method to use in which situation. The overarching principle is that the rules of program operation provide a guide to which method is best suited to which program and that those rules can and should drive the evaluation method, not vice versa. The evaluation should not drastically change key elements of the intervention for the sake of a cleaner evaluation design.

Key Concept:

The rules of program operation determine which impact evaluation method can be applied (not vice versa).

Randomized assignment is often the method preferred by evaluators. When properly implemented, it generates comparability between the treatment and comparison groups in observed and unobserved characteristics, with low risk for bias. Because randomized assignment is fairly intuitive, requires limited use of econometrics, and generates an average treatment effect for the population of interest, it also makes communicating results to policy makers straightforward. However, randomized designs are not always feasible, especially when they conflict with the operational rules of the program.

The operational rules most relevant for the evaluation design are those that identify who is eligible for the program and how they are selected for participation. Comparison groups come from those that are eligible but cannot be incorporated at a given moment (for example, when excess demand exists) or those near the threshold for participation in the program based on targeting or eligibility rules. It is difficult to find valid comparison groups unless the program rules that determine beneficiaries' eligibility and selection are equitable, transparent, and accountable.

Targeting Rule Principles

We can almost always find valid comparison groups if the operational rules for selecting beneficiaries are equitable, transparent, and accountable:

- *Equitable* targeting criteria are rules that rank or prioritize eligibility based on a commonly agreed indicator of need, or under which everyone is offered program benefits, or at least has an equal chance of being offered benefits.

- *Transparent* targeting criteria are rules that are made public, so that civil society can implicitly agree to them and can monitor that they were actually followed. Transparent rules should be quantitative and easily observed by outside parties.

- *Accountable* rules are rules that are the responsibility of program officials and whose implementation is the basis of those officials' job performance and reward.

Equitable rules, as we discuss later, translate in most cases into either randomized assignment or regression discontinuity designs. Transparency and accountability ensure that targeting criteria are quantitatively verifiable and are actually implemented as designed. When the operational rules violate these three principles of good governance, we face challenges both to creating a well-designed program and to conducting the evaluation.

The operational rules of eligibility are transparent and accountable when the government uses quantifiable criteria that can be externally verified and makes those criteria public. These principles of good governance improve the likelihood that the program actually benefits the target population and are the key to a successful evaluation. If the rules are not quantifiable and verifiable, then the evaluation team will have difficulty making sure that assignment to treatment and comparison groups happens as designed or, at minimum, documenting how it actually happened. If the evaluators cannot actually verify assignment, then they cannot correctly analyze the data to calculate impacts. Understanding the program assignment rules is critical to identifying the proper impact evaluation method.

Operational Targeting Rules

Rules of operation typically govern what the program benefits are, how they are financed and distributed, and how the program selects beneficiaries. The rules governing program financing and the incorporation of beneficiaries are key to finding valid comparison groups. The rules governing incorporation cover eligibility, allocation rules in the case of limited resources, and the phasing in of beneficiaries. More specifically, the key rules that generate a road map to comparison groups answer three fundamental operational questions related to money, targeting, and timing:

1. *Money: Does the program have sufficient resources to achieve scale and reach full coverage of all eligible beneficiaries?* Governments and nongovernmental organizations do not always have enough money to provide program services to everyone who is eligible and applies for benefits. In that case, the government has to decide which of the eligible applicants receive program benefits and which are excluded. Many times, programs are limited to specific geographic regions, to rural areas, or to small communities, even though there may be eligible beneficiaries in other regions or in larger communities.

2. *Targeting Rules: Who is eligible for program benefits? Is the program targeted based on an eligibility cutoff, or is it available to everyone?* Public school and primary health care are usually offered universally. Many programs use operational targeting rules that rely on a continuous ranking with a cutoff point. For example, pension programs set an age limit above which elderly individuals become eligible. Cash transfer programs often rank households based on their estimated poverty status, and households below a predetermined cutoff are deemed eligible.

3. *Timing: How are potential beneficiaries enrolled in the program—all at once or in phases over time?* Many times, administrative and resource constraints prevent a government from immediately providing benefits to everyone in its target group. It must roll out the program over time, and thus, it must decide who gets the benefits first and who is incorporated later. A common approach is to phase in a program geographically, over time, incorporating all eligible beneficiaries in one village or region before moving to the next.

Identifying and Prioritizing Beneficiaries

A critical operational issue embedded in all three questions is how beneficiaries are selected. This, as we will see below, is the key to identifying valid comparison groups. Comparison groups are naturally found among the noneligible populations and more frequently among the populations who are eligible but are incorporated later. How beneficiaries are prioritized depends in part on the objectives of the program. Is it a pension program for the elderly, a poverty alleviation program targeted to the poor, or an immunization program available to everyone?

To prioritize beneficiaries, the program must choose an indicator that is both quantifiable and verifiable. Once an indicator of need is agreed on, then how it is applied largely depends on the ability of the government to measure and rank need. If the government can accurately rank beneficiaries based on relative need, it may feel ethically obligated to roll out the program in order of need. However, ranking based on need requires not only a quantifiable measure, but also the ability and resources to measure that indicator on an individual basis.

In some cases, eligibility can be based on a continuous indicator that is cheap and easy to collect, such as age for pensions. For example, age 70 as a cutoff for eligibility for a pension is simple to measure and easy to apply. However, many times the eligibility indicator does not rank relative need within the eligible population. For example, a person 69 years old does not necessarily need a pension less than a person 70 years old, or a person 75 years old, does not necessarily need a pension more than a 72-year-old. In this case, the program can identify the eligible population but cannot easily rank relative need with the eligible population.

Other programs use eligibility criteria that could in principle be used both to determine eligibility and to rank relative need. For example, many programs are targeted to poor individuals, though accurate poverty indicators that reliably rank households are often hard to measure and costly to collect. Collecting income or consumption data on all potential beneficiaries to rank them by poverty level is a complex and costly process. Instead, many programs use some sort of proxy means tests to estimate poverty levels. These are indexes of simple measures such as assets and sociodemographic characteristics (Grosh et al. 2008). Proxy means tests can suffer from measurement error, are costly to implement, and may not always permit fine-tuned ranking of socioeconomic status or need, especially in the lower part of the poverty distribution. Proxy means tests can help determine reasonably well whether a household is above or below some gross cutoff, but they may be less precise when identifying distance from the cutoff. Their use enables programs to identify the eligible poor but not necessarily to rank need within an eligible population.

Rather than confront the cost and complexity of ranking households, many programs choose to rank at a higher level of aggregation, such as at the community level. The underlying assumption is that households within communities are basically homogenous, that the vast majority of the population is likely eligible, and that ranking households would not be worth the cost of identifying and excluding the few ineligibles. In this case, everyone within a community would be eligible for the program. Although this strategy works for small, rural communities, it works less well as programs move into more urbanized areas that are more heterogeneous. Targeting at an aggregate level has obvious operational benefits, but it often does not obviate the need to rank individual beneficiaries based on some objective and quantifiable indicator of need.

In cases when the agency funding a program chooses not to rank need because the process is too costly and error prone, it must use other criteria to decide how to sequence program rollout. One criterion that is consistent with good governance is equity. An equitable rule would be to give everyone who is eligible an equal chance of going first and to randomly assign potential beneficiaries their place in the sequence. This is a fair and equitable allocation rule, and it also produces a randomized evaluation design with both internal and external validity.

Translating Operational Rules into Comparison Groups

In table 10.1, we map the possible comparison groups to the type of program, based on operational rules and the three fundamental operational questions related to money, targeting, and timing that we formulated earlier. The columns are split by whether or not the program has sufficient resources to cover all potentially eligible beneficiaries eventually *(money)* and are further subdivided into programs that have targeted versus universal eligibility *(targeting rules)*. The rows are divided into phased versus immediate rollout of

Table 10.1 Relationship between a Program's Operational Rules and Impact Evaluation Methods

	MONEY →	Excess demand for program (limited resources)		No excess demand for program (fully resourced)	
	TARGETING RULES →	**Continuous targeting or ranking & cutoff (1)**	**No continuous targeting or ranking & cutoff (2)**	**Continuous targeting or ranking & cutoff (3)**	**No continuous targeting or ranking & cutoff (4)**
TIMING	**Phased implementation over time (A)**	**CELL A1** (3.1) Randomized assignment (4) RDD	**CELL A2** (3.1) Randomized assignment (3.2) Randomized promotion (5) DD with (6) Matching	**CELL A3** (3.1) Randomized assignment to phases (4) RDD	**CELL A4** (3.1) Randomized assignment to phases (3.2) Randomized promotion to early take-up (5) DD with (6) Matching
	Immediate implementation (B)	**CELL B1** (3.1) Randomized assignment (4) RDD	**CELL B2** (3.1) Randomized assignment (3.2) Randomized promotion (5) DD with (6) Matching	**CELL B3** (4) RDD	**CELL B4** If less than full takeup: (3.2) Randomized promotion (5) DD with (6) Matching

Source: Authors.

Note: The number in parentheses refers to the chapter of the book where the method is discussed. RDD = regression discontinuity design; DD = difference-in-differences.

the program *(timing)*. Each cell lists the potential sources of valid comparison groups. Each cell is labeled with an index whose first place indicates the row in the table (A, B) and whose second place indicates the column (1–4). For example, cell A1 refers to the cell in the first row and first column of the table. Cell A1 identifies the evaluation methods that are most adequate for programs that have limited resources, are targeted, and are phased in over time.

Most programs need to be phased in over time because of either financing constraints or logistical and administrative limitations. This group or category covers the first row of the chart—that is, cells A1, A2, A3, and A4. In this case, the equitable, transparent, and accountable operational rule is to give everyone an equal chance of getting the program first, second, third, and so on, implying randomized rollout of the program.

In the cases in which resources are limited—that is, in which there will never be enough resources to achieve full scale-up (in cells A1 and A2, and B1 and B2)—excess demand for those resources may emerge very quickly. Then a lottery to decide who gets into the program may be a viable alternative. In this case also, everyone gets an equal chance to benefit from the program. A lottery is an equitable, transparent, and accountable operational rule to allocate program benefits.

Another class of programs comprises those that are phased in over time and for which administrators can rank the potential beneficiaries by need—cells A1 and A3. If the criteria used to prioritize the beneficiaries are quantitative and available and have a cutoff for eligibility, the program can use a regression discontinuity design.

The other broad category consists of programs that have the administrative capability to be implemented immediately—that is, the cells in the bottom row of the chart. When the program has limited resources and is not able to rank beneficiaries (cell B2), then one could use randomized assignment based on excess demand. If the program has sufficient resources to achieve scale and no targeting criteria (cell B4), then the only solution is to use randomized promotion, under the assumption of less than full take-up of the program. If the program can rank beneficiaries and is targeted, one can again use regression discontinuity.

Finding the Minimum Scale of Intervention

The rules of operation also determine the minimum scale of intervention. The scale of intervention is the scale at which the program is being implemented. For example, if a health program is implemented at the district level, then all villages in the district would either receive the program (as a group) or not receive it. Some programs can be efficiently implemented at the individual, household, or institution level, whereas others need to be implemented at a community or administrative district level. Implementing an intervention at one of these higher levels (for example, by province or state) can be problematic for the evaluation for three main reasons:

1. The size of the evaluation sample and the cost of the evaluation increase with the scale of the intervention.

2. As the scale of the intervention increases, it is harder to find a sufficient number of units to include in the evaluation.

3. The internal validity of the evaluation is more likely to be threatened with large-scale units of intervention.

First, evaluations of interventions implemented at higher levels, such as the community or administrative district, require larger sample sizes and will be more costly, compared to evaluations of interventions at a lower level, such as at the individual or household level.[1] The level of intervention is important because it defines the unit of assignment to the treatment and comparison groups, and that has implications for the size of the evaluation sample and its cost. For interventions implemented at higher levels, you will need a larger sample to be able to detect the program's true impact. The intuition behind this will be discussed in chapter 11, which reviews power calculations and how to establish the sample size required for an evaluation.

A slightly distinct point is that the sample size needed for the randomized assignment to successfully balance the treatment and comparison groups becomes problematic at large levels of aggregation. Intuitively, if the level of aggregation is at the province level and the country only has six provinces, then randomization is unlikely to achieve balance between the treatment and comparison groups. In this case, say that the evaluation design allocates three states to the treatment group and three to the comparison group. It is very unlikely that the states in the treatment group would be similar to the comparison group, even if the number of households within each state is large. The key to balancing the treatment and comparison groups is the number of units assigned to the treatment and comparison groups, not the number of individuals or households in the sample.

The third problem with using large-scale units of intervention is that differential changes over time are more likely to compromise the internal validity of the randomized selection even if the groups' characteristics are balanced at baseline. Consider again the example of using states as the level of intervention for a health insurance program. The evaluation randomly assigns one group of states to the treatment group and another to the comparison group. Assume that you are lucky and the two groups are balanced at baseline—that is, households in the treatment and comparison groups have the same level of out-of-pocket medical expenditures, on average. After the baseline data are collected, some individual states may introduce other health policies, such as immunization programs or water and sanitation programs, that improve the health status of the population and thereby lower demand for medical care and out-of-pocket expenditures. If these policy changes are not balanced across the comparison and treatment groups, then the impact of health insurance on out-of-pocket expenditures is confounded with the change in other state health policies. Similarly, some states may experience faster economic growth than others. Health care expenditures most likely rise faster in states with faster income growth. Again, if those differential changes in local economic growth are not balanced across the comparison and treatment groups, then the impact of health insurance on out-of-pocket expenditures will be confounded with the change in the local economy. In general, it is harder to control for these types of temporal changes at larger scales of intervention. Performing randomized assignment on small units of implementation mitigates those threats to internal consistency.

To avoid the problems associated with implementing an intervention at a high geographical or administrative unit level, program managers need to find the minimum scale at which the program can be implemented. Various factors determine the minimum feasible scale of intervention:

- Economies of scale and administrative complexity in the delivery of the program

- Administrative ability to assign benefits at the individual or household level

- Concerns about potential civil conflicts

- Concerns about contamination of the comparison group.

The minimum scale of intervention is typically based on economies of scale and the administrative complexity of delivering the program. For example, a health insurance program may require a local office for beneficiaries to submit claims and to pay providers. The fixed costs of the office need to be spread over a large number of beneficiaries, so it might be inefficient to roll out the program at the individual level and more efficient to do so at the community level. However, in situations with new and untested types of interventions, it may be worth absorbing short-run inefficiencies and rolling out the program within administrative districts, so as to better ensure credibility of the evaluation and lower the costs of data collection.

Some governments argue that locally administered programs, such as health insurance programs, do not have the administrative capabilities to roll out programs at the individual level. They worry that it would be a burden to set up systems to deliver different benefits to different beneficiaries within local administrative units and that the program would not be able to guarantee that the assignment of treatment and comparison groups would be implemented as designed. The latter problem is a serious threat to the ability of the government to implement the evaluation design and therefore to the success of the study.

Sometimes governments prefer to implement programs at more aggregate levels, such as the community, because they worry about potential civil conflict when members of the comparison group observe their neighbors in the treatment group getting benefits early. In reality, little evidence has been put forward to substantiate these claims. A large number of programs have been successfully implemented at the individual or household level within communities without generating civil conflict, when benefits have been assigned in an equitable, transparent, and accountable way.

Finally, when a program is implemented at a very low level, such as at the household or individual level, contamination of the comparison group may compromise the internal validity of the evaluation. For example, say that you are evaluating the effect on households' health of providing tap water. If you install the taps for a household, but not for its neighbor, the treatment household may well share the use of the tap with their comparison neighbor; the neighboring household then would not be a true comparison, since it would benefit from a spillover effect.

In practice, program managers therefore need to find the minimum scale of intervention that (1) allows a large-enough sample for the evaluation, (2) mitigates the risks to internal validity, and (3) fits the operational context. Box 10.1 illustrates the choice and implications of the minimum scale of intervention in the context of cash transfer programs.

Box 10.1: Cash Transfer Programs and the Minimum Scale of Intervention

The majority of conditional cash transfers use communities as the minimum scale of intervention, for administrative and program design reasons, as well as out of concern about spillovers and potential conflict in the community if treatment were to be assigned at a lower level.

For example, the evaluation of Progresa/ Oportunidades, Mexico's conditional cash transfer program, relied on the rollout of the program at the community level in rural areas to randomly assign communities to the treatment and comparison groups. All eligible households in the treatment communities were offered the opportunity to enroll in the program in spring 1998, and all of the eligible households in the comparison communities were offered the same opportunity 18 months later, in winter 1999. However, the evaluators found substantial correlation in outcomes between households within communities. Therefore, to generate sufficient statistical power for the evaluation, they needed more households in the sample than would have been needed if they had been able to assign individual households to the treatment and comparison groups. The impossibility of implementing the program at the household level therefore led to larger sample size requirements and increased the cost of the evaluation. Similar constraints apply to a large proportion of programs in the human development sector.

Sources: Behrman and Hoddinott 2001; Gertler 2004; Levy and Rodríguez 2005; Schultz 2004; Skoufias and McClafferty 2001.

Is the Evaluation Ethical?

Ethics questions are often raised about conducting impact evaluations. One point of departure for this debate is to consider the ethics of investing substantial public resources in programs whose effectiveness is unknown. In this context, the lack of evaluation can itself be seen as unethical. The information on program effectiveness that impact evaluations generate can lead to more effective and ethical investment of public resources.

When the decision is made to design an impact evaluation, some important ethical issues must be considered. They relate to the rules used to assign program benefits, as to well as to the methods by which human subjects are studied.

The most basic principle in the assignment of program benefits is that the delivery of benefits should never be denied or delayed solely for the purpose of an evaluation. In this book, we have argued that evaluations should not dictate how benefits are assigned, but that instead evaluations should be fitted to program assignment rules. In this context, any ethical concerns do not stem from the impact evaluation itself but directly from the program assignment rules.

Key Concept:

Benefits should never be denied or delayed solely for the purpose of an evaluation.

Randomized assignment of program benefits often raises ethical concerns about denying program benefits to eligible beneficiaries. Yet most programs operate with limited financial and administrative resources, making it impossible to reach all eligible beneficiaries at once. From an ethical standpoint, all subjects that are equally eligible to participate in any type of social program should have the same chance of receiving the program. Randomized assignment fulfills this ethical requirement. In situations where a program will be phased in over time, rollout can be based on randomly selecting the order in which equally deserving beneficiaries will receive the program. In these cases, beneficiaries who enter the program later can be used as a comparison group for earlier beneficiaries, generating a solid evaluation design as well as a transparent and fair method for allocating scarce resources.

In many countries and international institutions, review boards or ethics committees have been set up to regulate research involving human subjects. These boards are charged with assessing, approving, and monitoring research studies, with the primary goals of protecting the rights and promoting the welfare of all subjects. Although impact evaluations are primarily operational undertakings, they also constitute research studies and as such should adhere to research guidelines for human subjects.

In the United States, the Office for Human Research Protections, within the Department of Health and Human Services, is responsible for coordinating and supporting the work of institutional review boards that are established in all research institutions and universities. The Office for Human Research Protections also publishes a compilation of over a thousand laws, regulations, and guidelines governing human subjects research in 96 countries and provides links to the ethical codes and regulatory standards currently used by the leading international and regional organizations.

For example, all research conducted in the United States or funded by U.S. federal agencies, such as the National Institutes of Health and the U.S. Agency for International Development, must comply with the ethical principles and regulatory requirements set forth in federal law.[2] The basic principles of the U.S. law pertaining to the protection of human subjects are based on the historic Belmont Report and include ensuring that

- selection of subjects is equitable,

- risks to subjects are minimized,

- risks to subjects are reasonable in relation to anticipated benefits,

- informed consent is sought from each prospective subject or his or her legal representative,

- adequate provisions are in place to protect the privacy of subjects and maintain confidentiality, and

- additional safeguards are included to protect more vulnerable subjects such as children, prisoners, and the economically disadvantaged.

Although the list stems from historical experience with medical trials, the basic principles of protecting the rights and promoting the welfare of all subjects are applicable to social research today. In the context of the evaluation of social programs, the first three points relate to the ethics of benefit assignments. The last three points relate to the protocols based on which subjects are studied for the sake of the evaluation.[3]

When designing, managing, or commissioning an impact evaluation, you should make sure that all stages adhere to any existing laws or review processes governing human subjects research, whether of the country where the evaluation is implemented or of the country where the funding agency is located.

How to Set Up an Evaluation Team?

An evaluation is a partnership between policy makers and evaluators, with each group dependent on the other for its success. Policy makers are responsible for guiding the work and ensuring the relevance of the evaluation—

formulating the evaluation questions, determining whether an impact evaluation is needed, supervising the evaluation, ensuring adequate resources for the work, and applying the results. Evaluators are responsible for the technical aspects—the evaluation methodology, sampling design, data collection, and analysis.

An evaluation is a balance between the technical expertise and independence brought to it by an external group of evaluators, and the policy relevance, strategic guidance, and operational coordination brought by the policy makers. In this partnership, a key element is determining what degree of institutional separation to establish between the evaluation providers and the evaluation users. Much can be gained from the objectivity provided by having the evaluation carried out independently of the institution responsible for the project that is being evaluated. However, evaluations can often have multiple goals, including building evaluation capacity within government agencies and sensitizing program operators to the realities of their projects once carried out in the field.

For an impact evaluation to be successful, evaluators and policy makers must work together. Whereas impact evaluations should be conducted by an external group to maintain objectivity and credibility, the process cannot be divorced from the operational rules, notably in assessing the rules of program implementation to determine the appropriate evaluation design and in ensuring that program implementation and evaluation are well coordinated, so that one does not compromise the other. Moreover, the results are less likely to be directly policy relevant or have policy impact without the engagement of policy makers from the beginning.

The Composition of an Evaluation Team

Policy makers can commission an evaluation using various contracting arrangements. First, the government unit commissioning the evaluation may decide to contract out the entire evaluation at once. It is then responsible for establishing at least a first draft of the evaluation plan, including the key objectives, policy questions, expected methodology, data to be collected, and budget ceilings. That plan provides the basic terms of reference to launch a call for technical and financial proposals from external evaluators. The terms can also specify a minimum team composition that the external evaluators must comply with. The preparation of technical proposals gives the external evaluators the chance to suggest improvements to the evaluation plan that the government has produced. Once the evaluation is contracted out, the external agency that has been contracted actively manages the evaluation and appoints an evaluation manager. In this model, the government team principally provides oversight.

Under a second type of contractual arrangement, the government unit commissioning the evaluation may decide to manage it directly. This involves developing an impact evaluation plan and sequentially contracting out its subcomponents. In this arrangement, the evaluation manager remains in the government unit commissioning the evaluation.

Regardless of the contracting arrangement, a key responsibility of the evaluation manager is to build the evaluation team, keeping in mind the interests of the clients and the steps needed to carry out the evaluation. Although each evaluation is different, the technical team of any impact evaluation effort that relies on collecting its own data, qualitative or quantitative, will almost always need certain members. They include the following:

- *An evaluation manager.* This person is responsible for establishing the key objectives, policy questions, indicators, and information needs of the evaluation (often in close collaboration with policy makers and using a theory of change such as a results chain); selecting the evaluation methodology; identifying the evaluation team; and drafting terms of reference for the parts of the evaluation to be contracted or subcontracted. It is important to designate an evaluation manager who will be able to work effectively with the data producers, as well as with the analysts and policy makers using the data and the results of the evaluation. If the person is not based locally, it is recommended that a local manager be designated to coordinate the evaluation effort in conjunction with the international manager.

- *A sampling expert.* This is someone who can guide work on power calculations and sampling. For quantitative impact evaluations, the sampling expert should be able to carry out power calculations to determine the appropriate sample sizes for the indicators established, select the sample, review the results of the actual sample versus the designed sample, and provide advice at the time of the analysis, for instance, on how to incorporate the sampling weights for the analysis, if needed. The sampling expert should also be tasked with selecting sites and groups for the pilot test. Particularly if the sampling expert is an international consultant, he or she will often need to be paired with a local information coordinator responsible for collecting the data from which the sample will be drawn.

- *A person or team responsible for designing the data collection instruments and accompanying manuals and codebooks.* This person works with the evaluation manager to ensure that the data collection instruments will indeed produce the data required for the analysis and is also involved in pilot testing the questionnaires.

- *A fieldwork team.* The team includes a fieldwork manager who can supervise the entire data collection effort, from planning the routes for the data collection to forming and scheduling the fieldwork teams, which are generally composed of supervisors and interviewers.

- *Data managers and processors.* They design the data entry programs, enter the data, check its validity, provide the needed data documentation, and produce the basic results that can be verified by the data analysts.

- *Data and policy analysts.* The analysts work with the data produced and with the evaluation manager to conduct the required analysis and write the evaluation reports.

Partners for the Evaluation

One of the first determinations that policy makers, together with the evaluation manager, must make is whether the evaluation—or parts of it—can be implemented locally and what kind of supervision and outside assistance will be needed. Evaluation capacity varies greatly from country to country. International contracts that allow firms in one country to carry out evaluations in another country are becoming more common. It is also becoming increasingly common for governments and multilateral institutions to implement evaluations locally, while providing a great deal of international supervision. It is up to the evaluation manager to critically assess local capacity and determine who will be responsible for what aspects of the evaluation effort.

Another question is whether to work with a private firm or a public agency. Private firms or research institutions can be more dependable in providing timely results, but capacity building in the public sector is lost, and private firms often are understandably less amenable to incorporating into the evaluation elements that will make the effort costlier. Research institutions and universities can also work as evaluators. The reputation and technical expertise of solid research institutions or universities can ensure that evaluation results are widely accepted by stakeholders. However, those institutions sometimes lack the operational experience or the ability to perform some aspects of the evaluation, such as data collection, so that those aspects may need to be subcontracted to another partner. Whatever combination of counterparts is finally crafted, a sound review of potential collaborators' past evaluation activities is essential to making an informed choice.

Particularly when working with a public agency, a conscientious evaluator should be aware of the capacity of the evaluation team in light of other activities that the unit is carrying out. This is particularly relevant when working with public sector agencies with multiple responsibilities and limited staff. Awareness of the unit's workload is important for assessing not only how it will affect the quality of the evaluation being conducted but also the opportunity cost of the evaluation with respect to other efforts for which the unit is responsible. In one example, an impact evaluation of an education reform was planned that required the efforts of the staff of the national assessment team responsible for the biannual national achievement tests. The team was selected as counterparts for the evaluation effort because they were the most professionally qualified to assume responsibility for the evaluation and because complementarities were sought between the evaluation and the national assessment. However, when the reform—and correspondingly the evaluation—was delayed, the delay derailed the entire survey effort; the achievement tests for the national assessment were not applied on schedule, and the country lost an opportunity to monitor educational progress. Such situations can be avoided through coordination with managers in the unit responsible for the evaluation to ensure that a balance is achieved in the timing of various activities, as well as the distribution of staff and resources across those activities.

How to Time the Evaluation?

We discussed in part 1 the advantages of prospective evaluations, designed during program preparation. Advance planning allows for a broader choice in generating comparison groups, facilitates the collection of baseline data, and helps stakeholders reach consensus about program objectives and questions of interest.

Though it is important to plan evaluations early in the project design phase, carrying them out should be timed to assess the program once it is mature. Pilot projects or nascent reforms are often prone to revision both of their content and in regard to how, when, where, and by whom they will be implemented. Program providers may need time to learn and consistently apply new operational rules. Because evaluations require clear rules of program operation to generate appropriate counterfactuals, it is important to apply evaluations to programs after they are well established.

Baseline data should always be collected, but another key timing issue is how much time is needed before results can be measured. The right balance is very much context specific: "If one evaluates too early, there is a risk of finding only partial or no impact; too late, and there is a risk that the program might lose donor and public support or that a badly designed program might be expanded" (King and Behrman 2009, p. 56). The following factors need to be weighted to determine when to collect follow-up data:[4]

- Program cycle, including program duration, time of implementation, and potential delays

- Expected time needed for the program to affect outcomes, as well as the nature of outcomes of interest

- Policy-making cycles

First, the impact evaluation needs to be fitted to the program implementation cycle. The evaluation cannot drive the program being evaluated. By their very nature, evaluations are subject to the program time frame; they must be aligned to the expected duration of the program. They also must be adapted to potential implementation lags when programs are slow to assign benefits or are delayed by external factors.[5] In general, although evaluation timing should be built into the project from the outset, evaluators should be prepared to be flexible and to make modifications as the project is implemented. In addition, provision should be made for tracking the interventions, using a strong monitoring system so that the evaluation effort is informed by the actual pace of the intervention.

The timing of *follow-up data collection* must take into account how much time is needed after the program is implemented for results to become apparent. The program results chain helps with identifying outcome indicators and the appropriate time to measure them. Some programs (such as income support programs) aim to provide short-term benefits, whereas others (such as basic education programs) aim for longer-term gains. Moreover, certain results by their nature take longer to appear (such as changes in life expectancy or fertility from a health reform) than others (such as earnings from a training program).

For example, in the evaluation of the Bolivian Social Investment Fund, which relied on baseline data collected in 1993, follow-up data were not collected until 1998 because of the time required to carry out the interventions (water and sanitation projects, health clinics, and schools) and for effects on the beneficiary population's health and education to emerge (Newman et al. 2002). A similar period of time has been required for the evaluation of a primary education project in Pakistan that used an experimental design with baseline and follow-up surveys to assess the impact of community schools on student outcomes, including academic achievement (King, Orazem, and Paterno 2008).

When to collect follow-up data will therefore depend on the program under study as well as on the outcome indicators of interest. Some evaluations will collect follow-up data while the program is still being implemented, to measure short-term changes and to maintain contact with the evaluation sample to reduce sample attrition over time. For programs that do not have continuous operations, additional rounds of follow-up data collected well after the program has been completed can help to measure longer-term changes. Follow-up data can be collected more than once, so that short-term and medium-term results can be considered and contrasted.

Follow-up data collected during program implementation may not capture full program impact if indicators are measured too early. Indeed, "programs do not necessarily attain full steady-state effectiveness after implementation commences. Learning by providers and beneficiaries may take time" (King and Behrman 2009, 65). Still, it is very useful to document short-term impacts. As already stated, some programs have only short-term objectives (such as income support). Evidence on how such a program performs in the short term can also provide information about expected longer-term outcomes. For instance, it is often valuable to measure shorter-term indicators that are good predictors of longer-term indicators (such as attended births as a shorter-term indicator of infant mortality). Follow-up data collected while the program is still being implemented are also useful to produce early impact evaluation results, which can invigorate dialogue between evaluators and policy makers.

Follow-up surveys that measure long-term outcomes after program implementation often produce the most convincing evidence regarding program effectiveness. For instance, the positive results from long-term impact evaluations of early childhood programs in the United States (Currie and Thomas 1995, 2000; Currie 2001) and Jamaica (Grantham-McGregor et al. 1994) have been influential in making the case for investing in early childhood interventions.

Long-term impacts sometimes constitute explicit program objectives, but they can also reflect unintended, indirect effects, such as those related to behavioral changes. The identification of longer-term impacts can nevertheless create difficulties. Impacts may simply vanish in the long term. A strong impact evaluation design also may not withstand the test of time. For example, units in the control group may begin to benefit from spillover effects from program beneficiaries.

Although short-term and longer-term follow-up data are complementary, the timing of an evaluation must also take into account when certain information is needed to inform decision making and must synchronize evaluation and data collection activities to key decision-making points. The production of results should be timed to inform budgets, program expansion, or other policy decisions.

How to Budget for an Evaluation?

Budgeting constitutes one of the last steps to operationalize the evaluation design. In this section, we review some existing impact evaluation cost data, discuss how to budget for an evaluation, and suggest some options for funding.

Review of Cost Data

Tables 10.2 and 10.3 contain cost data on impact evaluations of a number of World Bank–supported projects. The sample in table 10.2 comes from a comprehensive review of programs supported by the Social Protection and Labor unit. The sample in table 10.3 was selected based on the availability of current budget statistics from the set of impact evaluations financed by the Spanish Impact Evaluation Fund (SIEF). Although the two samples are not necessarily representative of all evaluations undertaken by the World Bank, as cost data are not yet consistently documented, they provide useful benchmarks on the costs associated with conducting rigorous impact evaluations.

Table 10.2 Cost of Impact Evaluations of a Selection of World Bank–Supported Projects

Impact evaluation	Country	Total cost of IE ($)	Total cost of program ($)	IE% of total program costs
Migrant Skills Development and Employment	China	220,000	50,000,000	0.4
Social Safety Net Project	Colombia	130,000	86,400,000	0.2
Social Sectors Investment Program	Dominican Republic	600,000	19,400,000	3.1
Social Protection	Jamaica	800,000	40,000,000	2.0
Social Safety Net Technical Assistance	Pakistan	2,000,000	60,000,000	3.3
Social Protection Project	Panama	1,000,000	24,000,000	4.2
1st Community Living Standards	Rwanda	1,000,000	11,000,000	9.1
Social Fund for Development 3	Yemen, Rep.	2,000,000	15,000,000	13.3
Average		**968,750**	**38,225,000**	**4.5**

Source: Authors' calculations from a sample of World Bank programs in the Social Protection Sector.

Note: IE = impact evaluation.

Table 10.3 Disaggregated Costs of a Selection of World Bank–Supported Projects

SIEF impact evaluation	Country	Total cost	Travel	World Bank staff	Consultants (national and int'l.)	Data collection (including filed staff)	Other (dissemination & workshops)
Poverty Reduction Support Credits and Maternal Health	Benin	1,690,000	270,000	200,000	320,000	840,000	60,000
Performance Pay Reform for School Teachers	Brazil	513,000	78,000	55,000	105,000	240,000	35,000
Nadie es Perfecto Program to Improve Parenting Skills	Chile	313,000	11,500	—	35,500	260,000	6,000
Paying for Performance in China's Health Sector: Evaluation of Health XI	China	308,900	60,000	35,000	61,000	152,900	—
National Rural Employment Guarantee Program	India	390,000	41,500	50,000	13,500	270,000	15,000
School Health and Nutrition: the Role of Malaria Control in Improving Education	Kenya	652,087	69,550	60,000	103,180	354,000	65,357
HIV Prevention Campaign for the Youth: Abstinence, Fidelity and Safe Sex	Lesotho	630,300	74,300	9,600	98,400	440,000	8,000
CCT, Schooling, and HIV Risk	Malawi	1,842,841	83,077	144,000	256,344	1,359,420	—
Contigo Vamos por Mas Oportunidades Program in the State of Guanajuato	Mexico	132,199	2,660	50,409	—	80,640	1,150

Randomized CCT Pilot in Rural Primary Education	Morocco	674,367	39,907	66,000	142,460	426,000	—
Learning and Growing in the Shadow of HIV/AIDS: Randomized ECD Program	Mozambique	838,650	86,400	31,000	62,500	638,750	20,000
Training of Community Distributors in the Prevention and Treatment of Malaria	Nigeria	1,024,040	64,000	35,000	106,900	817,740	—
School Health and Nutrition: the Role of Malaria Control in Improving Education	Senegal	644,047	61,800	60,000	102,890	354,000	65,357
CCTs to Prevent HIV and Other Sexually Transmitted Infections	Tanzania	771,610	60,000	62,000	100,000	518,611	30,999
Average		**744,646**	**71,621**	**66,031**	**115,975**	**482,290**	**30,686**

Source: Authors' calculations from a sample of impact evaluations financed by the Spanish Impact Evaluation Fund.

Note: CCT = conditional cash transfer; ECD = early childhood development; — = not available.

The direct costs of the evaluation activities range between $130,000 and $2 million, with an average cost of $968,750. Although those costs vary widely and may seem high in absolute terms, in relative terms they amounted to between 0.2 percent and 13.3 percent of total program costs,[6] with an average of 4.5 percent. Based on this sample, impact evaluations constitute only a small percentage of overall program budgets. In addition, the cost of conducting an impact evaluation must be compared to the opportunity costs of not conducting a rigorous evaluation and thus potentially running an ineffective program. Evaluations allow researchers and policy makers to identify which programs or program features work, which do not, and which strategies may be the most effective and efficient in achieving program goals. In this sense, the resources needed to implement an impact evaluation constitute a relatively small but significant investment.

Table 10.3 disaggregates the costs of the sample of SIEF-supported impact evaluations. The total costs of an evaluation include World Bank staff time, national and international consultants, travel, data collection, and dissemination activities.[7] In these, as in almost all evaluations for which existing data cannot be used, the highest cost is new data collection, accounting for over 60 percent of the cost, on average.

It is important to keep in mind that these numbers reflect different sizes and types of evaluations. The relative cost of evaluating a pilot program is generally higher than the relative cost of evaluating a nationwide or universal program. In addition, some evaluations require only one follow-up survey or may be able to use existing data sources, whereas others may need to carry out multiple rounds of data collection. The Living Standards Measurement Study Manual (Grosh and Glewwe 2000) provides estimations of the cost of collecting data through household surveys, based on experience in countries all over the world. However, the manual also emphasizes that costs depend largely on the capabilities of the local team, the resources available, and the length of time in the field. To learn more about how to cost a survey in a particular context, it is recommended that evaluators first contact the national statistical agency.

Budgeting for an Impact Evaluation

Clearly, many resources are required to implement a rigorous impact evaluation. Budget items include staff fees for at least one principal investigator/researcher, a research assistant, a field coordinator, a sampling expert, survey enumerators, and project staff, who may provide support throughout the evaluation. These human resources may consist of researchers and technical experts from international organizations, international or local consultants, and client country program staff. The costs of travel and subsistence (hotels and per diems) must also be budgeted. Resources for dissemination, often in the form of workshops, reports, and academic papers, should also be considered in the evaluation planning.

As we have said, the largest costs in an evaluation are usually those of data collection (including creating and pilot testing the survey) data collection materials and equipment, training for the enumerators, daily wages for the enumerators, vehicles and fuel, and data entry operations. Calculating the costs of all of these inputs requires making some assumptions about, for example, how long the questionnaire will take to complete and travel times between sites. A work sheet is provided in table 10.4 to help with estimating the costs of the data collection stage.

The costs of an impact evaluation may be spread out over several fiscal years. A sample budget in table 10.5 shows how the expenditures at each stage of an evaluation can be disaggregated by fiscal year for accounting and reporting purposes. Again, budget demands will likely be higher during the years when the data are collected.

Funding for Evaluations

Financing for an evaluation can come from many sources, including a project loan, direct program budgets, research grants, or donor funding. Often, evaluation teams look to a combination of sources to generate the needed funds. Although funding for evaluations used to come primarily from research budgets, a growing emphasis on evidence-based policy making has increased funding from other sources. In cases where an evaluation is likely to fill a substantial knowledge gap that is of interest to the development community more broadly, and where a credible, robust evaluation can be applied, policy makers should be encouraged to look for outside funding, given the public-good nature of the evaluation results. Sources of funding include the government, development banks, multilateral organizations, United Nations agencies, foundations, philanthropists, and research and evaluation organizations such as the International Initiative for Impact Evaluation.

Table 10.4   Work Sheet for Impact Evaluation Cost Estimation

Tasks and resources	Number	Rate/unit	No. of units	Total
Staff				
Program evaluation staff (evaluation manager, etc.)				
International and/or national consultants (researcher/principal investigator)				
Research assistant				
Statistical expert				
Field coordinator				
Travel				
International and local airfare				
Local ground transport				
Subsistence (hotel and per diem)				
Data collection[a]				
Instrument design				
Piloting				
Training				
Travel and per diems				
Survey material, equipment				
Printing questionnaires				
Field staff				
Enumerators				
Supervisors				
Transport (vehicles and fuel)				
Drivers				
Data entry and cleaning				
Data analysis and dissemination				
Workshops				
Papers, reports				
Other				
Office space				
Communications				
Software				

Source: Authors.

a. Data collection calculations must reflect assumptions such as the number of rounds of data collection required, how long the data collection will take, the number of villages in the sample, the number of households per village, the length of the questionnaire, travel time, and so on.

Table 10.5   Sample Impact Evaluation Budget

	Unit	Design Stage			Unit	Baseline Data Stage		
		Cost per unit (US$)	No. of units	Total cost (US$)		Cost per unit (US$)	No. of units	Total cost (US$)
A. Staff salaries	Weeks	7,500	2	15,000	Weeks	7,500	2	15,000
B. Consultant fees				10,250				27,940
International consultant (1)	Days	450	15	6,750	Days	450	0	0
International consultant (2)	Days	350	10	3,500	Days	350	10	3,500
Research assistant/field coordinator	Days	188	0	0	Days	188	130	24,440
C. Travel & subsistence				14,100				15,450
Staff: international airfare	Trips	3,350	1	3,350	Trips	3,350	1	3,350
Staff: hotel & per diem	Days	150	5	750	Days	150	5	750
International airfare: international consultants	Trips	3,500	2	7,000	Trips	3,500	2	7,000
Hotel & per diem: international consultants	Days	150	20	3,000	Days	150	20	3,000
International airfare: field coordinator	Trips		0	0	Trips	1,350	1	1,350
Hotel & per diem: field coordinator	Days		0	0	Days	150	0	0
D. Data collection								126,000
Data type 1: consent					School	120	100	12,000
Data type 2: education outcomes					Child	14	3,000	42,000
Data type 3: health outcomes					Child	24	3,000	7,200
V. Other								
Workshop(s)								
Dissemination / reporting								
Other 1 (clusterwide coordination overhead)								
Total costs per stage		Design stage:		39,350		Baseline stage:		184,390

(continued)

Table 10.5 *(continued)*

		Follow-up Data Stage I				Follow-up Data Stage II		
	Unit	Cost per unit (US$)	No. of units	Total cost (US$)	Unit	Cost per unit (US$)	No. of units	Total cost (US$)
A. Staff salaries	Weeks	7,500	2	15,000	Weeks	7,500	2	15,000
B. Consultant fees				32,550				32,440
International consultant (1)	Days	450	15	6,750	Days	450	10	4,500
International consultant (2)	Days	350	20	7,000	Days	350	10	3,500
Research assistant/field coordinator	Days	188	100	18,800	Days	188	130	24,440
C. Travel & subsitence				20,000				20,000
Staff: International airfare	Trips	3,350	2	6,700	Trips	3,350	2	6,700
Staff: hotel & per diem	Days	150	10	1,500	Days	150	10	1,500
International airfare: international consultants	Trips	3,500	2	7,000	Trips	3,500	2	7,000
Hotel & per diem: international consultants	Days	150	20	3,000	Days	150	20	3,000
International airfare: field coordinator	Trips	1,350	1	1,350	Trips	1,350	1	1,350
Hotel & per diem: field coordinator	Days	150	3	450	Days	150	3	450
D. Data Collection				114,000				114,000
Data type 1: consent								
Data type 2: education outcomes	Child	14	3,000	42,000	Child	14	3,000	42,000
Data type 3: health outcomes	Child	24	3,000	72,000	Child	24	3,000	72,000
V. Other								**65,357**
Workshop(s)						20,000	2	40,000
Dissemination / reporting						5,000	3	15,000
Other 1 (clusterwide coordination overhead)						5,179	2	10,357
Total costs per stage		Follow-up stage I		181,550		Follow-up stage II		246,797
						Total evaluation costs:		652,087

Source: Authors.

Notes

1. The discussion in this section applies most directly to a randomized assignment design, but the same principles hold for evaluations based on other methodologies.
2. See Kimmel 1988; NIH 2006; USAID 2008; U.S. Department of Health and Human Services 2010; and U.S. National Archives 2009.
3. Potential risk in collecting data for the evaluation of social programs include failing to obtain informed consent from subjects; testing children's cognitive development in front of their parents, which may lead to assumptions about the children's future capabilities; asking to speak with women alone or interviewing women about sensitive subjects in front of male family members; failing to understand the time or opportunity costs of interviewing subjects and providing compensation or a token of appreciation when appropriate.
4. See King and Behrman (2009) for a detailed discussion of timing issues in relation to the evaluation of social programs.
5. "There are several reasons why implementation is neither immediate nor perfect, why the duration of exposure to a treatment differs not only across program areas but also across ultimate beneficiaries, and why varying lengths of exposure might lead to a different estimates of program impact" (King and Behrman 2009, 56).
6. In this case, cost is calculated as a percentage of the portion of the project cost financed by the World Bank.
7. This cost does not include the costs of local project staff, who were often heavily engaged in the design and supervision of the evaluation, as accurate data on these costs are not regularly recorded.

References

Behrman, Jere R., and John Hoddinott. 2001. "An Evaluation of the Impact of PROGRESA on Pre-school Child Height." FCND Briefs 104, International Food Policy Research Institute, Washington, DC.

Currie, Janet. 2001. "Early Childhood Education Programs." *Journal of Economic Perspectives* 15 (2): 213–38.

Currie, Janet, and Duncan Thomas. 1995. "Does Head Start Make a Difference?" *American Economic Review* 85 (3): 341–64.

———. 2000. "School Quality and the Longer-Term Effects of Head Start." *Journal of Economic Resources* 35 (4): 755–74.

Gertler, Paul J. 2004. "Do Conditional Cash Transfers Improve Child Health? Evidence from PROGRESA's Control Randomized Experiment." *American Economic Review* 94 (2): 336–41.

Grantham-McGregor, S., C. Powell, S. Walker, and J. Himes. 1994. "The Long-Term Follow-up of Severely Malnourished Children Who Participated in an Intervention Program." *Child Development* 65: 428–93.

Grosh, Margaret, and Paul Glewwe, eds. 2000. *Designing Household Survey Questionnaires for Developing Countries: Lessons from 15 Years of the Living Standards Measurement Study*, vols. 1, 2, and 3. Washington, DC: World Bank.

Grosh, Margaret, Carlo del Ninno, Emil Tesliuc, and Azedine Ouerghi. 2008. *For Protection and Promotion: The Design and Implementation of Effective Safety Nets*. Washington, DC: World Bank.

Jalan, Jyotsna, and Martin Ravallion. 2003a. "Estimating the Benefit Incidence of an Antipoverty Program by Propensity-Score Matching." *Journal of Business & Economic Statistics* 21 (1): 19–30.

———. 2003b. "Does Piped Water Reduce Diarrhea for Children in Rural India?" *Journal of Econometrics* 112 (1): 153–73.

Kimmel, Allan. 1988. *Ethics and Values in Applied Social Research*. California: Sage Publications.

King, Elizabeth M., and Jere R. Behrman. 2009. "Timing and Duration of Exposure in Evaluations of Social Programs." *World Bank Research Observer* 24 (1): 55–82.

King, Elizabeth M., Peter F. Orazem, and Elizabeth M. Paterno. 2008. "Promotion with and without Learning: Effects on Student Enrollment and Dropout Behavior." Policy Research Working Paper Series 4722. World Bank, Washington, DC.

Levy, Santiago, and Evelyne Rodríguez. 2005. *Sin Herencia de Pobreza: El Programa Progresa-Oportunidades de México*. Washington, DC: Inter-American Development Bank.

NIH (U.S. National Institutes of Health). 2006. "Regulations and Ethical Guidelines" and "Belmont Report." Office of Human Subjects Research. http://ohsr.od.nih.gov/index.html.

Newman, John, Menno Pradhan, Laura B. Rawlings, Geert Ridder, Ramiro Coa, and Jose Luis Evia. 2002. "An Impact Evaluation of Education, Health, and Water Supply Investments by the Bolivian Social Investment Fund." *World Bank Economic Review* 16 (2): 241–74.

Rosenbaum, Paul. 2002. *Observational Studies*. Springer Series in Statistics.

Rosenbaum, Paul, and Donald Rubin. 1983. "The Central Role of the Propensity Score in Observational Studies of Causal Effects." *Biometrika* 70 (1): 41–55.

Schultz, Paul. 2004. "School Subsidies for the Poor: Evaluating the Mexican Progresa Poverty Program." *Journal of Development Economics* 74 (1): 199–250.

Skoufias, Emmanuel, and Bonnie McClafferty. 2001. "Is *Progresa* Working? Summary of the Results of an Evaluation by IFPRI." International Food Policy Research Institute, Washington, DC.

USAID (U.S. Agency for International Development). 2008. "Procedures for Protection of Human Subjects in Research Supported by USAID." http://www.usaid.gov/policy/ads/200/humansub.pdf.

U.S. Department of Health and Human Services. 2010. "International Compilation of Human Research Protections." Office for Human Research Protections. http://www.hhs.gov/ohrp/ international/HSPCompilation.pdf.

U.S. National Archives. 2009. "Protection of Human Subjects." *U.S. Code of Federal Regulations*, Title 22, Part 225.

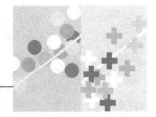

CHAPTER 11

Choosing the Sample

Once you have chosen a method to select the comparison group, the next step in planning an impact evaluation is to determine what data you need and the sample required to precisely estimate differences in outcomes between the treatment group and the comparison group. You must determine both the size of the sample and how to draw the units in the sample from a population of interest.

What Kinds of Data Do I Need?

Good quality data are required to assess the impact of the intervention on the outcomes of interest. The results chain discussed in chapter 2 provides a basis to define which indicators should be measured and when. The first and foremost need is data on outcome indicators directly affected by the program. However, the impact evaluation should not measure only outcomes for which the program is directly accountable. Data on outcome indicators that the program indirectly affects or indicators capturing unintended program impact will maximize the value of the information that the impact evaluation generates. As discussed in chapter 2, outcome indicators should preferably be selected so that they are "SMART": specific, measurable, attributable, realistic, and targeted.

Impact evaluations are typically conducted over several time periods, and you must determine when to measure the outcome indicators. Following the results chain, you can establish a hierarchy of outcome indicators, ranging from short-term indicators, such as school attendance in the context of an education program, to longer-term ones, such as student achievement or labor market outcomes. To measure impact convincingly over time, data are needed starting at the baseline. The section in chapter 10 on the timing of evaluations sheds light on when to collect data.

As we shall see, some indicators may not be amenable to impact evaluation in relatively small samples. Detecting impacts for outcome indicators that are extremely variable, rare events, or that are likely to be only marginally affected by an intervention may require prohibitively large samples. For instance, identifying the impact of an intervention on maternal mortality rates will be feasible only in a sample that contains many pregnant women. In such a case, it may be wise to focus the impact evaluation on indicators for which there is sufficient power to detect effect.

Apart from outcome indicators, it is also useful to consider the following:

- *Administrative data on the delivery of the intervention.* At a minimum, monitoring data are needed to know when a program starts and who receives benefits, as well as to provide a measure of the "intensity" of the intervention in cases when it may not be delivered to all beneficiaries with the same content, quality, or duration.

- *Data on exogenous factors that may affect the outcome of interest.* These make it possible to control for outside influences. This aspect is particularly important when using evaluation methods that rely on more assumptions than do randomized methods. Accounting for these factors also helps increase statistical power.

- *Data on other characteristics.* Including additional controls or analyzing the heterogeneity of the program's effects along certain characteristics makes possible a finer estimation of treatment effects.

In short, indicators are required throughout the results chain, including final outcome indicators, intermediate outcomes indicators, measures of the delivery of the intervention, exogenous factors, and control characteristics.[1]

The design selected for the impact evaluation will also affect the data requirements. For example, if either the matching or the difference-in-differences method is chosen, it will be necessary to collect data on a very broad array of characteristics for both treatment and comparison groups, making it possible to carry out a range of robustness tests, as described in part 2.

For each evaluation, it is useful to develop a matrix that lists the question of interest, the outcome indicators for each question, the other types of indicators needed, and the source of data, as outlined in figure 2.3 (chapter 2).

Can I Use Existing Data?

Some existing data are almost always needed at the outset of a program to estimate benchmark values of indicators or to conduct power calculations, as we will further discuss below. Beyond the planning stages, the availability of existing data can substantially diminish the cost of conducting an impact evaluation.

Existing data alone are rarely sufficient, however. Impact evaluations require comprehensive data covering a sufficiently large sample that is representative of both the treatment and comparison groups. *Population census data* covering the entire treatment and comparison groups are rarely available. Even when these censuses exist, they may contain only a limited set of variables or be fielded infrequently. Nationally representative household surveys may contain a comprehensive set of outcome variables, but they rarely contain enough observations from both the treatment and comparison groups to conduct an impact evaluation. Assume, for example, that you are interested in evaluating a large, national program that reaches 10 percent of the households in a given country. If a nationally representative survey is carried out on 5,000 households every year, it may contain roughly 500 households that receive the program in question. Is this sample large enough to conduct an impact evaluation? Power calculations can answer this question, but in most cases the answer is no.

Still, the possibility of using existing *administrative data* to conduct impact evaluations should be seriously considered. Administrative data are data collected by program agencies, often at the point of service delivery, as part of their regular operations. In some cases, monitoring data contain outcome indicators. For instance, schools may record students' enrollment, attendance, or test scores, and health centers may record patients' anthropometrics and vaccination or health status. Some influential retrospective evaluations have relied on administrative records (for instance Galiani, Gertler, and Schargrodsky 2005 on water policy in Argentina).

To determine whether existing data can be used in a given impact evaluation, the following questions must be considered:

- *Size*. Are existing data sets large enough to detect changes in the outcome indicators with sufficient power?

- *Sampling*. Are existing data available for both the treatment group and comparison group? Are existing samples drawn from a sampling frame that coincides with the population of interest? Were units drawn from the sampling frame based on a probabilistic sampling procedure?

- *Scope*. Do existing data contain all of the indicators needed to answer the policy questions of interest?

- *Frequency*. Are the existing data collected frequently enough? Are they available for all units in the sample over time?

Only in relatively rare cases are existing data suitable for impact evaluations. As a result, you will most likely have to budget for the collection of new data. Although data collection is often a major cost, it is also a high-return investment upon which the quality of the evaluation depends.

In some cases, the data required for impact evaluation can be collected by rolling out new information systems. This must be done in accordance with an evaluation design, so that outcome indicators are collected for a treatment and a comparison group at multiple times. New information systems may be required before new interventions, so that administrative centers in the comparison group use the new information system before receiving the intervention to be evaluated. Because the quality of administrative data can vary, auditing and external verification are required to guarantee the reliability of the evaluation. Collecting impact evaluation data through administrative sources instead of through surveys can dramatically reduce the cost of an evaluation but may not always be feasible.

If administrative data are not sufficient for your evaluation, you will likely have to rely on *survey data*. In addition to exploring whether you can use existing surveys, you should also find out if any new national data collection efforts (such as demographic and health surveys or a Living Standards Measurement Survey) are being planned. If a survey measuring the required indicators is planned, it may be possible to oversample the population of interest. For instance, the evaluation of the Nicaraguan Social Fund complemented a national living standards measurement survey with an extra sample of beneficiaries (Pradhan and Rawlings 2002). If a survey is planned that will cover the population of interest, you may also be able to introduce a question or series of questions as part of that survey.

Most impact evaluations require the collection of survey data, including at least a *baseline* and a *follow-up survey*. Survey data may be of various types depending on the program to be evaluated and the unit of analysis. Most evaluations rely on individual or household surveys as a primary data source. Here, we review some general principles of survey data collection. Even though they primarily relate to household surveys, the same principles also apply to most other types of survey data.[2]

The first step in deciding whether to use existing data or collect new survey data will be to determine the size of the sample that is needed. If the existing data contain a sufficient number of observations, you may be able to use them. If not, additional data will need to be collected. Once it is determined that you need to collect survey data for the evaluation, you must

- determine who will collect the data,

- develop and pilot questionnaires,

- conduct fieldwork and quality control, and

- process and store the data,

The remainder of this chapter will discuss how to determine the necessary sample size and how to sample. The remaining steps in data collection are dealt with in chapter 12. The implementation of those various steps is usually commissioned, but understanding their scope and key components is essential to effectively managing a quality impact evaluation.

Power Calculations: How Big a Sample Do I Need?

The first step in determining whether existing data can be used or in preparing to collect new data for the evaluation will be to determine how large the sample must be. The associated calculations are called *"power calculations."* We discuss the basic intuition behind power calculations by focusing on the simplest case—an evaluation conducted using a randomized assignment method and assuming that noncompliance is not an issue. (Compliance assumes that all of the units assigned to the treatment group are treated and all of the units assigned to the comparison group are not.)

Why Power Calculations?

Power calculations indicate the minimum sample size needed to conduct an impact evaluation and to answer convincingly the policy question of interest. In particular, power calculations can be used to do the following:

- Assess whether existing data sets are large enough for the purpose of conducting an impact evaluation.

- Avoid collecting too much information, which can be very costly.

- Avoid collecting too few data. Say that you are estimating a program that has a positive impact on its recipients. If the sample is too small, you may not be able to detect positive impact and may thus conclude that the

Key Concept:
Power calculations indicate the sample size required for an evaluation to estimate precisely the impact of a program (the difference in outcomes between the treatment and comparison groups).

program has no effect. That, of course, could lead to a policy decision to eliminate the program, and that would be detrimental to potential beneficiaries and to society.

Power calculations provide an indication of the smallest sample (and lowest budget) with which it is possible to measure the impact of a program, that is, the smallest sample that will allow meaningful differences in outcomes between the treatment and comparison groups to be detected. Power calculations are thus crucial for determining which programs are successful and which are not.

Is the Program's Impact Different from Zero?

Most impact evaluations test a simple hypothesis embodied in the question, *Does the program have an impact?* In other words, *Is the program impact different from zero?* Answering this question requires two steps:

1. Estimate the average outcomes for the treatment and comparison groups.

2. Assess whether a difference exists between the average outcome for the treatment group and the average outcome for the comparison group.

Estimating Average Outcomes for the Treatment and Comparison Groups

Let us assume that you are interested in estimating the impact of a nutrition program on the weight of children at age 5. We assume that 100,000 children participated in the program, that 100,000 children did not participate, and that the children who were chosen to participate were randomly drawn from among the country's 200,000 children. As a first step, you will need to estimate the average weight of the children who participated and the average weight of those who did not.

To determine the average weight of participating children,[3] one could weigh every one of the 100,000 participating children, and then average the weights. Of course, doing that would be extremely costly. Luckily, it is not necessary to measure every child. The average can be estimated using the average weight of a sample drawn from the population of participating children.[4] The more children in the sample, the closer the sample average will be to the true average. When a sample is small, the average weight constitutes a very imprecise estimate of the average in the population; for example, a sample of two children will not give a precise estimate. In contrast, a sample of 10,000 children will produce a more precise estimate that is much closer to the true average weight. In general, the more observations in the sample, the more reliable the statistics obtained from the sample will be.[5]

Figure 11.1 illustrates this intuition. Suppose you are drawing a sample from a population of interest, in this case, the children that participated in the program. First, you draw a sample of just two observations. This does not guarantee that the sample will have the same characteristics as the population. It may be that you happen to draw two individuals with unusual characteristics. For example, even if in the population of interest only 20 percent of children wear round hats, you might easily draw a sample of two children that wear round hats. Clearly, you were unlucky when drawing this sample. Drawing larger samples diminishes your chances of being unlucky. A large sample is more likely than a small sample to look just like the population of interest. Figure 11.1 illustrates what happens when you draw a large sample. A large sample is very likely to have roughly the same characteristics as the population: in this example, 20 percent wear round hats, 10 percent wear square hats, and 70 percent wear triangular hats.

So now we know that with a larger sample we will have a more accurate image of the population of participating children. The same will be true for nonparticipating children: as the sample of nonparticipating children gets larger, we will know more precisely what that population looks like. But why should we care? If we are able to estimate the average outcome (weight) of participating and nonparticipating children more precisely, we will also be able to tell more precisely the difference in weight between the two

Figure 11.1 A Large Sample Will Better Resemble the Population

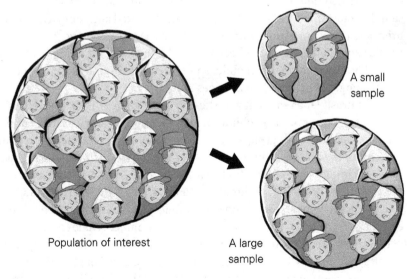

Population of interest

A small sample

A large sample

Source: Authors.

groups—and that is the impact of the program. To put it another way, if you only have a vague idea of the average weight of children in the participating (treatment) and nonparticipating (comparison) groups, then how can you have a precise idea of the difference in the weight of the two groups? That's right; you can't. In the following section, we will explore this idea in a slightly more formal way.

Comparing the Average Outcomes for the Treatment and Comparison Groups

Once you have estimated the average outcome (weight) for the treatment group (participating children selected by randomized assignment) and the comparison group (nonparticipating children selected by randomized assignment), you can proceed to determine whether the two outcomes are different. This part is clear: you subtract the averages and check what the difference is. Formally, the impact evaluation tests the *null (or default) hypothesis,*

H_0 : impact = 0   (The hypothesis is that the program does not have an impact),

against the alternative hypothesis:

H_a : impact $\neq$ 0   (The alternative hypothesis is that the program has an impact).

Imagine that in the nutrition program example, you start with a sample of two treated children and two comparison children. With such a small sample, your estimate of the average weight of treated and comparison children, and thus your estimate of the difference between the two groups, will not be very reliable. You can check this by drawing different samples of two treated and two comparison children. What you will find is that the estimated impact of the program bounces around a lot.

By contrast, let us say that you start with a sample of 1,000 treated children and 1,000 comparison children. As we have said, your estimates of the average weight of both groups will be much more precise. Therefore, your estimate of the difference between the two groups will also be more precise.

For example, say that you find that the average weight in the sample of treatment (participating) children is 25.2 kilograms (kg), and the average in the sample of comparison (nonparticipating) children is 25 kg. The difference between the two groups is 0.2 kg. If these numbers came from samples of two observations each, you would not be very confident that the impact of the program is truly positive because the entire 0.2 kg could be due to the lack of precision in your estimates. However, if these numbers come from samples of 1,000 observations each, you would be confident that you are quite close to the true program impact, which in this case would be positive.

The key question then becomes, *Exactly how large must the sample be to allow you to know that a positive estimated impact is due to true program impact, rather than to lack of precision in your estimates?*

Two Potential Errors in Impact Evaluations

When testing whether a program has an impact, two types of error can be made. A *type I error* is made when an evaluation concludes that a program has had an impact, when in reality it had no impact. In the case of the hypothetical nutrition intervention, this would happen if you, as the evaluator, were to conclude that the average weight of the children in the treated sample is higher than that of the children in the comparison sample, even though the average weight of the children in the two populations is in fact equal. In this case, the positive impact you saw came purely from the lack of precision of your estimates.

A *type II error* is the opposite kind of error. A type II error occurs when an evaluation concludes that the program has had no impact, when in fact it has had an impact. In the case of the nutrition intervention, this would happen if you were to conclude that the average weight of the children in the two samples is the same, even though the average weight of the children in the treatment population is in fact higher than that of the children in the comparison population. Again, the impact should have been positive, but because of lack of precision in your estimates, you concluded that the program had zero impact.

Key Concept:

The power is the probability of detecting an impact if there is one. An impact evaluation has high power if there is a low risk of not detecting real program impacts, that is, of committing a type II error.

When testing the hypothesis that a program has had an impact, statisticians can limit the size of type I errors. Indeed, the likelihood of a type I error can be set by a parameter called the *"confidence level."* The confidence level is often fixed at 5 percent, meaning that you can be 95 percent confident in concluding that the program has had an impact. If you are very concerned about committing a type I error, you can conservatively set a lower confidence level, for instance, 1 percent so that you are 99 percent confident in concluding that the program has had an impact.

However, type II errors are also worrying for policy makers. Many factors affect the likelihood of committing a type II error, but the sample size is crucial. If the average weight of 50,000 treated children is the same as the average weight of 50,000 comparison children, then you probably can confidently conclude that the program has had no impact. By contrast, if a sample of two treatment children weigh on average the same as a sample of two comparison children, it is harder to reach a reliable conclusion. Is the average weight similar because the intervention has had no impact or because the data are not sufficient to test the hypothesis in such a small sample? Drawing large samples makes it less likely that you will only observe children who weigh the same simply by luck (or bad luck). In large samples, the difference in mean between the treated sample and comparison sample provides a better estimate of the true difference in mean between all treated and all comparison units.

The *power (or statistical power)* of an impact evaluation is the probability that it will detect a difference between the treatment and comparison groups, when in fact one exists. An impact evaluation has a high power if there is a low risk of not detecting real program impacts, that is, of committing a type II error. The examples above show that the size of the sample is a crucial determinant of the power of an impact evaluation. The following sections will further illustrate this point.

Why Power Calculations Are Crucial for Policy

The purpose of power calculations is to determine how large a sample is required to avoid concluding that a program has had no impact, when it has in fact had one (a type II error). The power of a test is equal to 1 minus the probability of a type II error.

An impact evaluation has *high power* if a type II error is unlikely to happen, meaning that you are unlikely to be disappointed by results showing that the program being evaluated has had no impact, when in reality it did have an impact.

From a policy perspective, *underpowered impact evaluations* with a high probability of type II errors are not only unhelpful but also very costly. A high probability of type II error jeopardizes the reliability of any negative impact evaluation results. Putting resources into these so-called underpowered impact evaluations is therefore a risky investment.

Underpowered impact evaluations can also have dramatic practical consequences. For example, in the hypothetical nutrition intervention mentioned earlier, if you were to conclude that the program was not effective, even though it was, policy makers would be likely to close down a program that, in fact, benefits children. It is therefore crucial to minimize the probability of type II errors by using large-enough samples in impact evaluations. That is why carrying out power calculations is so crucial and relevant.

Power Calculations Step by Step

We now turn to the basic principles of power calculations, focusing on the simple case of a randomly assigned program. Carrying out power calculations requires examining the following six questions:

1. Does the program create *clusters*?

2. What is the *outcome* indicator?

3. Do you aim to compare program impacts between *subgroups*?

4. What is the *minimum level of impact* that would justify the investment that has been made in the intervention?

5. What is a reasonable *level of power* for the evaluation being conducted?

6. What are the baseline *mean and variance of the outcome indicators*?

Each of these steps must relate to the specific policy context in which you have decided to conduct an impact evaluation.

We have already mentioned that the minimum scale of intervention for a program influences the size of the sample required for the evaluation. The first step in power calculations is to determine whether the program that you want to evaluate creates any *clusters*. An intervention whose level of intervention is different from the level at which you would like to measure outcomes creates cluster. For example, it may be necessary to implement a program at the hospital, school, or village level (in other words, through clusters), but you measure its impact on patients, students, or villagers (see table 11.1).[6]

The nature of any sample data built from programs that are clustered is a bit different from that of samples obtained from programs that are not. As a result, power calculations will involve slightly different steps, depending on whether the program in question randomly assigns benefits among clusters or simply assigns benefits randomly among all units in a population. We will discuss each situation in turn. We start with the principles of power calculations when there are no clusters, that is, when the treatment is assigned at the level at which outcomes are observed, and then go on to discuss power calculations when clusters are present.

Table 11.1 Examples of Clusters

Benefit	Level at which benefits are assigned (cluster)	Unit at which outcome is measured
Conditional cash	Village	Households
Malaria treatment	School	Individuals
Training program	Neighborhood	Individuals

Source: Authors.

Power Calculations without Clusters

Let us assume that you have solved the first question by establishing that the program's benefits are not assigned by clusters. In other words, the program to be evaluated randomly assigns benefits among all units in an eligible population. In this case, the evaluation sample can be constructed by taking a simple random sample of the entire *population of interest*.

The second and third steps relate to the objectives of the evaluation. In the second step, you must identify the most important *outcome indicators* that the program was designed to improve. These indicators derive from the fundamental evaluation research question and the conceptual framework, as discussed in part 1. The present discussion will also yield insights into the type of indicators that are most amenable to being used in impact evaluations.

Third, the main policy question of the evaluation may entail comparing program impacts between *subgroups*, such as age or income categories. If this is the case, then sample size requirements will be larger, and power calculations will need to be adjusted accordingly. For instance, it may be that a key policy question is whether an education program has a larger impact on female students than on male students. Intuitively, you will need a sufficient number of students of each sex in the treatment group and in the comparison group to detect an impact for each subgroup. Setting out to compare program impacts between two subgroups can double the required sample size. Considering heterogeneity between more groups (for example, by age) can also substantially increase the size of the sample required.

Fourth, you must determine the minimum impact that would justify the investment that has been made in the intervention. This is fundamentally a policy question rather than a technical one. Is a conditional cash transfer program a worthwhile investment if it reduces poverty by 5 percent, 10 percent, or 15 percent? Is an active labor market program worth implementing if it increases earnings by 5 percent, 10 percent, or 15 percent? The answer is highly context specific, but in all contexts it is necessary to determine the change in the outcome indicators that would justify the investment made in the program. Put another way, *what is the level of impact below which an intervention should be considered unsuccessful?* Answering this question will depend not only on the cost of the program and the type of benefits that it provides, but also on the opportunity cost of not investing funds in an alternative intervention.

Carrying out power calculations makes it possible to adjust the sample size to detect the minimum desired effect. For an evaluation to identify a small impact, estimates of any difference in mean outcomes between the treatment and comparison groups will need to be very precise, requiring a large sample. Alternatively, for interventions that are judged to be worthwhile only if they lead to large changes in outcome indicators, the samples needed to conduct an impact evaluation will be smaller. Nevertheless, the *minimum detectable effect* should be set conservatively, since any impact smaller than the minimum desired effect is unlikely to be detected.

Fifth, the evaluator needs to consult statistical experts to determine a reasonable *power level* for the planned impact evaluation. As stated earlier, the power of a test is equal to 1 minus the probability of any type II error. Therefore, the power ranges from 0 to 1, with a high value indicating less risk of failing to identify an existing impact. A power of 80 percent is a widely used benchmark for power calculations. It means that you will find an impact in 80 percent of the cases where one has occurred. A higher level of power of 0.9 (or 90 percent) often provides a useful benchmark but is more conservative, increasing the required sample sizes.[7]

Sixth, you must ask a statistical expert to estimate some basic parameters, such as a *baseline mean and variance, of the outcome indicators.* These benchmark values should preferably be obtained from existing data collected in a setting similar to the one where the program under study will be implemented.[8] It is very important to note that the more variable the outcomes of interest prove to be, the more difficult it will be to estimate a reliable treatment effect. In the example of the hypothetical nutrition intervention, children's weight is the outcome of interest. If all individuals weigh the same at the baseline, it will be feasible to estimate the impact of the nutrition intervention in a relatively small sample. By contrast, if baseline weights among children are widely variable, then a much larger sample will be required to estimate the program's impact.

Once these six steps have been completed, the statistical expert can carry out a power calculation using standard statistical software.[9] The resulting power calculation will indicate the required sample size, depending on the parameters established in steps 1 to 6. The computations themselves are straightforward, once policy-relevant questions have been answered (particularly in steps 3 and 4).[10]

When seeking advice from statistical experts, the evaluator should ask for an analysis of the *sensitivity* of the power calculation to changes in the assumptions. That is, it is important to understand how much the required sample size will have to increase under more conservative assumptions (such as lower expected impact, higher variance in the outcome indicator, or a higher power level). It is also good practice to commission power calculations for various outcome indicators, as the required sample sizes can vary substantially if some outcome indicators are much more variable than others.

Finally, power calculations provide the minimum required sample size. In practice, implementation issues often imply that the actual sample size is smaller than the planned sample size. Any such deviations need to be considered carefully, but it is advisable to add a margin of 10 percent or 20 percent to the sample size predicted by power calculations to account for such factors.[11]

How Big a Sample Do I Need to Evaluate an Expanded Health Insurance in Subsidy Program?

Let us say that the president and the minister of health were pleased with the quality and results of the evaluation of the Health Insurance Subsidy Program (HISP), our example in previous chapters. However, before scaling up the HISP, they decide to pilot an expanded version of the program (which they call HISP+). HISP pays for part of the cost of health insurance for poor rural households, covering costs of primary care and drugs, but it does not cover hospitalization. The president and the minister of health wonder whether an expanded HISP+ that also covers hospitalization would further lower out-of-pocket health expenditures. They ask you to design an impact evaluation to assess whether HISP+ further lowers health expenditures for poor rural households.

In this case, choosing an impact evaluation design is not a challenge for you: HISP+ has limited resources and cannot be implemented universally immediately. As a result, you have concluded that randomized assignment would be the most viable and robust impact evaluation method. The president and the minister of health understand how well the randomized assignment method works and are very supportive.

To finalize the design of the impact evaluation, you have commissioned a statistician who will help you establish how big a sample is needed. Before he starts working, the statistician asks you for some key input. He uses a checklist of six questions.

1. The statistician asks whether the HISP+ program will generate clusters. At this point, you are not totally sure. You believe that it might be possible to randomize the expanded benefit package at the household level among all poor rural households who already benefit from HISP. However, you are aware that the president and the minister of health may prefer to assign the expanded program at the village level, and that would create clusters. The statistician suggests conducting power calculations for a benchmark case without clusters and then considering how results change if clusters exist.

2. The statistician asks what the outcome indicator is. You explain that the government is interested in a well-defined indicator: household out-of-pocket health expenditures. The statistician looks for the most up-to-

date source to obtain benchmark values for this indicator and suggests using the follow-up survey from the HISP evaluation. He notes that among households who received HISP, yearly per capita out-of-pocket health expenditures average $7.84.

3. The statistician double-checks that you are not interested in measuring program impacts for subgroups, such as regions of the country or specific subpopulations.

4. The statistician asks about the minimum level of impact that would justify the investment in the intervention. In other words, what additional decrease in out-of-pocket health expenditures below the benchmark average of $7.84 would make this intervention worthwhile? He stresses that this is not a technical consideration but truly a policy question; that is why a policy maker such as you has to set the minimum effect that the evaluation should be able to detect. You remember having heard the president mentioning that the HISP+ program would be considered effective if it reduced household out-of-pocket health expenditures by $2. Still, you know that for the purpose of the evaluation, it may be better to be conservative in determining the minimum detectable impact, since any smaller impact is unlikely to be captured. To understand how the required sample size varies based on the minimum detectable effect, you suggest that the statistician perform calculations for a minimum reduction of out-of-pocket health expenditures of $1, $2, and $3.

5. The statistician asks what would be a reasonable level of power for the evaluation being conducted. He adds that power calculations are usually conducted for a power of 0.9 but offers to perform robustness checks later for a less-conservative level of 0.8.

6. Finally, the statistician asks what is the variance of the outcome indicator in the population of interest. He goes back to the data set of treated HISP households, pointing out that the standard deviation of out-of-pocket health expenditures is $8.

Equipped with all this information, the statistician undertakes the power calculations. As agreed, he starts with the more conservative case of a power of 0.9. He produces the results shown in table 11.2.

The statistician concludes that to detect a $2 decrease in out-of-pocket health expenditures with a power of 0.9, the sample needs to contain at least 672 units (336 treated units and 336 comparison units, with no clustering). He notes that if you were satisfied to detect a $3 decrease in out-of-pocket health expenditure, a smaller sample of at least 300 units (150 units in each group) would be sufficient. By contrast, a much larger sample of at least

Table 11.2 Sample Size Required for Various Minimum Detectable Effects (Decrease in Household Health Expenditures), Power = 0.9, No Clustering

Minimum detectable effect	Treatment group	Comparison group	Total sample
$1	1,344	1,344	2,688
$2	336	336	672
$3	150	150	300

Source: Authors.

Note: The minimum detectable effect describes the minimum reduction of household out-of-pocket health expenditures to be detected by the impact evaluation.

2,688 units (1,344 in each group) would be needed to detect a $1 decrease in out-of-pocket health expenditures.

The statistician then produces another table for a power level of 0.8. Table 11.3 shows that the required sample sizes are smaller for a power of 0.8 than for a power of 0.9. To detect a $2 reduction in household out-of-pocket health expenditures, a total sample of at least 502 units would be sufficient. To detect a $3 reduction, at least 224 units are needed. However, to detect a $1 reduction, at least 2,008 units would be needed in the sample.

The statistician stresses that the following results are typical of power calculations:

• The higher (more conservative) the level of power, the larger the required sample size.

• The smaller the impact to be detected, the larger the required sample size.

Table 11.3 Sample Size Required for Various Minimum Detectable Effects (Decrease in Household Health Expenditures), Power = 0.8, No Clustering

Minimum detectable effect	Treatment group	Comparison group	Total sample
$1	1,004	1,004	2,008
$2	251	251	502
$3	112	112	224

Source: Authors.

Note: The minimum detectable effect describes the minimum reduction of household out-of-pocket health expenditures to be detected by the impact evaluation.

Table 11.4 Sample Size Required to Detect Various Minimum Desired Effects (Increase in Hospitalization Rate), Power = 0.9, No Clustering

Minimum detectable effect (percentage point)	Treatment group	Comparison group	Total sample
1	9,717	9,717	19,434
2	2,430	2,430	4,860
3	1,080	1,080	2,160

Source: Authors.

Note: The minimum desired effect describes the minimum change in the hospital utilization rate (expressed as percentage point) to be detected by the impact evaluation.

The statistician asks whether you would like to conduct power calculations for other outcomes of interest. You suggest also considering the sample size required to detect whether HISP+ affects the hospitalization rate. In the sample of treated HISP villages, 5 percent of households have a member visiting the hospital in a given year. The statistician produces a new table, which shows that relatively large samples would be needed to detect even large changes in the hospitalization rate (table 11.4) of 1, 2, or 3 points from the baseline rate of 5 percent.

The table shows that sample size requirements are larger for this outcome (the hospitalization rate) than for out-of-pocket health expenditures. The statistician concludes that if you are interested in detecting impacts on both outcomes, you should use the larger sample sizes implied by the power calculations performed on the hospitalization rates. If sample sizes from the power calculations performed for out-of-pocket health expenditures are used, the statistician suggests letting the president and the minister of health know that the evaluation will not have sufficient power to detect policy-relevant effects on hospitalization rates.

QUESTION 8
A. Which sample size would you recommend to estimate the impact of HISP+ on out-of-pocket health expenditures?
B. Would that sample size be sufficient to detect changes in the hospitalization rate?

Power Calculations with Clusters

The discussion above introduced the principles of carrying out power calculations for programs that do not create clusters. However, as discussed in part 2, some programs assign benefits at the cluster level. We now briefly describe how the basic principles of power calculations need to be adapted for clustered samples.

In the presence of clustering, an important guiding principle is that the number of clusters matters much more than the number of individuals within the clusters. A sufficient number of clusters is required to test convincingly whether a program has had an impact by comparing outcomes in samples of treatment and comparison units.

If you randomly assign treatment among a small number of clusters, the treatment and comparison clusters are unlikely to be identical. Randomized assignment between two districts, two schools, or two hospitals will not guarantee that the two clusters are similar. By contrast, randomly assigning an intervention among 100 districts, 100 schools, or 100 hospitals is more likely to ensure that the treatment and the comparison groups are similar. In short, a sufficient number of clusters is necessary to ensure that balance is achieved. Moreover, the number of clusters also matters for the precision of the estimated treatment effects. A sufficient number of clusters is required to test the hypothesis that a program has an impact with sufficient power. It is, therefore, very important to ensure that the number of clusters available for randomized assignment is large enough.

Following the intuition discussed above, you can establish the number of clusters required for precise hypothesis testing by conducting power calculations. Carrying out power calculations for cluster samples requires an extra step beyond the basic procedure:

1. Does the program create clusters?

2. What is the outcome indicator?

3. Do you aim to compare program impacts between subgroups?

4. What is the minimum level of impact that would justify the investment that has been made in the program?

5. What are the baseline mean and variance of the outcome indicator?

6. How variable is the outcome indicator in the population of interest?

7. How variable is the outcome indicator within clusters?

Compared to power calculations without cluster, only the last step is new: you now also have to ask your statistical expert what is the degree of correlation between outcomes within clusters. At the extreme, all outcomes within a cluster are perfectly correlated. For instance, it may be that household income is not especially variable within villages but that significant inequalities in income occur between villages. In this case, if you consider adding an individual to your evaluation sample, adding an individual from a new village will provide much more additional power than adding an individual from a village that is already represented.

Indeed, in this case the second villager is likely to look very similar to the original villager already included. In general, higher *intra-cluster correlation* in outcomes increases the number of clusters required to achieve a given power level.

In clustered samples, power calculations highlight the trade-offs between adding clusters and adding observations within clusters. The relative increase in power from adding a unit to a new cluster is almost always larger than that from adding a unit to an existing cluster. Although the gain in power from adding a new cluster can be dramatic, adding clusters may also have operational implications and increase the cost of data collection. The next section shows how to conduct power calculations with clusters in the case of HISP+ and discusses some of the trade-offs involved.

In many cases, at least 30 to 50 clusters in each treatment and comparison group are required to obtain sufficient power and guarantee balance of baseline characteristics when using randomized assignment methods. However, the number may vary depending on the various parameters discussed above, as well as the degree of intra-cluster correlation. Furthermore, the number will likely increase when using methods other than randomized assignment (assuming all else is set constant).

Key Concept:

The number of clusters matters much more for power calculations than does the number of individuals within the clusters. At least 30 clusters are often required in each of the treatment and comparison groups.

How Big a Sample Do I Need to Evaluate an Expanded Health Insurance Subsidy Program with Clusters?

After your first discussion with the statistician about power calculations for HISP+, you decided to talk briefly to the president and the minister of health about the implications of randomly assigning the expanded HISP+ benefits among all individuals in the population receiving the basic HISP plan. That consultation revealed that such a procedure would not be politically feasible: it would be hard to explain why one person would receive the expanded benefits, while her neighbor would not.

Instead of randomization at the individual level, you therefore suggest randomly selecting a number of HISP villages to pilot HISP+. All villagers in the selected village would then become eligible. This procedure will create clusters and thus require new power calculations. You now want to determine how large a sample is required to evaluate the impact of HISP+ when it is randomly assigned by cluster.

You consult with your statistician again. He reassures you: only a little more work is needed. On his checklist, only one question is left unanswered. He needs to know how variable the outcome indicator is within clusters. Luckily, this is also a question he can answer using the HISP follow-up data, where he finds that the within-village correlation of out-of-pocket health expenditures is equal to 0.04.

He also asks whether an upper limit has been placed on the number of villages in which it would be feasible to implement the new pilot. Since the program now has 100 HISP villages, you explain that you could have, at most, 50 treatment villages and 50 comparison villages for HISP+. With that information, the statistician produces the power calculations shown in table 11.5 for a power of 0.9.

The statistician concludes that to detect a $2 decrease in out-of-pocket health expenditures, the sample must include at least 900 units, that is, 9 units per cluster in 100 clusters. He notes that this number is higher than that in the sample under randomized assignment at the household level, which required only a total of 672 units. To detect a $3 decrease in out-of-pocket health expenditures, the sample would need to include at least 340 units, or 4 in each of 85 clusters.

However, when the statistician tries to establish the sample required to detect a $1 decrease in out-of-pocket health expenditures, he finds that it would not be possible to detect such an effect with 100 clusters. At least 109 clusters would be needed, and even then the number of observations within each cluster would be extremely high. As he notes, this finding highlights that a large number of clusters is needed for an evaluation to have enough power to detect relatively small impacts, regardless of the number of observations within clusters.

The statistician then suggests considering how these numbers vary with a power of only 0.8 (table 11.6). The required sample sizes are again smaller for a power of 0.8 than for a power of 0.9, but they are still larger for the clustered sample than for the simple random sample.

The statistician then shows you how the total number of observations required in the sample varies with the total number of clusters. He decides

Table 11.5 Sample Size Required for Various Minimum Detectable Effects (Decrease in Household Health Expenditures), Power = 0.9, Maximum of 100 Clusters

Minimum detectable effect	Number of clusters	Units per cluster	Total sample with clusters	Total sample without clusters
$1	Not feasible	Not feasible	Not feasible	2,688
$2	100	9	900	672
$3	85	4	340	300

Source: Authors.

Note: The minimum desired effect describes the minimum reduction of household out-of-pocket health expenditures to be detected by the impact evaluation.

Impact Evaluation in Practice

Table 11.6 Sample Size Required for Various Minimum Detectable Effects (Decrease in Household Health Expenditures), Power = 0.8, Maximum of 100 Clusters

Minimum detectable effect	Number of clusters	Units per cluster	Total sample with clusters	Total sample without Clusters
$1	100	102	10,200	2,008
$2	90	7	630	502
$3	82	3	246	224

Source: Authors.

Note: The minimum detectable effect describes the minimum reduction of household out-of-pocket health expenditures to be detected by the impact evaluation.

to repeat the calculations for a minimum detectable effect of $2 and a power of 0.9. The size of the total sample required to estimate such an effect increases strongly when the number of clusters diminishes (table 11.7). With 100 clusters, a sample of 900 observations was needed. If only 30 clusters were available, the total sample would need to contain 6,690 observations. By contrast, if 157 clusters were available, only 785 observations would be needed.

QUESTION 9
A. Which total sample size would you recommend to estimate the impact of HISP+ on out-of-pocket health expenditures?
B. In how many villages would you advise the president and minister of health to roll out HISP+?

Table 11.7 Sample Size Required to Detect a $2 Minimum Impact for Various Numbers of Clusters, Power = 0.9

Minimum detectable effect	Number of clusters	Units per cluster	Total sample with clusters
$2	30	223	6,690
$2	60	20	1,200
$2	86	11	946
$2	100	9	900
$2	120	7	840
$2	135	6	810
$2	157	5	785

Source: Authors.

In Summary

To summarize, the quality of an impact evaluation depends directly on the quality of the data on which it is based. In this regard, properly constructed samples of adequate size are absolutely crucial. We have reviewed the basic principles of carrying out power calculations. When performed while planning an evaluation, power calculations are an essential tool for containing data collection costs by avoiding the collection of more data than needed, while also minimizing the risk of reaching the costly and erroneous conclusion that a program has had no impact because too little information was collected. Although power calculations require technical and statistical underpinnings, they also require a clear policy foundation. In general, increasing sample size produces decreasing returns, so that determining the adequate sample will often require balancing the need for precise impact estimates with budget considerations.

Key Concept:

Quasi-experimental impact evaluation methods almost always require larger samples than the randomized assignment benchmark.

We have focused on the benchmark case of an impact evaluation implemented using the randomized assignment method. This is the simplest scenario and therefore the most suitable to convey the intuition behind power calculations. Still, many practical aspects of our power calculations have not been discussed, and deviations from the basic cases discussed here need to be considered carefully. For instance, quasi-experimental impact evaluation methods almost always require larger samples than the randomized assignment benchmark. Sample size requirements also increase if a risk of bias is present in the estimated treatment effects or when imperfect compliance arises. Those topics are beyond the scope of this book, but Spybrook et al. (2008) and Rosenbaum (2009, chapter 14) discuss them in more detail. A number of tools are available for those interested in exploring sample design further. For example, the W.T. Grant Foundation developed the freely available Optimal Design Software for Multi-Level and Longitudinal Research, which is useful for statistical power analysis in the presence of clusters. In practice, many agencies commissioning an evaluation hire an expert to perform power calculations, and the expert should be able to provide advice when methods other than randomized assignment are used.

Deciding on the Sampling Strategy

Size is not the only relevant factor in ensuring that a sample is appropriate for an impact evaluation. The process by which a sample is drawn from the population of interest is also crucial. The principles of sampling can be guides to drawing representative samples. Sampling requires three steps:

1. Determine the *population of interest*.

2. Identify a *sampling frame*.

3. *Draw* as many units from the sampling frame as required by power calculations.

First, the *population of interest* needs to be very clearly defined.[12] To do that requires accurately defining the observational unit for which outcomes will be measured, with clear specification of the geographic coverage or any other relevant attributes that characterize the population. For example, if you are managing an early childhood development program, you may be interested in measuring cognitive outcomes for young children between ages 3 and 6 in the entire country, only for such children in rural areas, or only for children enrolled in preschool.

Second, once the population of interest has been defined, a *sampling frame* must be established. The sampling frame is the most comprehensive list that can be obtained of units in the population of interest. Ideally, the sampling frame should exactly coincide with the population of interest. For instance, a full and totally up-to-date census of the population of interest would constitute an ideal sampling frame. In practice, existing lists, such as population censuses, facility censuses, or enrollment listings are often used as sampling frames.

An adequate sampling frame is required to ensure that the conclusions reached from analyzing a sample can be generalized to the entire population. Indeed, a sampling frame that does not exactly coincide with the

Figure 11.2   A Valid Sampling Frame Covers the Entire Population of Interest

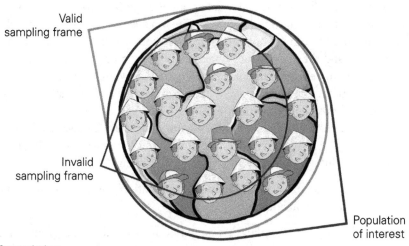

Source: Authors.

population of interest creates a *coverage bias*, as illustrated in figure 11.2. In the presence of coverage bias, results from the sample do not have full external validity for the entire population of interest but only for the population included in the sampling frame. As a result, coverage biases blur the interpretation of impact evaluation results, since it is unclear from which population they were obtained.

When considering drawing a new sample or assessing the quality of an existing sample, it is important to determine whether the best available sampling frame coincides with the population of interest. The degree to which statistics computed from the sample can be generalized to the population of interest as a whole depends on the magnitude of the coverage bias, in other words, the lack of overlap between the sampling frame and the population of interest.

Coverage bias can occur, for example, if you are interested in all households in a country but use a phone book as the sampling frame, so that any households without a phone will not be sampled. That can bias the evaluation results if the households without a phone also have other characteristics that differ from those of the population of interest and if those characteristics affect how households would benefit from the intervention. For instance, households without a phone may be in remote rural areas. If you are interested in evaluating the impact of a vocational training program, omitting the most isolated population will affect the results of the evaluation because those households are likely to have more difficulty accessing the labor market.

Coverage biases constitute a real risk, and the construction of sampling frames requires careful effort. For instance, census data may contain the list of all units in a population. However, if much time has elapsed between the census and the time the sample data are collected, the sampling frame may no longer be fully up-to-date, creating a coverage bias. Moreover, census data may not contain sufficient information on specific attributes to build a sampling frame. If the population of interest consists of children attending preschool, and the census does not contain data on preschool enrollment, complementary enrollment data or facility listings would be needed.[13]

Once you have identified the population of interest and a sampling frame, you must choose a method to draw the sample. Various alternative procedures can be used. *Probability sampling* methods are the most rigorous, as they assign a well-defined probability of each unit's being drawn. The three main probability sampling methods are the following:[14]

- *Random sampling.* Every unit in the population has exactly the same probability of being drawn.[15]

- *Stratified random sampling.* The population is divided into groups (for example, male and female) and random sampling is performed within

Impact Evaluation in Practice

each group. As a result, every unit in each group (or stratum) has the same probability of being drawn. Provided that each group is large enough, stratified sampling makes it possible to draw inferences about outcomes not only at the level of the population but also within each group. Stratification is essential for evaluations that aim to compare program impacts between subgroups.

• *Cluster sampling.* Units are grouped in clusters, and a random sample of clusters is drawn, after which either all units in those clusters constitute the sample or a number of units within the cluster are randomly drawn. This means that each cluster has a well-defined probability of being selected, and units within a selected cluster also have a well-defined probability of being drawn.

In the context of an impact evaluation, the procedure for drawing a sample often derives from the eligibility rules of the program under evaluation. As described in the discussion on sample size, if the smallest viable unit of implementation is larger than the unit of observation, randomized assignment of benefits will create clusters. For this reason, cluster sampling often arises in impact evaluation studies.

Nonprobabilistic sampling can create serious sampling errors. Sometimes, *purposive sampling* or *convenience sampling* is used instead of the well-defined probabilistic sampling procedures discussed above. In those cases sampling errors can occur even if the sampling frame captures the entire population and no coverage bias is present. To illustrate, suppose that a national survey is undertaken by asking a group of interviewers to collect household data from the dwelling closest to the school in each village. When such a nonprobabilistic sampling procedure is used, it is likely that the sample will not be representative of the population of interest as a whole. In particular, a coverage bias will arise, as remote dwellings will not be surveyed.

In the end, it is necessary to pay careful attention to the sampling frame and the sampling procedure to determine whether results obtained from a given sample have external validity for the entire population of interest. Even if the sampling frame has perfect coverage and a probability sampling procedure is used, nonsampling errors can also limit the external validity of the sample. We discuss nonsampling errors in the next chapter.

Notes

1. Cost data are also needed for cost-benefit analysis.
2. For detailed reference on household surveys, see Grosh and Glewwe (2000)

and UN (2005). Dal Poz and Gupta (2009) discusses some issues specific to collecting data in the health sector.

3. At this point, the discussion can apply to any population—the entire population of interest, the treatment population, or the comparison population.

4. In this context, the term "population" does not refer to the population of the country but rather to the entire group of children that we are interested in, the "population of interest."

5. This intuition is formalized by a theorem called the "central limit theorem." Formally, for an outcome y, the central limit theorem states that the sample mean $\bar{y}$ on average constitutes a valid estimate of the population mean. In addition, for a sample of size n and for a population variance σ, the variance of the sample mean is inversely proportional to the size of the sample:

$$\text{var}(\bar{y}) = \frac{\sigma^2}{n}.$$

As the size of the sample n increases, the variance of sample estimates tends to 0. In other words, the mean is more precisely estimated in large samples than in small samples.

6. The allocation of benefits by cluster is often made necessary by social or political considerations that make randomization within clusters impossible. In the context of an impact evaluation, clustering often becomes necessary because of likely spillovers, or contagion of program benefits between individuals within clusters.

7. Together with power, a confidence level fixing an acceptable probability of type I error also needs to be set, typically at 0.05 (or 0.01 for a conservative level).

8. When computing power from a baseline, the correlation between outcomes over time should also be taken into account in power calculations.

9. For instance, Spybrook et al. (2008) introduced Optimal Design, a user-friendly software to conduct power calculations.

10. Having treatment and comparison groups of equal size is generally desirable. Indeed, for a given number of observations in a sample, power is maximized by assigning half the observations to the treatment group and half to the comparison group. However, treatment and comparison groups do not always have to be of equal size. Let your statistician know of any constraints against having two groups of equal size or any reasons to have two groups of unequal size.

11. Chapter 12 will discuss the issues of nonresponse and attrition in more details.

12. In the context of a program evaluation, the total population of interest may be assigned to the treatment group or the comparison group. This section discusses in general terms how to draw a sample from the total population of interest.

13. If cluster sampling is used and the list of units within the clusters is outdated, you should consider the possibility of conducting a full enumeration of units within each cluster. For instance, if a community is sampled, the agency in charge of data collection could start by listing all of the households in the villages before conducting the survey itself.

14. See Cochran (1977); Lohr (1999); Kish (1995); Thompson (2002); or at a more basic level, Kalton (1983) for detailed discussions of sampling (including other methods such as systematic sampling or multistage sampling) beyond the basic concepts discussed here. Grosh and Muñoz (1996); Fink (2008); Iarossi (2006); and UN (2005) all provide practical guidance for sampling.

15. Strictly speaking, samples are drawn from sampling frames. In our discussion we assume that the sampling frame perfectly overlaps with the population.

References

Cochran, William G. 1977. *Sampling Techniques*. 3rd ed. New York: John Wiley.

Dal Poz, Mario, and Neeru Gupta. 2009. "Assessment of Human Resources for Health Using Cross-National Comparison of Facility Surveys in Six Countries." *Human Resources for Health* 7: 22.

Fink, Arlene G. 2008. *How to Conduct Surveys: A Step by Step Guide*. 4th ed. Beverly Hills, CA: Sage Publications.

Galiani, Sebastian, Paul Gertler, and Ernesto Schargrodsky. 2005. "Water for Life: The Impact of the Privatization of Water Services on Child Mortality." *Journal of Political Economy* 113(1): 83–120.

Grosh, Margaret, and Paul Glewwe, eds. 2000. *Designing Household Survey Questionnaires for Developing Countries: Lessons from 15 Years of the Living Standards Measurement Study*. Washington, DC: World Bank.

Grosh, Margaret, and Juan Muñoz. 1996. "A Manual for Planning and Implementing the Living Standards Measurement Study Survey." LSMS Working Paper 126, World Bank, Washington, DC.

Iarossi, Giuseppe. 2006. *The Power of Survey Design: A User's Guide for Managing Surveys, Interpreting Results, and Influencing Respondents*. Washington, DC: World Bank.

Kalton, Graham. 1983. *Introduction to Survey Sampling*. Beverly Hills, CA: Sage Publications.

Kish, Leslie. 1995. *Survey Sampling*. New York: John Wiley.

Lohr, Sharon. 1999. *Sampling: Design and Analysis*. Pacific Grove, CA: Brooks Cole.

Pradhan, Menno, and Laura B. Rawlings. 2002. "The Impact and Targeting of Social Infrastructure Investments: Lessons from the Nicaraguan Social Fund." *World Bank Economic Review* 16 (2): 275–95.

Rosenbaum, Paul. 2009. *Design of Observational Studies*. New York: Springer Series in Statistics.

Spybrook, Jessaca, Stephen Raudenbush, Xiaofeng Liu, Richard Congdon, and Andrés Martinez. 2008. *Optimal Design for Longitudinal and Multilevel Research: Documentation for the "Optimal Design" Software*. New York: William T. Grant Foundation.

Thompson, Steven K. 2002. *Sampling*. 2nd ed. New York: John Wiley.

UN (United Nations). 2005. *Household Sample Surveys in Developing and Transition Countries*. New York: United Nations.

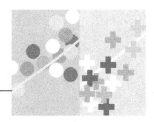

CHAPTER 12

Collecting Data

In chapter 11, we discussed the type of data needed for an evaluation and noted that most evaluations require the collection of new data. We then discussed how to determine the necessary sample size and how to draw a sample. In this chapter, we review the steps in collecting data. A clear understanding of these steps will help you ensure that the impact evaluation is based on quality data that do not compromise the evaluation design. As a first step, you will need to hire help from a firm or government agency that specializes in data collection. In parallel, you will commission the development of an appropriate questionnaire. The data collection entity will recruit and train field staff and pilot test the questionnaire. After making the necessary adjustments, the firm or agency will be able to proceed with fieldwork. Finally, the data that are collected must be digitized or processed and validated before they can be delivered and used.

Hiring Help to Collect Data

You will need to designate the agency in charge of collecting data early on. Some important trade-offs have to be considered when you are deciding who should collect impact evaluation data. Potential candidates for the job include

- the institution in charge of implementing the program,

- another government institution with experience collecting data (such as the local statistical agency), or

- an independent firm or think tank that specializes in data collection.

The data collection entity always needs to work in close coordination with the *agency implementing the program*. Because baseline data must be collected before any program operations begin, close coordination is required to ensure that no program operations are implemented before data collection is done. When baseline data are needed for the program's operation (for instance, data for a targeting index, in the context of an evaluation based on a regression discontinuity design), the entity in charge of data collection must be able to process it quickly and transfer it to the institution in charge of program operations. Close coordination is also required in timing the collection of follow-up survey data. For instance, if you have chosen a randomized rollout, the follow-up survey must be implemented before the program is rolled out to the comparison group, to avoid contamination.

An extremely important factor in deciding who should collect data is that the same data collection procedures should be used for both the comparison and treatment groups. The implementing agency often has contact only with the treatment group and so is not in a good position to collect data for the comparison groups. But using different data collection agencies for the treatment and comparison groups is risky, as it can create differences in the outcomes measured in the two groups simply because the data collection procedures differed. If the implementing agency cannot collect data effectively for both the treatment and comparison groups, the possibility of engaging a partner to do so should be strongly considered.

In some contexts, it may also be advisable to commission data collection to an independent agency to ensure that it is perceived as objective. Concerns that the program implementing agency does not collect objective data may not be warranted, but an independent data collection body that has no stake in the evaluation results can add credibility to the overall impact evaluation effort.

Because data collection involves a complex sequence of operations, it is recommended that a specialized and experienced entity be responsible for it. Few program-implementing agencies have sufficient experience to collect the large-scale, high-quality data necessary for an impact evaluation. In most cases, you will have to consider commissioning a local institution such as the national statistical agency or a specialized firm or think tank.

Commissioning a local institution such as the *national statistical agency* can give the institution exposure to impact evaluation studies and help it build capacity. However, local statistical agencies may not always have the capacity to take on extra mandates in addition to their regular activities. They may also lack the necessary experience in fielding surveys for impact evaluations, for instance, experience in successfully tracking individuals over time. If such constraints appear, contracting an *independent firm* or think tank specialized in data collection may be more practical.

You do not necessarily have to use the same entity to collect information at baseline and in follow-up surveys. For instance, for an impact evaluation of a training program, for which the population of interest comprises the individuals who signed up for the course, the institution in charge of the course could collect the baseline data when individuals enroll. It is unlikely, however, that the same agency will also be the best choice to collect follow-up information for both the treatment and comparison groups. In this context, contracting rounds of data collection separately has its advantages, but efforts should be made not to lose between rounds any information that will be useful in tracking households or individuals, as well as to ensure that baseline and follow-up data are measured consistently.

To determine the best institution for collecting impact evaluation data, all of these factors—experience in data collection, ability to coordinate with the program's implementing agency, independence, opportunities for capacity building, adaptability to the impact evaluation context—must be weighed, together with the likely quality of the data collected in each case. One effective way to identify the organization best placed to collect quality data is to write terms of reference and ask organizations to submit technical and financial proposals.

Because the prompt delivery and the quality of the data are crucial for the reliability of the impact evaluation, the contract for the agency in charge of data collection must be structured carefully. The scope of the expected work and deliverables must be made extremely clear. In addition, it is often advisable to introduce incentives into contracts and link those incentives to clear indicators of data quality. For instance, as we will stress below, the nonresponse rate is a key indicator of data quality. To create incentives for data collection agencies to minimize nonresponse, the contract can stipulate one unit cost for the first 90 percent of the sample, a higher unit cost for the units between 90 percent and 95 percent, and again a higher unit cost for units between 95 percent and 100 percent. Alternatively, a separate contract can be written for the survey firm to track nonrespondents.

Developing the Questionnaire

When commissioning data collection, you should have several clear objectives in mind and give specific guidance on the content of the data collection instrument or questionnaire. Data collection instruments must elicit all the information required to answer the policy question set out by the impact evaluation.

Developing Indicators

As we have discussed, *indicators* must be measured throughout the results chain, including final impact indicators, intermediate impact indicators, measures of the delivery of the intervention, exogenous factors, and control characteristics.

It is important to be selective about which indicators to measure. Being selective helps to limit data collection costs, simplifies the task of the data collection agency, and improves the quality of the data collected by minimizing demands on the respondents' time. Collecting information that is either irrelevant or unlikely to be used has a very high cost. Having a data analysis plan written in advance will help you to identify priorities and necessary information.

Data on outcome indicators and control characteristics must be collected consistently at the *baseline* and in the *follow-up survey*. Collecting baseline data is highly desirable. Even if you are using randomized assignment or a regression discontinuity design, where simple postintervention differences can in principle be used to estimate a program's impact, baseline data are essential for testing whether the design of the impact evaluation is adequate (see the checklist in box 8.1 of chapter 8). Having baseline data also gives you an insurance policy when randomization does not work, in which case difference-in-difference methods can be used instead. Baseline data are also useful during the impact analysis stage, since baseline control variables can help increase statistical power and allow you to analyze impacts on different subpopulations. Finally, baseline data can be used to enhance the design of the program. For instance, baseline data sometimes make it possible to analyze the effectiveness of the targeting or to provide additional information about beneficiaries to the program-implementing agency.

Measuring Indicators

Once you have defined the core data that need to be collected, the next step is to determine exactly how to measure those indicators. *Measurement* is an art in itself and is best commissioned to the agency hired to collect data, the survey experts, or the evaluators. Entire books have been written about how best to measure particular indicators in specific contexts, for example, the exact phrasing of the questions asked in household surveys (see references in Grosh and Glewwe [2000] and UN [2005])[1] or the detailed procedures that should be followed to collect test score or health data. Though these discussions may appear cumbersome, they are extremely important. We here provide some general guiding principles to guide you in commissioning data collection.

Outcome indicators should be as consistent as possible with local and international best practice. It is always useful to consider how indicators of interest have been measured in best-practice surveys both locally and internationally. Using the same indicators (including the same survey modules or questions) ensures comparability between the preexisting data and the data collected for the impact evaluation. If you decide to choose an indicator that is not fully comparable or not well measured, that may limit the usefulness of the evaluation results.

All of the indicators should be measured in exactly the same way for all units in both the treatment group and comparison group. Using different data collection methods (for example, using a phone survey for one and an in-person survey for the other) creates the risk of generating bias. The same is true of collecting data at different times for the two groups (for example, collecting data for the treatment group during the rainy season and for the comparison group during the dry season). That is why the procedures used to measure any outcome indicator should be formulated very precisely. The data collection process should be exactly the same for all units. Within the questionnaire, each module related to the program should be introduced without affecting the flow or framing of responses in other parts of the questionnaire.

Formatting Questionnaires

Because different ways of asking the same survey question can yield different answers, both the framing and the format of the questions should be the same for all units to prevent any respondent or enumerator bias. Glewwe (UN 2005) makes six specific recommendations regarding the formatting of questionnaires for household surveys. These recommendations apply equally to most other data collection instruments:

1. Each question should be written out in full on the questionnaire, so that the interviewer can conduct the interview by reading each question word for word.

2. The questionnaire should include precise definitions of all of the key concepts used in the survey, so that the interviewer can refer to the definition during the interview if necessary.

3. Each question should be as short and simple as possible and should use common, everyday terms.

4. The questionnaires should be designed so that the answers to almost all questions are precoded.

5. The coding scheme for answers should be consistent across all questions.

6. The survey should include skip codes, which indicate which questions are not to be asked based on the answers given to the previous questions.

Once a questionnaire has been drafted by the person commissioned to work on the instrument, it should be presented to a team of experts for discussion. Everybody involved in the evaluation (policy makers, researchers, data analysts, and data collectors) should be consulted about whether the questionnaire collects all of the information desired in an appropriate fashion.

Testing the Questionnaire

It is very important that the questionnaire be piloted and field-tested extensively before it is finalized. Extensive *piloting* of the questionnaire will test its format, as well as any alternative formatting and phrasing options. *Field-testing* the full questionnaire in real-life conditions is critical for checking its length and for verifying that its format is sufficiently consistent and comprehensive to produce precise measures of all relevant information. Field-testing is an integral part of the questionnaire design work that is commissioned.

Conducting Fieldwork

Even when you commission data collection, a clear understanding of all the steps involved in that process is crucial to help you ensure that the required *quality control mechanisms* and the right *incentives* are in place. The entity in charge of collecting data will need to coordinate the work of a large number of different actors, including enumerators, supervisors, field coordinators, and logistical support staff, in addition to a data entry team composed of programmers, supervisors, and the data entry operators. A clear work plan should be put in place to coordinate the work of all these teams, and the *work plan* is a key deliverable.

At the start, the work plan must include proper *training* for the data collection team before collection begins. A complete *reference manual* should be prepared for training and used throughout fieldwork. Training is key to ensuring that data are collected consistently by all involved. The training process is also a good opportunity to identify the best-performing enumerators and to conduct a last pilot of instruments and procedures under normal conditions. Once the sample has been drawn, the instruments have been designed and piloted, and the teams have been trained, the data collection can begin. It is good practice to ensure that the fieldwork plan has each survey team collect data on the same number of treatment and comparison units.

As discussed in chapter 11, proper sampling is essential to ensuring the quality of the sample. However, many *nonsampling errors* can occur while the data are being collected. In the context of an impact evaluation, a particular concern is that those errors may not be the same in the treatment and comparison groups.

Nonresponse arises when it becomes impossible to collect complete data for some sampled units. Because the actual samples are restricted to those units for which data can be collected, units that choose not to respond to a survey may make the sample less representative and can create bias in the evaluation results. *Attrition* is a common form of nonresponse that occurs when some units drop from the sample between data collection rounds, for example, because migrants are not fully tracked.

Nonresponse and attrition are particularly problematic in the context of impact evaluations because they may create differences between the treatment group and the comparison group. For example, attrition may be different in the two groups: if the data are being collected after the program has begun to be implemented, the response rate among treatment units can be higher than the rate among comparison units. That may happen because the comparison units are unhappy not to have been selected or are more likely to migrate. Nonresponses can also occur within the questionnaire itself, typically because some indicators are missing or the data are incomplete for a particular unit.

Measurement error is another type of problem that can generate bias if it is systematic. Measurement error is the difference between the value of a characteristic as provided by the respondent and the true (but unknown) value (Kasprzyk 2005). Such difference can be traced to the way the questionnaire is worded or to the data collection method that is chosen, or it can occur because of the interviewers who are fielding the survey or the respondent who is giving the answers.

The quality of the impact evaluation depends directly on the quality of the data that are collected. *Quality standards* need to be made clear to all stakeholders in the data collection process; the standards should be particularly emphasized during the training of enumerators and in the reference

Key Concept:
Nonresponse arises when data are missing or incomplete for some sampled units. Nonresponse can create bias in the evaluation results.

Key Concept:
Best-practice impact evaluations aim to keep nonresponse and attrition below 5 percent.

manuals. For instance, detailed procedures to minimize nonresponse or (if acceptable) to replace units in the sample are essential. The data collection agency must understand clearly the acceptable nonresponse and attrition rates. Best-practice impact evaluations aim to keep nonresponse and attrition below 5 percent. That may not always be feasible in very mobile populations but nevertheless provides a useful benchmark. Survey respondents are sometimes compensated to minimize nonresponse. In any case, the contract for the data collection agency must contain clear incentives, for instance, higher compensation if the nonresponse rate is below 5 percent or another acceptable threshold.

Well-defined *quality assurance procedures* must be established for all stages of the data collection process, including the designing of the sampling procedure and questionnaire, the preparation stages, data collection, data entry, and data cleaning and storage.

Quality checks during the fieldwork should be given a very high priority to minimize nonresponse errors for each unit. Clear procedures must exist for revisiting units that have provided no information or incomplete information. Multiple filters should be introduced in the quality control process, for instance, by having enumerators, supervisors, and if necessary, field coordinators revisit the nonresponse units to verify their status. The questionnaires from nonresponse interviews should still be clearly coded and recorded. Once the data have been completely digitized, the nonresponse rates can be summarized and all sampled units fully accounted for.

Quality checks should also be made on any incomplete data for a particular surveyed unit. Again, the quality control process should include multiple filters. The enumerator is responsible for checking the data immediately after they have been collected. The supervisor and the field coordinator should perform random checks at a later stage.

Quality checks for measurement errors are more difficult but are crucial for assessing whether information has been collected accurately. Consistency checks can be built into the questionnaire. In addition, supervisors need to conduct *spot checks* and cross-checks to ensure that the enumerators collect data in accordance with the established quality standards. Field coordinators should also contribute to those checks to minimize potential conflicts of interests within the survey firm.

It is critical that all steps involved in checking quality are requested explicitly when commissioning data collection. You may also consider contracting with an external agency to audit the quality of the data collection activities. Doing that can significantly limit the range of problems that can arise as a result of lack of supervision of the data collection team.

Processing and Validating the Data

Household surveys are typically collected using paper and pencil, although more recently electronic data collection using laptop computers, handhelds, and other devices has become more commonplace. In either case, data must be digitized and processed. *A data entry software* program has to be developed and a system put in place to manage the flow of data to be digitized. Norms and procedures must be established, and data entry operators must be carefully trained to guarantee that data entry is consistent. As much as possible, data entry should be integrated into data collection operations (including during the pilot-testing phase), so that any problems with the data collected can be promptly identified and verified in the field.

When working with paper-and-pencil surveys, the quality benchmark for the data entry process should be that the raw physical data are exactly replicated in the digitized version, with no modifications made to them while they are being entered. To minimize data entry errors, it is advisable to commission a *double-blind data entry* procedure that can be used to identify and correct for any remaining errors.

In addition to these quality checks during the data entry process, software can be developed to perform automatic checks for many nonsampling errors (both item nonresponse and inconsistencies) that may occur in the field. If the data entry process is integrated into the fieldwork procedures, incomplete or inconsistent data can be referred back to the field workers for on-site verification (Muñoz 2005, chapter 15). This kind of integration is not without challenges for the organizational flow of fieldwork operation, but it can yield substantial quality gains, diminishing measurement error and increasing the power of the impact evaluation. The possibility of using such an integrated approach should be considered explicitly when data collection is being planned. New technologies can facilitate those quality checks.

As we have seen, data collection comprises a set of operations whose complexity should not be underestimated. Box 12.1 discusses how the data collection process for the evaluation of the Nicaraguan Atención a Crisis pilots yielded high-quality data with remarkably low attrition and item nonresponse and few measurement and processing errors. Such high-quality data can be obtained only when data quality procedures and proper incentives are put in place at the moment of commissioning data collection.

At the end of the data collection process, the data set should be delivered with detailed documentation, including a complete codebook and data dictionary, and stored in a secure location. If the data are being collected for an impact evaluation, then the data set should also include complementary

Box 12.1: Data Collection for the Evaluation of the Nicaraguan Atención a Crisis Pilots

In 2005, the Nicaraguan government launched the Atención a Crisis pilots. Its objective was to evaluate the impact of combining a conditional cash transfer (CCT) program with productive transfers, such as grants for investment in nonagricultural activities or vocational training. The Atención a Crisis pilot was implemented by the ministry of the family, with support from the World Bank.

A randomized assignment in two stages was used for the evaluation. First, 106 target communities were randomly assigned to either the comparison group or the treatment group. Second, within treatment communities, eligible households were randomly assigned one of three benefit packages: (1) a conditional cash transfer; (2) the CCT plus a scholarship that allowed one of the household members to choose among a number of vocational training courses; and (3) the CCT plus a productive investment grant to encourage recipients to start a small nonagricultural activity, with the goal of asset creation and income diversification (Macours and Vakis 2009).

A baseline survey was collected in 2005, a first follow-up survey in 2006, and a second follow-up survey in 2008, 2 years after the intervention ended. Rigorous quality checks were put in place at all stages of the data collection process. First, questionnaires were thoroughly field-tested, and enumerators were trained both in class and in field conditions. Second, field supervision was set up, so that all questionnaires were revised multiple times by enumerators, supervisors, field coordinators, and other reviewers. Third, a double-blind data entry system was used, together with a comprehensive quality check program that could identify incomplete or inconsistent questionnaires. Questionnaires with item nonresponse or inconsistencies

were systematically sent back to the field for verification. These procedures and requirements were explicitly specified in the terms of reference of the data collection firm.

In addition, detailed tracking procedures were put in place to minimize attrition. At the start, a full census of households residing in the treatment and control communities in 2008 was undertaken in close collaboration with community leaders. In the presence of substantial geographical mobility, the survey firm was given incentives to track individual migrants throughout the country. As a result, only 2 percent of the original 4,359 households could not be interviewed in 2009. The survey firm was also commissioned to track all individuals from the households surveyed in 2005. Again only 2 percent of the individuals to whom program transfers were targeted could not be tracked (another 2 percent had died). Attrition was 3 percent for all children of households surveyed in 2005 and 5 percent for all individuals in households surveyed in 2005.

Attrition and nonresponse rates provide a good indicator of survey quality. Reaching those remarkably low attrition rates required intense efforts by the data collection firm, as well as explicit incentives. The per unit cost of a tracked household or individual is also much higher, and that needs to be accounted for. In addition, thorough quality checks had a cost and increased data collection time. Still, in the context of the Atención a Crisis pilot, the sample remained representative at both the household and the individual levels 3 to 4 years after the baseline, measurement error was minimized, and the reliability of the evaluation was ensured. As a result, the Atención a Crisis pilot is one of the safety net programs whose sustainability can be most convincingly studied.

Source: Macours and Vakis 2009; authors.

information on treatment status and program participation. A complete set of documentation will speed up the analysis of the impact evaluation data, which will produce results that can be used for policy making in a timely fashion. It will also facilitate information sharing.

Note

1. See also Fink and Kosecoff (2008); Iarossi (2006); and Leeuw, Hox, and Dillman (2008), which provide a wealth of practical guidance for data collection.

References

Fink, Arlene G., and Jacqueline Kosecoff. 2008. *How to Conduct Surveys: A Step by Step Guide*. 4th ed. London: Sage Publications.

Glewwe, Paul. 2005. "An Overview of Questionnaire Design for Household Surveys in Developing Countries." In *Household Sample Surveys in Developing and Transition Countries*, chapter 3. New York: United Nations.

Grosh, Margaret, and Paul Glewwe, eds. 2000. *Designing Household Survey Questionnaires for Developing Countries: Lessons from 15 Years of the Living Standards Measurement Study*. Washington, DC: World Bank.

Iarossi, Giuseppe. 2006. *The Power of Survey Design: A User's Guide for Managing Surveys, Interpreting Results, and Influencing Respondents*. Washington, DC: World Bank.

Kasprzyk, Daniel. 2005. "Measurement Error in Household Surveys: Sources and Measurement." In *Household Sample Surveys in Developing and Transition Countries*, chapter 9. New York: United Nations.

Leeuw, Edith, Joop Hox, and Don Dillman. 2008. *International Handbook of Survey Methodology*. New York: Taylor & Francis Group.

Macours, Karen, and Renos Vakis. 2009. "Changing Household Investments and Aspirations through Social Interactions: Evidence from a Randomized Experiment." Policy Research Working Paper 5137, World Bank, Washington, DC.

Muñoz, Juan. 2005. "A Guide for Data Management of Household Surveys." In *Household Sample Surveys in Developing and Transition Countries*, chapter 15. New York: United Nations.

UN (United Nations). 2005. *Household Sample Surveys in Developing and Transition Countries*. New York: United Nations.

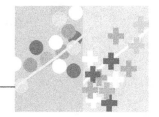

CHAPTER 13

Producing and Disseminating Findings

In this chapter, we discuss the content and use of the various reports that are produced during an impact evaluation. During the preparation phase, the evaluation manager will normally prepare an *impact evaluation plan*, which details the objectives, design, and sampling and data collection strategies for the evaluation (box 13.1 presents a suggested outline of the process). The various elements of the evaluation plan are discussed in chapters 1 through 12.

Once the evaluation is under way, the evaluators will produce a number of reports, including the *baseline report*, the *impact evaluation report*, and *policy briefs*. The evaluators should also produce fully documented data sets as final products. Once the impact evaluation report is available and the results are known, it is then time to think how to best disseminate the findings among policy makers and other development stakeholders. The production and dissemination of impact evaluation findings are the topic of this chapter.

What Products Will the Evaluation Deliver?

The main outputs of an evaluation are an impact evaluation report and a number of policy briefs that summarize the key findings. It can take several

Box 13.1: Outline of an Impact Evaluation Plan

1. Introduction
2. Description of the intervention
3. Objectives of the evaluation
   3.1 Hypotheses, theory of change, results chain
   3.2 Policy questions
   3.3 Key outcome indicators
4. Evaluation design
5. Sampling and data
   5.1 Sampling strategy
   5.2 Power calculations
6. Data collection plan
   6.1 Baseline survey
   6.2 Follow-up survey(s)
7. Products to be delivered
   7.1 Baseline report
   7.2 Impact evaluation report
   7.3 Policy brief
   7.4 Fully documented data sets
8. Dissemination plan
9. Ethical issues
10. Time line
11. Budget and funding
12. Composition of evaluation team

years from the start of the evaluation to complete such a report, since evaluation findings can be produced only once the follow-up data are available. Because of this lag, policy makers often request intermediary evaluation products, such as a baseline report, to make available preliminary information to sustain policy dialogue and decisions.[1]

As discussed in chapter 10, the evaluation manager will work with data analysts to produce the baseline and final reports. Data analysts are experts in statistics or econometrics who will program the impact evaluation analysis in statistical software such as Stata, SPSS, or R. Data analysts are responsible for ensuring the quality, scientific rigor and credibility of the results. Here, we do not discuss how to analyze data,[2] but rather outline the scope of the reports to which the data will contribute.

Intermediate Product: Baseline Report

The main objectives of a *baseline report* are to assess whether the chosen impact evaluation design will be valid in practice and to describe the baseline (preprogram) characteristics and outcomes of the eligible population. A baseline report also generates information about the program and its beneficiaries that can be useful to enhance both the implementation of the program and its evaluation. Box 13.2 outlines the suggested content of a baseline report.[3]

The baseline report is produced from the analysis of a clean baseline data set complemented by administrative data on each unit's treatment status. The assignment of households, individuals, or facilities to the treatment or

---

Box 13.2: Outline of a Baseline Report

1. Introduction
2. Description of the intervention (benefits, eligibility rules, and so on)
3. Objectives of the evaluation
    3.1 Hypotheses, theory of changes, results chain
    3.2 Policy questions
    3.3 Key outcome indicators
4. Evaluation design
    4.1 Original design
    4.2 Actual program participants and nonparticipants
5. Sampling and data
    5.1 Sampling strategy
    5.2 Power calculations
    5.3 Data collected
6. Validation of evaluation design
7. Comprehensive descriptive statistics
8. Conclusion and recommendations for implementation

---

the comparison group is generally performed after the baseline data have been collected. As a result, treatment status is often registered in a separate administrative data set. For instance, a public lottery may be organized to determine which communities, among all the eligible communities where a baseline survey has been collected, will benefit from a cash transfer program. If that is to be done, data analysts must merge the administrative data with the baseline data. If the evaluation includes more than, say, 100 eligible units, it will not be practical to match the baseline data with the administrative data by name. Each eligible unit will need to be assigned a unique number or *identifier,* which will identify it in all sources of data, including the baseline and administrative databases.

The first sections of the baseline report build on the impact evaluation plan by presenting the motivation for the evaluation, the description of the intervention (including benefits and benefit assignment rules), the objectives of the evaluation (including the theory of change, core policy questions, hypotheses, and indicators), and the evaluation design. The section on the evaluation design should discuss whether the assignment of program benefits was implemented in a manner consistent with the planned design. Because the assignment is normally done just after completion of the baseline survey, it is good practice to include information on actual assignment in the baseline report. The section on sampling generally starts by outlining the sampling strategy and the power calculations produced for the evaluation plan, before describing in detail how baseline data were collected and the type of information that is available. The report should discuss any challenges faced during baseline data collection, and it should present key indicators of data quality, such as nonresponse rates. In that regard, the baseline report will highlight key issues that need to be addressed at follow-up. For instance, if the rate of nonresponse was high at baseline, the evaluators will need to develop new field or tracking procedures to ensure that that does not happen again during the follow-up survey.

As we have said, the first main objective of the baseline report is to provide an early assessment of the validity of the evaluation design in practice. In chapter 8, we highlighted that most impact evaluation methods produce valid estimates of the counterfactual only under specific assumptions. Box 8.1 (chapter 8) presents a checklist of tests that can be used to assess whether a method is appropriate in a given context. Some of those tests do not require follow-up data and can be applied as soon as baseline data are available. For example, if the randomized assignment or randomized offering method is used, the baseline report should state whether the treatment and comparison groups have similar baseline characteristics. If the evaluation is based on the regression discontinuity method, the baseline report should report tests of the continuity of the eligibility index around the threshold. Although these falsification checks do not guarantee that the comparison group will remain valid until the follow-up survey, it is crucial that the baseline report document them.

In addition to testing the validity of the evaluation design, the baseline report should include tables that describe the characteristics of the evaluation sample. They can enhance program implementation by allowing the program managers to better understand the profile of beneficiaries and to tailor the program intervention to their needs. For example, by knowing the level of education or average work experience of participants in a training program, program managers may be able to fine-tune the content of the training courses.

From the evaluation standpoint, the baseline survey often yields information that was unavailable at the time the evaluation plan was being written. Say that you are evaluating the impact of a village health program on child diarrhea. When writing the evaluation plan, you may not know what the incidence of diarrhea is in the village. So in the evaluation plan, you would have only an estimate, and you would base your power calculations on that estimate. However, once you have baseline data, you are able to verify the actual baseline incidence of diarrhea and, thus, whether your original sample size is adequate. If you find that baseline values of outcome indicators are different from the ones used to perform the original power calculations, the baseline report should include updated power calculations.

To ensure the credibility of the final evaluation results, it is good practice to let external experts review the baseline report. Disseminating the baseline report can also reinforce the policy dialogue among stakeholders throughout the evaluation cycle.

Final Products: Impact Evaluation Report, Policy Brief, and Data Sets

The *final impact evaluation report* is the main product of an evaluation and is produced after follow-up data have been collected.[4] The main objectives of the evaluation report are to present evaluation results and answer all the policy questions that were set out initially. As a complement, the report also needs to show that the evaluation is based on valid estimates of the counterfactual and that the estimated impacts are fully attributable to the program.

The final impact evaluation report is a comprehensive one that summarizes all the work connected with the evaluation and includes detailed descriptions of the data analysis and econometric specifications, as well as discussion of results, tables, and appendixes. Box 13.3 outlines the content of a full impact evaluation report. Many good examples of final impact evaluation reports are available, such as Maluccio and Flores (2005), Levy and Ohls (2007), or Skoufias (2005) for conditional cash transfer programs; Card et al. (2007) for a youth training program; Cattaneo et al. (2009) for a housing program; and Basinga et al. (2010) for a results-based financing program for the health sector.

As for the baseline report, the evaluators will work with data analysts to produce the final impact evaluation report. The analyst will start by producing a master data set containing the baseline data set, the follow-up data set, administrative data on actual program implementation, and data on the original assignment to treatment and comparison groups. All of these sources should be merged, using a unique identifier for each unit.

Because the final impact evaluation report is the main output of the evaluation, it should incorporate the key information presented in the evaluation plan and the baseline report, before turning to analysis and discussion

---

Box 13.3: Outline of an Evaluation Report

1. Introduction
2. Description of the intervention (benefits, eligibility rules, and so on)
   2.1. Design
   2.2 Implementation
3. Objectives of the evaluation
   3.1 Hypotheses, theory of change, results chain
   3.2 Policy questions
   3.3 Key outcome indicators
4. Evaluation design
   4.1 In theory
   4.2 In practice
5. Sampling and data
   5.1 Sampling strategy
   5.2 Power calculations
   5.3 Data collected
6. Validation of evaluation design
7. Results
8. Robustness checks
9. Conclusion and policy recommendations

of the results. In particular, the introductory part of the final report should present the full rationale for the intervention and the evaluation and describe the intervention (benefits and benefit assignment rules), the objectives of the evaluation (including the theory of change, core policy questions, hypotheses, and indicators), the original evaluation design, and how it was implemented in practice.

In general, the interpretation of results depends crucially on how well an intervention was implemented. The final evaluation report should therefore discuss the implementation of the intervention in detail. This can be done before presenting results, by describing data on program implementation obtained from follow-up surveys or complementary administrative sources.

The sampling and data section is the place to describe the sampling strategy and power calculations, before the extensive discussion of the baseline and follow-up data collected. Key indicators of data quality, such as nonresponse and attrition, must be presented for each data round. If nonresponse and attrition rates are high, it becomes crucial for the data analysts to discuss how that may affect the interpretation of the results. For example, testing whether attrition and nonresponse are balanced between the comparison and treatment groups is a must.

Once the data have been described, the report can turn to the presentation of results for all key policy questions and outcome indicators identified as objectives of the evaluation. The structure of the results section will depend on the types of policy questions under study. For instance, does the evaluation test various program alternatives, or does it test only whether or not an intervention works? Did policy makers request an analysis of how results vary among subgroups? For evaluations that were well designed and implemented, rigorous evaluation results can often be presented in an intuitive way.

As we have said, the impact evaluation report should provide strong evidence that the estimated impacts are indeed fully attributable to the program. Therefore, the report must carefully scrutinize the validity of the evaluation design. To demonstrate the validity of the impact evaluation design, a first step is to present the results of falsification tests performed with baseline data (box 8.1, chapter 8). The report should also contain the results of any tests that can be performed with follow-up data. For instance, if a difference-in-differences approach is chosen, the series of falsification tests described in box 8.1 can be performed only in the presence of follow-up data.

The introductory section of the evaluation report should document any new challenges with the evaluation method that arose between the baseline and follow-up surveys. For example, noncompliance with assignment to the treatment and comparison groups has important implications for the analysis and interpretation of results and must be discussed up front in the report. The report must also contain information on how many units assigned to the treatment group indeed received the program and how many of those assigned to the comparison group did not receive the program. If any deviation from the original assignment has occurred, the analysis has to be adjusted to account for noncompliance (refer to the techniques discussed in part 2).

Parallel with tests of the validity of the evaluation design, the final report is the place to provide a comprehensive discussion of the nature, reliability, and robustness of the results. It should contain a series of robustness tests relevant to the evaluation methodology being used. For instance, when matching methods are applied, the report needs to present results from applying alternative techniques to find the best match for each treated observation. It is the responsibility of the data analysts to identify and present the robustness checks most appropriate for a specific evaluation. The final parts of the report should clearly answer each policy question that the evaluation set out to answer and provide detailed policy recommendations based on the results.

Understanding how the intervention was implemented is particularly crucial when evaluation results show a limited or negative impact. Non-results or negative results are no reason to punish program or evaluation managers. Rather, they provide an opportunity for program and evaluation managers to explain clearly what did not work as intended; that, in itself, can lead to large policy gains and should be rewarded. Continuous communication between the evaluation team and the policy makers responsible for the program is particularly critical when signs appear that an evaluation will produce non-results or negative results. Complementary process evaluations or qualitative work can provide valuable explanation for why a program did not achieve the intended results. Lack of results traceable to imperfect program implementation should be clearly distinguished from lack of results from a well-implemented program that had a weak design.[5] In general, evaluations that test program alternatives are most useful in illuminating which program design features work and which do not.

Overall, the final data analysis should provide convincing evidence that the estimated program impacts are indeed caused by the intervention. To guarantee that results are fully objective and thus ensure their legitimacy, all reports should be peer reviewed and subject to broad consultations before being finalized. The content of the final impact evaluation report may subsequently be transformed into more technical academic papers for publication in peer-reviewed journals, lending additional credibility to the evaluation results.

In addition to the comprehensive evaluation report, evaluators should produce one or more shorter policy briefs to help communicate the results to policy makers and other stakeholders. A policy brief concentrates on presenting the core findings of the evaluation through graphs, charts, and other accessible formats and on discussing the policy recommendations. It also contains a short summary of the technical aspects of the evaluation. The policy brief can be made publicly available in paper and Web formats and circulated to politicians, civil society, and the media. Good examples of policy briefs can be found on the Poverty Action Lab (J-PAL) or World Bank Human Development Web site (for example, Poverty Action Lab 2008; World Bank Human Development Network 2010).

The last major product of an impact evaluation is a set of relevant data and their documentation. Tools such as the Microdata Management Toolkit of the International Household Survey Network (http://www.ihsn.org) can assist in this process. Policy makers and impact evaluators will typically agree on a time line in which the initial impact analysis is conducted and evaluation data are released into the public domain. Making data publicly available enhances transparency because impact results can be replicated and externally validated. Public access will also encourage external researchers to conduct additional analysis with the same data, which can provide valuable information and learning for the program. When making data publicly available, it is important to guarantee anonymity to all research subjects; any information that could identify survey respondents (such as names, addresses, or location information) must be removed from the publicly available data sets. This type of sensitive information should be kept secure and made available only for authorized future data collection activities.

How to Disseminate Findings?

Beyond delivering evaluation results, the ultimate goal of impact evaluations is to make public policies more effective and improve development outcomes. To ensure that an impact evaluation informs policy decisions, it must communicate clearly with all of its stakeholders, including policy makers, civil society, and the media. Influential evaluations often include a detailed dissemination plan that outlines how key stakeholders will be kept informed and engaged throughout the evaluation cycle. Such a dissemination plan can facilitate the use of results in policy making and ensure that impact evaluations truly achieve results.

At the initial stages of the evaluation design, evaluators have their first opportunity to build strong communication channels with policy makers.

As should be clear from our discussion of evaluation methods, an evaluation design depends directly on how the program itself is designed and implemented, and so it is critical that external evaluators and the policy makers doing the commissioning collaborate during the program design stage. A well-functioning evaluation team will ensure that the evaluation is fully aligned to the needs of policy makers and that its progress and results are regularly communicated to them.

The *dissemination plan* should outline how the evaluation team will increase the demand for the evaluation results and maximize their use in decision making. At minimum, the evaluators should foster awareness about the evaluation by effectively communicating the results to internal and external stakeholders throughout the evaluation cycle. At the inception of the evaluation, a pre-study and launch workshop with implementers and key stakeholders can help achieve consensus on its main objectives, policy questions, and design features. In addition to providing a platform for consultations and ensuring that the evaluation is fully aligned to stakeholder needs, such an event is important to raise awareness about the evaluation and reinforce interest in learning its results.

During the evaluation, periodic meetings of an interinstitutional committee or permanent discussion roundtable can help ensure that the work of the evaluation team remains fully policy relevant. Such discussion forums can provide feedback and guidance on the production of terms of reference, the content of the survey instrument, the dissemination of results, or the most appropriate channels to reach high-level decision makers.

The organization of dissemination events for intermediary products, such as a baseline report, is important to maintain an active policy dialogue with evaluation users. Fostering early discussion around the baseline report is beneficial in both disseminating policy-relevant intermediary results and ensuring continued awareness about the nature of impact evaluation results to come.

Before finalizing the evaluation report, some evaluators choose to organize a final consultation event to give stakeholders the opportunity to comment on the results. These consultations can contribute to improving the quality of evaluation results, as well as their acceptance. Once the final impact evaluation report and associated policy briefs are available, high-visibility dissemination events are critical to ensure wide awareness of the results among stakeholders. An in-country consultation and dissemination workshop with a broad set of stakeholders provides a platform to discuss results, gather feedback, and outline policy changes that could be made as a result of the evaluation. That workshop can be followed by a high-level dissemination workshop involving top policy makers (see box 13.4). Outside

> **Box 13.4: Disseminating Evaluation Findings to Improve Policy**
>
> The evaluation of results-based financing for health care in Rwanda provides a good example of a successful dissemination strategy. Under the leadership of the ministry of health, a team composed of local academics and World Bank experts was formed to lead the evaluation. Various stakeholders were involved throughout the evaluation, beginning with its launch, and that proved key to ensuring its success and strong political buy-in. Final results of the evaluation (Basinga et al. 2010) were unveiled during a daylong public dissemination event involving high-level decision makers and multiple stakeholders. Thanks to these communication channels, the findings strongly influenced the design of health policy in Rwanda. The results were also disseminated at international health conferences and through a Web site.
>
> *Source:* Morgan 2010.

the country, the results can be disseminated at conferences, seminars, and other gatherings, if the evaluation results can be useful for policy making in other countries. Other innovative dissemination channels, such as Web interfaces, are also helpful to increase the visibility of findings.

Overall, the dissemination of impact evaluation outputs, according to a well-thought-out plan spanning the evaluation cycle, is important to ensure that results effectively feed the policy dialogue. Only when evaluation results are adequately shared with policy makers and fully used in the decision-making process can impact evaluations fulfill their ultimate objective of improving the effectiveness of social programs.

Notes

1. An evaluation may generate other intermediary products. For instance, qualitative fieldwork or process evaluations provide highly valuable complementary information before the final impact evaluation report is produced. We focus on the baseline report because it constitutes the main intermediary product of quantitative impact evaluations, the subject of this book.
2. Khandker et al. (2009) present an introduction to evaluation that includes a review of data analysis and the relevant Stata commands for each impact evaluation method.
3. The outline is indicative and can be tailored depending on the nature of each evaluation, for instance, by modifying the order or content of the various sections.

4. In cases when multiple rounds of follow-up data are collected, an impact evaluation report can be produced for each round, and the results compared, to highlight whether program impacts are sustainable or vary with duration of exposure.

5. As discussed in chapter 1, this is a reason why efficacy trials to minimize implementation challenges are useful in determining whether a particular program design works under ideal circumstances. Once proof of concept has been documented, the pilot can be scaled up.

References

Basinga, Paulin, Paul J. Gertler, Agnes Binagwaho, Agnes L. B. Soucat, Jennifer R. Sturdy, and Christel M. J. Vermeersch. 2010. "Paying Primary Health Care Centers for Performance in Rwanda." Policy Research Working Paper Series 5190, World Bank, Washington, DC.

Card, David, Pablo Ibarraran, Ferdinando Regalia, David Rosas, and Yuri Soares. 2007. "The Labor Market Impacts of Youth Training in the Dominican Republic: Evidence from a Randomized Evaluation." NBER Working Paper 12883, National Bureau of Economic Research, Washington, DC.

Cattaneo, Matias, Sebastian Galiani, Paul Gertler, Sebastian Martinez, and Rocio Titiunik. 2009. "Housing, Health and Happiness." *American Economic Journal: Economic Policy* 1 (1): 75–105.

Khandker, Shahidur R., Gayatri B. Koolwal, and Hussein A. Samad. 2009. *Handbook on Impact Evaluation: Quantitative Methods and Practices.* Washington, DC: World Bank.

Levy, Dan, and Jim Ohls. 2007. "Evaluation of Jamaica's PATH Program: Final Report." Ref. No. 8966-090, Mathematica Policy Research, Inc., Washington, DC.

Maluccio, John, and Rafael Flores. 2005. "Impact Evaluation of a Conditional Cash Transfer Program: The Nicaraguan Red de Proteccion Social." Research Report 141, International Food Policy Research Institute, Washington, DC.

Morgan, Lindsay. 2010. "Signed, Sealed, Delivered? Evidence from Rwanda on the Impact of Results-Based Financing for Health." HRBF Policy Brief, World Bank, Washington, DC.

Poverty Action Lab. 2008. "Solving Absenteeism, Raising Test Scores." Policy Briefcase 6. http://www.povertyactionlab.org.

Skoufias, Emmanuel. 2005. "PROGRESA and Its Impacts on the Welfare of Rural Households in Mexico." Research Reports 139, International Food Policy Research Institute, Washington, DC.

World Bank Human Development Network. 2010. "Does Linking Teacher Pay to Student Performance Improve Results?" Policy Note Series 1, World Bank, Washington DC. http://www.worldbank.org/hdchiefeconomist.

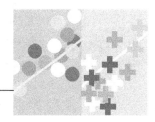

CHAPTER 14

Conclusion

This book is a practical guide to designing and implementing impact evaluations. We expect that its content will appeal to three main audiences: (1) policy makers who consume the information generated from impact evaluations, (2) project managers and development practitioners who commission evaluations, and (3) technicians who design and implement impact evaluations. Essentially, impact evaluation is about generating evidence on which social policies work, and which do not. That can be done in a classic impact evaluation framework, comparing outcomes with and without the program. Impact evaluations can also be conducted to explore implementation alternatives within a program or to look across programs to assess comparative performance.

We argue that impact evaluations are a worthwhile investment for many programs and that, coupled with monitoring and other forms of evaluation, they allow for a clear understanding of the effectiveness of particular social policies. We present a menu of impact evaluation methodologies, each with its own set of costs and benefits with respect to implementation, political economy, financial requirements, and interpretation of results. We argue that the best method should be chosen to fit the operational context, and not the other way around. Finally, we provide practical tips, tools, and guidance to assist during the evaluation process and to facilitate getting the most out of an evaluation's results.

Impact evaluations are complex undertakings with many moving parts. The following checklist highlights the core elements of a well-designed impact evaluation, which should include the following:

✓ A concrete policy question—grounded in a theory of change—that can be answered with an impact evaluation

✓ A valid identification strategy, consistent with the operational rules of the program, that shows the causal relation between the program and outcomes of interest

✓ A well-powered sample that allows policy-relevant impacts to be detected and a representative sample that allows results to be generalized to a larger population of interest

✓ A high-quality source of data that provides the appropriate variables required by the analysis, of both treatment and comparison groups, using both baseline and follow-up data

✓ A well-formed evaluation team that works closely with policy makers and program staff

✓ An impact report and associated policy briefs, disseminated to key audiences in a timely manner and feeding both program design and policy dialogues

We also highlight some key tips that can help mitigate common risks inherent in the process of conducting an impact evaluation:

✓ Impact evaluations are best designed early in the project cycle, ideally as part of the program design. Early planning allows for a prospective evaluation design based on the best available methodology and will provide the time necessary to plan and implement baseline data collection prior to the start of the program in evaluation areas.

✓ Impact results should be informed by process evaluation and rigorous monitoring data that give a clear picture of program implementation. When programs succeed, it is important to understand why. When programs fail, it is important to distinguish between a poorly implemented program and a flawed program design.

✓ Collect baseline data and build a backup methodology into your impact evaluation design. If the original evaluation design is invalidated, for example if the original comparison group receives program benefits, having a backup plan can help you avoid having to throw out the evaluation altogether.

✓ Maintain common identifiers among different data sources, so that they can be easily linked during the analysis. For example, a particular household should have the same identifier in the monitoring systems and in baseline and follow-up surveys.

✓ Impact evaluations are as useful for learning about how programs work and for testing programmatic alternatives as they are for evaluating the overall impact of a single bundle of goods and services. By unbundling a program, even large, universal programs can learn a lot by testing innovations through well-designed impact evaluations. Embedding an additional program innovation as a small pilot in the context of a larger evaluation can leverage the evaluation to produce valuable information for future decision making.

✓ Impact evaluations should be thought of as another component of a program's operation and should be adequately staffed and budgeted with the required technical and financial resources. Be realistic about the costs and complexity of carrying out an impact evaluation. The process of designing an evaluation and collecting a baseline from scratch will typically take a year or more. Once the program starts, the intervention needs a sufficient exposure period to affect outcomes. Depending on the program, that can take anywhere from a year to five years, or more. Collecting one or more follow-up surveys, conducting the analysis, and dissemination will also involve substantial effort over a number of months. Altogether, a complete impact evaluation cycle from start to finish typically takes at least three to four years of intensive work and engagement. Adequate financial and technical resources are necessary at each step of the way.

Ultimately, individual impact evaluations provide concrete answers to specific policy questions. Although these answers provide information that is customized for the specific entity commissioning and paying for the evaluation, they also provide information that is of value to others around the world who can learn and make decisions based on the evidence. For example, more recent conditional cash transfer programs in Africa, Asia, and Europe have drawn lessons from the original evaluations of Colombia's Familias en Acción, Mexico's Progresa, and other Latin American conditional cash transfer programs established in years past. In that way, impact evaluations are partly a global public good. Evidence generated through one impact evaluation adds to global knowledge on that subject. This knowledge base can then inform policy decisions in other countries and contexts as well. Indeed, the international community is moving toward scaling up support for rigorous evaluation.

At the country level, more sophisticated and demanding governments are looking to demonstrate results and to be more accountable to their core constituencies. Increasingly, evaluations are being conducted by national and subnational line ministries and government bodies set up to lead a national evaluation agenda, such as the National Council for Evaluation of Social Development Policies (CONEVAL) in Mexico and the Department of Performance Monitoring and Evaluation in South Africa. Evidence from impact evaluations is increasingly informing budgetary allocations made by congresses at the national level. In systems where programs are judged based on hard evidence and final outcomes, programs with a strong evidence base will be able to thrive, while programs lacking such proof will find it more difficult to sustain funding.

Multilateral institutions such as the World Bank and regional development banks, as well as national development agencies, donor governments, and philanthropic institutions, are also demanding more and better evidence on the effective use of development resources. Such evidence is required for accountability to those lending or donating the money, as well as for decision making about where best to allocate scarce development resources. The number of impact evaluations undertaken by development institutions has risen sharply in recent years. To illustrate, figure 14.1 depicts the number of impact evaluations completed or active at the World Bank between 2004 and 2010, by region. The positive trend is likely to continue.

A growing number of institutions dedicated primarily to the production of high-quality impact evaluations are emerging, including ones from the academic arena, including the Poverty Action Lab, Innovations for Poverty Action, and the Center of Evaluation for Global Action, and independent agencies that support impact evaluations, such as the International Initiative for Impact Evaluation. A number of impact evaluation–related associations now bring together groups of evaluation practitioners and researchers and policy makers interested in the topic, including the Network of Networks on Impact Evaluation and regional associations such as the African Evaluation Association and the Latin American and Caribbean Economics Association Impact Evaluation Network. All of these efforts reflect the increasing importance of impact evaluation in international development policy.[1]

Given this growth in impact evaluation, whether you run evaluations for a living, contract impact evaluations, or use the results of impact evaluations for decision making, being conversant in the language of impact evaluation is an increasingly indispensable skill for any development practitioner. Rigorous evidence of the type generated through impact evaluations can be one of the drivers of development policy dialogue, providing the basis to support

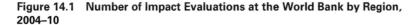

**Figure 14.1   Number of Impact Evaluations at the World Bank by Region,
2004–10**

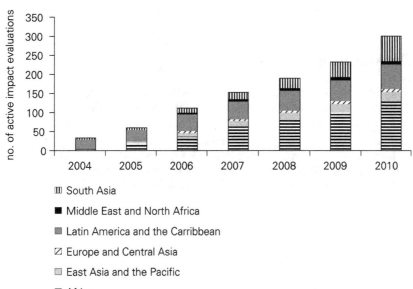

▥ South Asia

■ Middle East and North Africa

▨ Latin America and the Carribbean

▨ Europe and Central Asia

▢ East Asia and the Pacific

≡ Africa

Source: World Bank.

or oppose investments in development programs and policies. Evidence from impact evaluations allows project managers to make informed decisions on how to achieve outcomes more cost-effectively. Armed with the evidence from an impact evaluation, the policy maker has the job of closing the loop by feeding those results into the decision-making process. This type of evidence can inform debates, opinions, and ultimately, the human and monetary resource allocation decisions of governments, multilateral institutions, and donors.

Evidence-based policy making is fundamentally about reprogramming budgets to expand cost-effective programs, curtail ineffective ones, and introduce improvements to program designs based on the best available evidence. Impact evaluation is not a purely academic undertaking. Impact evaluations are driven by the need for answers to policy questions that affect people's lives daily. Decisions on how best to spend scarce resources on antipoverty programs, health, education, safety nets, microcredit, agriculture, and myriad other development initiatives have the potential to improve the welfare of people across the globe. It is vital that those decisions be made using the most rigorous evidence possible.

Note

1. For additional reading, see Savedoff, Levine, and Birdsall (2006).

References

Legovini, Arianna. 2010. "Development Impact Evaluation Initiative: A World Bank–Wide Strategic Approach to Enhance Development Effectiveness." Draft Report to the Operational Vice Presidents, World Bank, Washington, DC.

Savedoff, William, Ruth Levine, and Nancy Birdsall. 2006. "When Will We Ever Learn? Improving Lives through Impact Evaluation." CGD Evaluation Gap Working Group Paper, Center for Global Development, Wahington, DC. http://www.cgdev.org/content/publications/detail/7973.

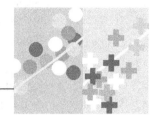

GLOSSARY

Italic indicates terms that are defined in the glossary.

Activity. Actions taken or work performed through which *input*s, such as funds, technical assistance, and other types of resources are mobilized to produce specific *output*s.

Alternative hypothesis. In *impact evaluation*, the alternative hypothesis is usually the hypothesis that the *null hypothesis* is false; in other words, that the intervention has an impact on *outcome*s.

Attrition. Attrition occurs when some units drop from the *sample* between one data collection round and another, for example, because migrants are not tracked. Attrition is a case of unit *nonresponse*. Attrition can create *bias* in *impact evaluation*s if it is correlated with treatment status.

Baseline. Preintervention, ex-ante. The situation prior to an intervention, against which progress can be assessed or comparisons made. Baseline data are collected before a program or policy is implemented to assess the "before" state.

Before-and-after comparison. Also known as "pre-post comparison" or "reflexive comparison," a before-and-after comparison attempts to establish the impact of a program by tracking changes in *outcome*s for program beneficiaries over time, using measurements before and after the program or policy is implemented.

Bias. The bias of an *estimator* is the difference between an estimator's expectation and the true value of the parameter being estimated. In *impact evaluation*, this is the difference between the impact that is calculated and the true impact of the program.

Census data. Data that cover all units in the population of interest (*universe*). Contrast with *survey data*.

Cluster. A cluster is a group of units that are similar in one way or another. For example, in a *sampling* of school children, children who attend the same school would belong to a cluster because they share the same school facilities and teachers and live in the same neighborhood.

Cluster sample. A *sample* obtained by drawing a *random sample* of clusters, after which either all units in the selected clusters constitute the sample, or a number of units within each selected *cluster* is randomly drawn. Each cluster has a well-defined probability of being selected, and units within a selected cluster also have a well-defined probability of being drawn.

Comparison group. Also known as a "control group." A valid comparison group will have the same characteristics as the group of beneficiaries of the program (*treatment group*), except that the units in the comparison group do not benefit from the program. Comparison groups are used to estimate the *counterfactual*.

Cost-benefit analysis. Ex-ante calculations of total expected costs and benefits, used to appraise or assess project proposals. Cost-benefit can be calculated ex-post in *impact evaluations* if the benefits can be quantified in monetary terms and the cost information is available.

Cost-effectiveness. Determining cost-effectiveness entails comparing similar interventions based on cost and effectiveness. For example, *impact evaluations* of various education programs allow policy makers to make more informed decisions about which intervention may achieve the desired objectives, given their particular context and constraints.

Counterfactual. The counterfactual is an estimate of what the *outcome* (Y) would have been for a program participant in the absence of the program (P). By definition, the counterfactual cannot be observed. Therefore, it must be estimated using *comparison groups*.

Difference-in-differences. Also known as "double difference" or "DD." Difference-in-differences estimates the *counterfactual* for the change in *outcome* for the *treatment group* by taking the change in outcome for the *comparison group*. This method allows us to take into account any differences between the treatment and comparison groups that are constant over time. The two differences are thus before and after, and between the treatment and comparison groups.

Effect. Intended or unintended change due directly or indirectly to an intervention

Estimator. In statistics, an estimator is a statistic (a function of the observable *sample* data) that is used to estimate an unknown population parameter; an estimate is the result from the actual application of the function to a particular sample of data.

Evaluation. Evaluations are periodic, objective assessments of a planned, ongoing, or completed project, program, or policy. Evaluations are used to answer specific questions, often related to design, implementation, and results.

External validity. To have external validity means that the causal impact discovered in the *impact evaluation* can be generalized to the universe of all eligible units. For an evaluation to be externally valid, it is necessary that the evaluation *sample* be a representative sample of the universe of eligible units.

Follow-up survey. Also known as "postintervention" or "ex-post" survey. A survey that is fielded after the program has started, once the beneficiaries have benefited from it for some time. An *impact evaluation* can include several follow-up surveys.

Hawthorne effect. The "Hawthorne *effect*" occurs when the mere fact that units are being observed makes them behave differently.

Hypothesis. A hypothesis is a proposed explanation for an observable phenomenon. See also, *null hypothesis* and *alternative hypothesis*.

Impact evaluation. An impact *evaluation* is an evaluation that tries to make a causal link between a program or intervention and a set of *outcomes*. An impact evaluation tries to answer the question of whether a program is responsible for changes in the outcomes of interest. Contrast with *process evaluation*.

Indicator. An indicator is a *variable* that measures a phenomenon of interest to the evaluator. The phenomenon can be an *input*, an *output*, an *outcome*, a characteristic, or an attribute.

Inputs. The financial, human, and material resources used for the development intervention.

Instrumental variable. An instrumental *variable* is a variable that helps identify the causal impact of a program when participation in the program is partly determined by the potential beneficiaries. A variable must have two characteristics to qualify as a good instrumental variable: (1) it must be correlated with program participation, and (2) it may not be correlated with *outcomes* Y (apart from through program participation) or with unobserved variables.

Intention-to-treat, or ITT, estimator. The ITT *estimator* is the straight difference in the *outcome indicator* Y for the group to whom we offered treatment and the same indicator for the group to whom we did not offer treatment. Contrast with *treatment-on-the-treated*.

Internal validity. To say that an *impact evaluation* has internal validity means that it uses a valid *comparison group*, that is, a comparison group that is a valid estimate of the *counterfactual*.

Intra-cluster correlation. Intra-cluster correlation is correlation (or similarity) in *outcomes* or characteristics between units that belong to the same cluster. For example, children that attend the same school would typically be similar or correlated in terms of their area of residence or socioeconomic background.

John Henry effect. The John Henry effect happens when comparison units work harder to compensate for not being offered a treatment. When one compares treated units to those "harder-working" comparison units, the estimate of the impact of the program will be biased; that is, we will estimate a smaller impact of the program than the true impact that we would find if the comparison units did not make the additional effort.

Matching. Matching is a nonexperimental *evaluation* method that uses large data sets and heavy statistical techniques to construct the best possible *comparison group* for a given *treatment group*.

Minimum desired effect. The minimum change in *outcome*s that would justify the investment that has been made in an intervention, counting not only the cost of the program and the benefits that it provides, but also the opportunity cost of not investing funds in an alternative intervention. The minimum desired *effect* is an input for *power calculations*; that is, *evaluation sample*s need to be large enough to detect at least the minimum desired effect with sufficient *power*.

Monitoring. Monitoring is the continuous process of collecting and analyzing information to assess how well a project, program, or policy, is performing. It relies primarily on administrative data to track performance against expected results, make comparisons across programs, and analyze trends over time. Monitoring usually tracks *input*s, activities, and *output*s, though occasionally it includes *outcome*s as well. Monitoring is used to inform day-to-day management and decisions.

Nonresponse. That data are missing or incomplete for some sampled units constitutes nonresponse. Unit nonresponse arises when no information is available for some *sample* units, that is, when the actual sample is different than the planned sample. *Attrition* is one form of unit nonresponse. Item nonresponse occurs when data are incomplete for some sampled units at a point in time. Nonresponse may cause *bias* in *evaluation* results if it is associated with treatment status.

Null hypothesis. A null *hypothesis* is a hypothesis that might be falsified on the basis of observed data. The null hypothesis typically proposes a general or default position. In *impact evaluation*, the default position is usually that there is no difference between the treatment and control groups, or in other words, that the intervention has no impact on *outcome*s.

Outcome. Can be intermediate or final. An outcome is a result of interest that comes about through a combination of supply and demand factors. For example, if an intervention leads to a greater supply of vaccination services, then actual vaccination numbers would be an outcome, as they depend not only on the supply of vaccines but also on the behavior of the intended beneficiaries: do they show up at the service point to be vaccinated? Final or long-term outcomes are more distant outcomes. The distance can be interpreted in a time dimension (it takes a long time to get to the outcome) or a causal dimension (many causal links are needed to reach the outcome).

Output. The products, capital goods, and services that are produced (supplied) directly by an intervention. Outputs may also include changes that result from the intervention that are relevant to the achievement of *outcome*s.

Population of interest. The group of units that are eligible to receive an intervention or treatment. The population of interest is sometimes called the universe.

Power. The power is the probability of detecting an impact if one has occurred. The power of a test is equal to 1 minus the probability of a *type II error*, ranging from 0 to 1. Popular levels of power are 0.8 and 0.9. High levels of power are more conservative and decrease the likelihood of a type II error. An *impact evaluation* has high power if there is a low risk of not detecting real program impacts, that is, of committing a type II error.

Power calculations. *Power* calculations indicate the *sample* size required for an *evaluation* to detect a given *minimum desired effect*. Power calculations depend on parameters such as power (or the likelihood of *type II error*), *significance level*, variance, and *intra-cluster correlation* of the *outcome* of interest.

Process evaluation. A process *evaluation* is an evaluation that tries to establish the level of quality or success of the processes of a program; for example, adequacy of the administrative processes, acceptability of the program benefits, clarity of the information campaign, internal dynamics of implementing organizations, their policy instruments, their service delivery mechanisms, their management practices, and the linkages among these. Contrast with *impact evaluation*.

Random sample. The best way to avoid a biased or unrepresentative *sample* is to select a random sample. A random sample is a probability sample in which each individual in the population being sampled has an equal chance (probability) of being selected.

Randomized assignment or randomized control designs. Randomized assignment is considered the most robust method for estimating *counterfactuals* and is often referred to as the "gold standard" of *impact evaluation*. With this method, beneficiaries are randomly selected to receive an intervention, and each has an equal chance of receiving the program. With large-enough *sample* sizes, the process of random assignment ensures equivalence, in both observed and unobserved characteristics, between the treatment and control groups, thereby addressing any *selection bias*.

Randomized offering. Randomized offering is a method for identifying the impact of an intervention. With this method, beneficiaries are randomly offered an intervention, and each has an equal chance of receiving the program. Although the program administrator can randomly select the units to whom to offer the treatment from the universe of eligible units, the administrator cannot obtain perfect compliance: she or he cannot force any unit to participate or accept the treatment and cannot refuse to let a unit participate if the unit insists on doing so. In the randomized offering method, the randomized offering of the program is used as an *instrumental variable* for actual program participation.

Randomized promotion. Randomized promotion is a method similar to *randomized offering*. Instead of random selection of the units to whom the treatment is offered, units are randomly selected for promotion of the treatment. In this way, the program is left open to every unit.

Randomized selection methods. "Randomized selection method" is a group name for several methods that use random assignment to identify the *counterfactual*. Among them are *randomized assignment* of the treatment, *randomized offering* of the treatment, and *randomized promotion*.

Regression. In statistics, regression analysis includes any techniques for modeling and analyzing several *variable*s, when the focus is on the relationship between a dependent variable and one or more independent variables. In *impact evaluation*, regression analysis helps us understand how the typical value of the *outcome indicator Y* (dependent variable) changes when the assignment to treatment or *comparison group P* (independent variable) is varied, while the characteristics of the beneficiaries (other independent variables) are held fixed.

Regression discontinuity design (RDD). Regression discontinuity design is a nonexperimental *evaluation* method. It is adequate for programs that use a continuous index to rank potential beneficiaries and that have a threshold along the index that determines whether potential beneficiaries receive the program or not. The cutoff threshold for program eligibility provides a dividing point between the *treatment* and *comparison group*s.

Results chain. The results chain sets out the program logic that explains how the development objective is to be achieved. It shows the links from *input*s to activities, to *output*s, to results.

Sample. In statistics, a sample is a subset of a population. Typically, the population is very large, making a *census* or a complete enumeration of all the values in the population impractical or impossible. Instead, researchers can select a representative subset of the population (using a sampling frame) and collect statistics on the sample; these may be used to make inferences or to extrapolate to the population. This process is referred to as *sampling*.

Sampling. Process by which units are drawn from the *sampling frame* built from the *population of interest* (universe). Various alternative sampling procedures can be used. Probability sampling methods are the most rigorous because they assign a well-defined probability for each unit to be drawn. Random sampling, stratified random sampling, and cluster sampling are all probability sampling methods. Nonprobabilistic sampling (such as purposive or convenience sampling) can create sampling errors.

Sampling frame. The most comprehensive list of units in the *population of interest* (universe) that can be obtained. Differences between the sampling frame and the population of interest create a coverage (*sampling*) *bias*. In the presence of coverage *bias*, results from the *sample* do not have *external validity* for the entire population of interest.

Selection bias. Selection bias occurs when the reasons for which an individual participates in a program are correlated with outcomes. This bias commonly occurs when the *comparison group* is ineligible or self-selects out of treatment.

Significance level. The significance level is usually denoted by the Greek symbol, α (alpha). Popular levels of significance are 5 percent (0.05), 1 percent (0.01), and 0.1 percent (0.001). If a test of significance gives a p value lower than the α level, the *null hypothesis* is rejected. Such results are informally referred to as "statistically significant." The lower the significance level, the stronger the evidence required. Choosing the level of significance is an arbitrary task, but for many applications, a level of 5 percent is chosen for no better reason than that it is conventional.

Spillover effect. Also known as contamination of the *comparison group*. A spillover effect occurs when the comparison group is affected by the treatment administered to the *treatment group*, even though the treatment is not administered directly to the comparison group. If the spillover effect on the comparison group is negative (that is, if they suffer because of the program), then the straight difference between *outcomes* in the treatment and comparison groups will yield an overestimation of the program impact. By contrast, if the spillover effect on the comparison group is positive (that is, they benefit), then it will yield an underestimation of the program impact.

Statistical power. The *power* of a statistical test is the probability that the test will reject the *null hypothesis* when the *alternative hypothesis* is true (that is, that it will not make a *type II error*). As power increases, the chances of a type II error decrease. The probability of a type II error is referred to as the false negative rate (β). Therefore power is equal to $1 - \beta$.

Stratified sample. Obtained by dividing the population of interest (*sampling frame*) into groups (for example, male and female), and then drawing a *random sample* within each group. A stratified *sample* is a probabilistic sample: every unit in each group (or stratum) has the same probability of being drawn.

Survey data. Data that cover a *sample* of the population of interest. Contrast with *census data*.

Treatment group. Also known as the treated group or the intervention group. The treatment group is the group of units that benefits from an intervention, versus the *comparison group* that does not.

Treatment-on-the-treated (effect of). Also known as the TOT *estimator*. The *effect* of treatment on the treated is the impact of the treatment on those units that have actually benefited from the treatment. Contrast with *intention-to-treat*.

Type I error. Error committed when rejecting a *null hypothesis* even though the null hypothesis actually holds. In the context of an *impact evaluation*, a type I error is made when an *evaluation* concludes that a program has had an impact (that is, the null hypothesis of no impact is rejected), even though in reality the program had no impact (that is, the null hypothesis holds). The *significance level* determines the probability of committing a type I error.

Type II error. Error committed when accepting (not rejecting) the *null hypothesis* even though the null hypothesis does not hold. In the context of an *impact evaluation*, a type II error is made when concluding that a program has no impact (that is, the null hypothesis of no impact is not rejected) even though the program did have an impact (that is, the null hypothesis does not hold). The probability of committing a type II error is 1 minus the *power* level.

Variable. In statistical terminology, a variable is a symbol that stands for a value that may vary.

INDEX

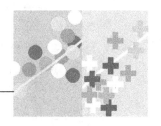

Boxes, figures, notes, and tables are indicated by *b, f, n,* and *t,* respectively.

"equal trends" assumption in DD method, 99–101, 100*f*

equitable targeting criteria, 144

estimating the counterfactual, 36–47
    before-and-after counterfeit estimate of counterfactual, 40–45, 41*f*, 44*t*, 96
    ITT and TOT estimates, 39–40, 231, 235
        perfect clones, 37*f*
    randomized selection. *See* randomized selection methods
    RDD. *See* regression discontinuity design
    valid comparison groups, 37–38, 39*b*
    with-and-without counterfeit estimate of counterfactual, 40, 45–47, 46*t*, 47*t*

estimator, 93*n*1, 229, 230, 231, 235

ethical nature of evaluation, determining, 153–54

evaluation, defined, 7

evaluation managers, 156

evaluation teams
    data managers, processors, and analysts, 157, 212–13
    dissemination of findings by, 219–21
    fieldwork team, 157, 204–6
    setting up, 154–58

evidence-based policy making, 3–6, 5*b*, 227

ex-post matching, 115

exogenous factors, data on, 172

external validity or generalizability, 14, 54–55, 57*f*, 230

F

fair and transparent rules for program assignment, 49–51

falsification tests, 117, 118–19*b*

fieldwork team, 157, 204–6

finances for impact evaluation. *See under* operationalizing an impact evaluating design

findings, 211–22
    baseline report, 212, 213–15, 213*b*
    dataset, 219
    dissemination of, 219–21, 221*b*
    final impact evaluation report, 211–12, 215–18, 216*b*
    implementation procedure, as step in, 140, 141*f*
    policy briefs, 211, 219

follow-up survey, timing of collection of, 159–60, 231

formatting questionnaires, 203–4

funding impact evaluations. *See under* operationalizing an impact evaluating design

G

generalizability or external validity, 14, 54–55, 57*f*, 230

glossary, 229–35

H

"Hawthorne effect," 126, 231

Health Insurance Subsidy Program (HISP) case study, 31–32
    before-and-after counterfeit estimate of counterfactual, 42–45, 44*t*
    DD in, 102*t*
    ITT and TOT estimates, 39–40, 231, 235
    matching, 111–12*t*
    power calculations for
        with clusters, 19*t*, 189–91, 191*t*
        without clusters, 184–87, 186*t*, 187*t*
    randomized assignment in, 61–63, 62*t*, 63*t*
    randomized promotion in, 76–77, 76*t*, 77*t*
    RDD in, 86–89, 87*f*, 88*f*, 88*t*
    with-and-without counterfeit estimate of counterfactual, 45–47, 46*t*, 47*t*

hypothesis
    alternative hypothesis, 178, 229, 231, 235
    formulating, 27, 176
    null hypothesis, 79*n*7, 178, 229, 231, 232, 234, 235

I

identifying beneficiaries of programs, 146–47

impact evaluation, 3–19, 223–28
    backup plans, importance of, 127
    causal inference in, 33–34
    collection of data, 199–209. *See also* collection of data
    combined with other studies, information sources, and evaluations, 15–17
    combining methods of, 95, 119–20, 121*b*, 127. *See also* combining methods
    core elements of, 224
    cost-effectiveness analysis and, 11–12, 12*b*
    counterfactual, 34–47. *See also* counterfactual
    DD, 95–105. *See also* difference-in-differences
    defined, 7–8, 231
    efficacy and effectiveness studies, 14–15
    evidence-based policy making, as element in, 3–6, 5*b*, 227
    findings, 211–22. *See also* findings
    glossary, 229–35

regression discontinuity design (RDD),
81–43
   agricultural subsidy program case study
      (fertilizers for rice production),
      82–84, 83*f*
   baseline data and, 91*b*
   CCT program case study, 84–86*f*
   continuous eligibility indexes, programs
      with, 81–82
   DD, combined with, 120
   defined, 234
   in HISP case study, 86–89, 87*f*, 88*f*, 88*t*
   imperfect compliance and, 122
   limitations of, 91–93
   real-world applications of, 89–90, 89*b*,
      90*b*, 91*b*
   verification and falsification tests, 118*b*
reports
   final impact evaluation report, 211–12,
      215–18, 216*b*
   intermediate baseline reports, 212,
      213–15, 213*b*
results chain, 24–26, 25*f*, 26*f*, 234
retrospective impact evaluation, 13–14
risks to subjects, minimizing, 154, 169*n*3
Rwanda, results-based health care
      financing in, 221*b*

S

sampling, 171–97
   coverage bias, avoiding, 194, 195
   defined, 234
   existing versus new data, 173–75
   implementation procedure, as step in,
      140, 141*f*
   methodologies, 194–95
   minimum required sample size, 183–84
   population of interest, 193–94
   power calculations for determining
      sample size. *See* power calculations
   principles and strategies, 192–95
   types of data required, determining,
      171–75
   valid sampling frame, 193–94, 193*f*, 234
sampling experts, on evaluation teams,
      156–57
sampling frame, 193–94, 193*f*, 234
selection bias, 45, 96, 102, 114–15, 234
setting up impact evaluations, 21–30
   hypotheses, formulating, 27
   M&E plan for performance indicators, 28*t*
   performance indicators, selecting, 27–28,
      28*t*

results chain, developing, 24–26, 25*f*, 26*f*,
      234
   study question, formulation of, 22
   theory of change, developing, 22–23, 23*b*
SIEF (Spanish Impact Evaluation Fund),
      161, 162–63*t*, 164
significance level, 233, 234, 235
SMART indicators, 27, 28*t*, 171
Spanish Impact Evaluation Fund (SIEF),
      161, 162–63*t*, 164
spillovers, 123–25, 125*b*, 125*f*, 235
statistical experts, consulting, 183
statistical power. *See* power calculations
stratified random sampling, 194–95
subgroups, comparing program impacts
      between, 126, 182
survey data, 165, 174–175, 200, 229, 235

T

targeting, operational. *See* operationalizing
      an impact evaluating design
testing questionnaires, 204
theories of change, 22–23, 23*b*
timing
   of data collection, 126
   long-term outcomes, measuring, 160
   as operational targeting rule, 146
   operationalization of, 158–60
TOT (treatment-on-the-treated) estimate,
      39–40, 65, 67*f*, 68, 72, 74, 121*b*, 235
training of fieldwork team, 204–5
transparency of targeting criteria, 144–45
transparent and fair rules for program
      assignment, 49–51
treatment groups
   average outcomes for treatment and
      comparison groups, estimating,
      176–78, 177*f*
   defined, 235
treatment-on-the-treated (TOT) estimate,
      39–40, 235
type I and type II errors, 179–80, 235

U

unintended behavioral responses, 126
United States
   early childhood programs, long-term
      impacts of, 160
universe. *See* population of interest

V

validation of data, 207–9
verification tests. *See* falsification tests

CPSIA information can be obtained
at www.ICGtesting.com
Printed in the USA
LVHW100952310821
696563LV00008B/42